EVA AND PERFORMANCE MEASUREMENT

Text and Case Studies of Indian Companies

EVA AND PERFORMANCE MEASUREMENT

Text and Case Studies of Indian Companies

DR. MADHU SEHRAWAT
Lecturer, Dyal Singh College (Day)
University of Delhi, Delhi

DEEP & DEEP PUBLICATIONS PVT. LTD.
F-159, Rajouri Garden, New Delhi - 110 027

EVA AND PERFORMANCE MEASUREMENT
Text and Case Studies of Indian Companies

ISBN 978-81-8450-154-4

Typeset by RAHUL COMPOSERS
358, Pocket-B, Phase-II, Sector-15B, Dwarka, New Delhi - 110 075

Printed in India at NEW ELEGANT PRINTERS
A-49/1, Mayapuri, Phase-I, New Delhi - 110 064

Published by DEEP & DEEP PUBLICATIONS PVT. LTD.,
F-159, Rajouri Garden, New Delhi - 110 027 • Phone : 25435369, 25440916
E-mail : ddpubs@gmail.com • ddpbooks@yahoo.co.in
Showroom :
2/13, Ansari Road, Daryaganj, New Delhi - 110 002 • Telefax : 23245122

Contents

KAMAL GUPTA
Ph.D. FCA
(Formerly, Technical Director, ICAI)

N-23, Sector XI
Noida - 201 301
Tel.: 0120-254 4572
0120-254 6986
Fax: 0120-433 5671
e-mail: kgupta@airtelmail.in

Foreword

As a unique subject aiming to present rational and credible measures of wealth, performance and liquidity of enterprises, accounting has assumed unprecedented significance in the modern economies. This has also resulted in questioning, review and thorough examination of the traditional concepts of accounting. Economic Value Added (EVA) is one of the most significant of the relatively new concepts in accounting. I am indeed very happy that Dr. (Mrs.) Madhu Sehrawat has chosen this subject for her empirical research in the Indian milieu. Knowledge about EVA has a bearing on incentive management, financial management policies as well as on investment strategies.

An important finding of the study is that in terms of measuring shareholders' value addition/destruction, EVA is superior to not only Return on Net Worth or Return on Capital Employed but also to the most widely used Earnings per Share. Another interesting fact brought out by the study is that progressive companies (e.g., Infosys, Hindustan Lever etc.) have already started publishing EVA statements.

Already, EVA measurements have assumed prime position in business valuations. One hopes that their use as a prime tool of investor-decision-making would also increase.

The author's presentation is lucid and analytical. The study should be of wide interest to financial analysts, executives, regulators and researchers. It is a useful addition to the existing literature on value management.

Noida

DR. KAMAL GUPTA

Preface

Management's obsession with measurement appears to grow unbounded. Companies are increasingly developing new metrics of measurement in order to quantify various tangible and intangible aspects of the business processes. In many of the cases it has been seen that the measurement systems of the companies dump abundant financial data on the executives with no actual information and insights. It is theme—*drowning in data*—that lies at the heart of the new measurement crisis. The problem is not that the wrong things were being measured, but that too much is being measured. Executives want everything to be described in numerical terms—customer satisfaction, customer loyalty, customer profitability, brand value, employee satisfaction, supplier performance, health and safety, efficiency, productivity, innovation, new product development, and so on. The list of things that would be nice to measure—in even a moderately-sized business—is endless!

This issue is becoming such a significant one that some executives are now starting to question what value they are getting from their organisation's measurement systems. These questions become even more frantic when the executives concerned think about how much their organisation's measurement systems cost them to run. It does not mean that they should stop or trim back their measurement initiatives. But it does mean that they should think carefully about how they can best utilize their measurement systems to ensure that they deliver maximum value. And it is to this issue—how to make measurement pay—that we must now turn our attention to value-based performance measurement. After reviewing recent writing and efforts in the field of performance measurement it becomes clear that significant effort has been devoted to improve measurement methodologies. People have sought and developed new methods of measuring financial performance—Activity-based costing, activity-based management, shareholder value analysis, economic value added, free cash flow analysis and new frameworks to balance financial and non-financial measures—the balanced scorecard, performance prism, etc.

The book is an attempt in this direction focused on introducing the concept of value-based management, designing and implementing the methodologies and frameworks for managing a business in the interest of maximizing its fundamental intrinsic value. Economic Value Added (EVA) is gaining ground as companies increasingly look to maximize the intrinsic value of their business rather than mere absolute profit or return figures. This is because there is empirical evidence that stock market prices do not reflect the intrinsic value of a business over a short, say 1-3 year period. Stock prices are driven largely by state-of-the-world factors, the vagaries of the capital market or industry-specific outlook, than by the actual performance of companies. Fundamental value means earning returns in excess of the opportunity cost of capital and how much financial capital is to be exposed to that ROCE, RONW, EPS, etc. are not the desired levers for value creation rather the new value-based levers, like, EVA, SVA, WA, CFROI, etc. are on cards today. The journey is intrinsic value maximizing rather than maximizing the absolute profits and EVA is a means to that end.

This book is based on the research work done as part of my doctoral dissertation and would not have been possible without the benign guidance of the senior colleagues and the selfless cooperation of peers. Through the following words, I wish to acknowledge the assistance of a number of persons and organizations, without whom, it would neither have been worthwhile nor possible to undertake this work. First and foremost, it's a proud privilege and the most pleasant duty to express my deep sense of gratitude and sincere appreciation to my research supervisor, Prof. Jawahar Lal, Department of

Commerce, University of Delhi for providing his valuable guidance, constant encouragement, inspiration, selfless cooperation and warm affection during the completion of the work. A work of research, especially of the magnitude as it is and on such a topic not very much in vogue amongst the research scholars would have been impossible to do without his constant advices, constructive comments and valuable suggestions at every stage. I owe much more than my words can render.

I am grateful to Prof. S.K. Jain, Head, Department of Commerce, University of Delhi for his kind interest, encouragement and support and also for providing necessary facilities at the Department of Commerce.

I am extremely thankful to Prof. A.K. Seth for his constant help, collaboration and guidance in the analysis part of the study. His friendly and unreserved help from the very outset proved very helpful for me to complete this work.

Thanks are also due to Dr. A.K. Saini, Incharge, FMS Computer Centre for providing access to his centre to collect the reliable financial data which is the basis of any research work of this kind. The officers and staff of following libraries and institutions are to be thanked for their assistance. Rattan Tata Library, Institute of Chartered Accountants of India, the Institute of Public Administration, the Faculty of Management Studies, the American Information Resource Centre, the Delhi University Computer Centre and the College Library of Dyal Singh College.

I express my gratitude towards Mr. G.S. Bhatia, of Deep & Deep Publications Pvt. Ltd. for readily agreeing to publish the book.

Last but not the least, I acknowledge my deep indebtedness to my parents for their constant encouragement and help throughout the study. I am thankful to my husband, Dr. Narendra Singh for his support and constructive help in every aspect of the study. Appreciation is also due towards our very lovely little angles, my daughter Manasvi and my son Naman for their patience.

MADHU SEHRAWAT

CHAPTER

1

Introduction to Performance Measurement

1.1 OVERVIEW

Performance system was developed as a means of monitoring and maintaining organizational control, which is the process of ensuring that an organization pursues strategies that lead to the achievement of overall goals and objectives, i.e., performance measurement is the method of assessing a company's progress towards achieving its present goals. Through key performance measures, an organisation's strategy is linked to its operations. Performance measurement plays a vital role in every organization as it is often viewed as a forward-looking system of measurements that assist managers to predict the company's economic performance and spot the need for changes in operations. In addition, it can provide managers, supervisors and operators with information required for making daily judgements and decisions. Performance measurement is increasingly used by organizations, as it enables them to ensure that they are achieving continuous improvements in their operations in order to sustain a Creation competitive edge, increased market share and increased profits.

Creation, management and distribution of shareholder wealth has now become a mandatory and ineluctable task for chief executives in New York, London, Tokyo, Sydney and yes, even, in Delhi, Mumbai, etc. With the globalisation of competition and capital markets and a tidal wave of privatisation, shareholder value creation is rapidly capturing the attention of executives. There are four major factors such as ownership position, compensation tied to shareholder return performance, threat of takeover and competitive labour markets for corporate executives, which have induced management to adopt a shareholder orientation.

Investors, nowadays, are no longer just a source of funds demanding high returns on the capital provided by them rather are more concerned with what the company is doing with their money—whether it is creating value for them or not. Greater concern about value rather than absolute profits brought about by a shifted focus from the earlier profit-maximisation to value-maximisation as corporate objective, disastrous consequences of assessing financial performance of company and relative attractiveness of an investment project using traditional profit-based measures, such as, EPS, ROI, ROE, Gross/Net Profit Margin, etc. has made the fund managers and investors more conscious of the need to crave new tools to assess corporate financial performance, to manage for shareholder value in a business. It is basically the dissatisfaction with traditional accounting-based performance measures that has spawned a number of alternatives e.g., Cash Value Added (CVA), Shareholder Value Added (SVA), Cash Flow Return On Investment (CFROI), Market Value Added (MVA), Economic Value Added (EVA) and Wealth Added[1] (WA), of which Economic Value Added (EVA) is currently the most prominent one.

It is commonly assumed that if a company produces "satisfactory" growth in EPS, then the market value of its shares will increase. But, EPS growth does not necessarily lead to an increase in the market value of the stock. This is enumerated by the shortcomings in earnings approach, Return on Investment (ROI) and Return on Equity (ROE) approaches. For instance, companies use alternative accounting methods of valuing inventories, computing depreciation and purchase *versus* pooling-of-interests accounting for mergers and acquisitions. A change in accounting method can materially impact earnings but does not alter the company's cash flow and therefore should not affect its economic value. The relationship between the change in economic value and earnings is further obscured by the fact that investments in working capital and fixed capital needed to sustain the firm are excluded from the earnings calculation.

Moreover, earnings fail to measure changes in economic value because the earnings calculation ignores the time value of money. Hurdle rates or ROI are often based on an estimate of the business unit's cost of capital or the corporate cost of capital. Comparing ROI, an accrual accounting return with the cost of capital measures, an economic return is clearly just like comparing apples with oranges. Moreover, ROI is a single period measurement which ignores events beyond the current period. Besides this, a business attempting to increase its market share and competitive position will likely to increase its new product development and marketing spending, price aggressively, and invest in expanded production capacity and working capital. While each of these activities is aimed at strengthening the organisation's longer-term strategic position, ROI may well decline over the next several years even though such actions increase value. In sharp contrast, harvesting strategy allows erosion in market share and thereby increases cash flow by minimising investment in fixed capital and freeing up working capital, it is typically appropriate for product with relatively low market shares only. All these shortcomings of ROI exists with ROE as ROE is so similar to ROI; in addition, ROE is also sensitive to leverage. All these shortcomings have paved the way towards value added measures and specifically towards Economic Value Added (EVA)—the Generic Value Driver as exhibited below in Figure 1.1.

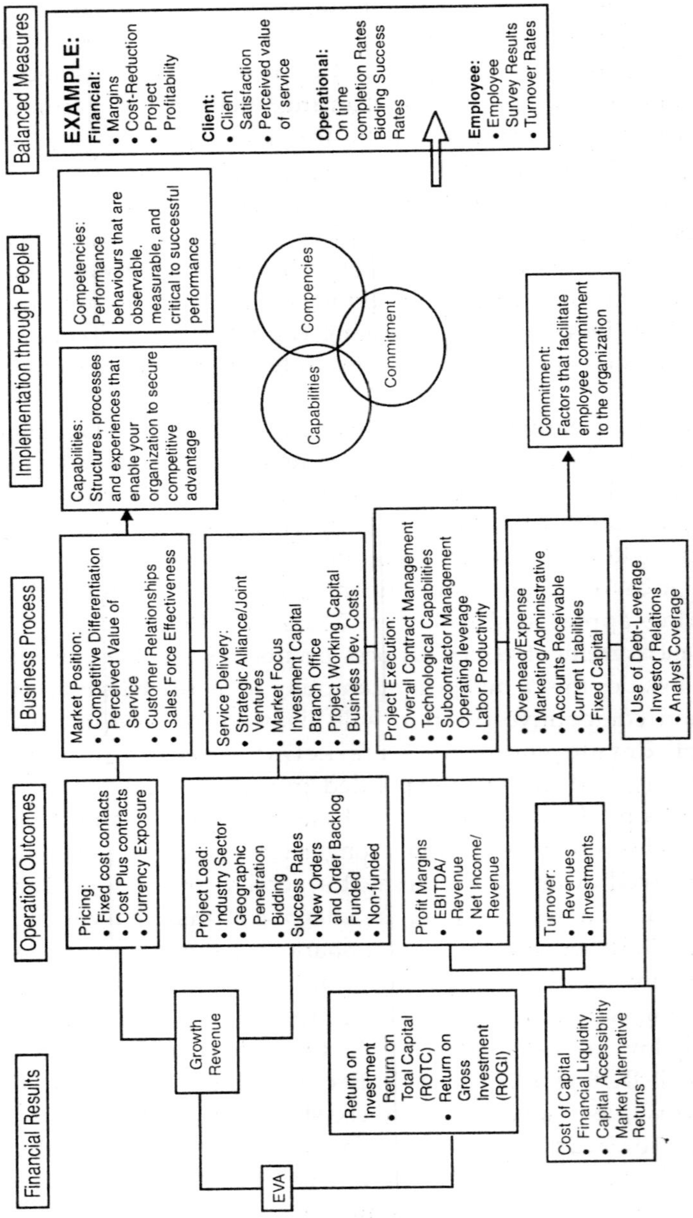

FIG. 1.1

EVA—The Generic Value Driver

1.2 MEASURING BUSINESS PERFORMANCE THROUGH VALUE-BASED MANAGEMENT FRAMEWORK

Corporate managers now face a challenge where a new economic framework, a Value-Based Management Framework that better reflects value and profitability must be implemented in their companies. The "Value Proposition" has become a buzzword in the corporate parlance. Value-based management is a consistent framework that aligns management action and strategic objectives with shareholder value creation. It instills a mindset where everyone in the organisation learns to prioritize decisions based on their understanding of how those decisions contribute to corporate world, to create a corporate mindset in which management decision-making and execution are focussed on the creation of shareholder value keeping into mind the fundamental drivers of shareholder value as exhibited below:

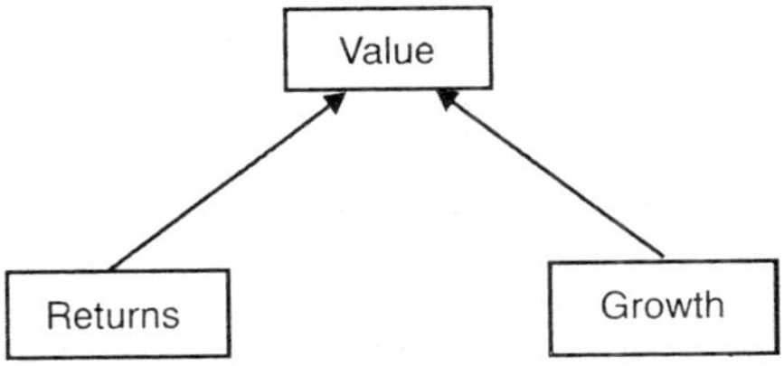

FIG. 1.2
Drivers of Shareholder Value

As shareholder activism intensifies, the primary questions that consume executives' time are: "How is my business doing, and how do I know whether my decisions today will create long-term value?" Today's managers are confused by conflicting priorities as they receive conflicting signals from the performance measures used in each of the management processes including strategic planning, budgeting, reporting and compensation. Rumours of the simplicity of measurement are grossly exaggerated, which may explain the profusion of new concepts in this area. Managers are skeptical about new initiatives and don't understand how to prioritize them. Further, the fast growing measurement systems of companies dump abundant financial data on the executives with no actual information and insights. They are provided access to so much data that effectively executives end up "drowning in data"! i.e., the problem is not that wrong things are measured but that too much is being measured. Managing for value addresses the conflicts by prioritizing each of the initiatives in the context of the company's goal to consistently create shareholder value as shown below:

THE BALANCE OF COMPETING OBJECTIVES

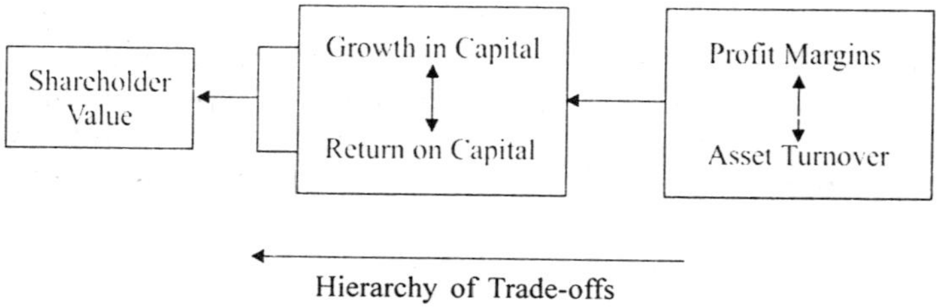

FIG. 1.3
Managing Shareholder Value

But the mindset of managing for value is not enough in itself. To achieve maximum value it must be translated into reality, that is, using it in frontline decision-making. Successful value management requires that a mindset of managing for value be integrated into the way decisions are made. James A. Knight discusses the issue of value management in five categories viz. goal, strategy, measures, processes and decisions. Making value management a reality requires management to agree that value maximisation is the company's goal and managing a company for value requires delivering maximum return to the investors while balancing the interest of other important constituents including customers and employees. Management must then develop a business strategy to achieve the goal of maximum value creation.

Value creation is the wealth created for a company's stockholders through price appreciation and dividends. It can be calculated in variety of ways wherever the information on stock price and dividends is readily available. Calculating value is a trivial exercise because value in the future is not easy to calculate and such calculations are subjective in nature. Value is an impressive term whose analysis is more an art than a science. Giving due consideration to this fact, value in the study stands for economic value added i.e., how much value has been added to wealth invested by shareholders? Whether the company's routine processes results into creation of value or the destruction of value. An attempt has been made in the study to find out whether the share prices of the value adding companies are high as compared to those of destroying value or not i.e., whether any link can be established between the traditional concept of value creation and that of latest one used in value-based management.

Creating value for shareholders means creating value that meets or exceeds their expectations for value creation. If management can beat the investors' expectations, as reflected in the return factor, so much the better. But, sometimes, the management may find itself in a position where the probability of beating the investors' expectations is low. In such situations, the management needs to manage the expectations of investors so they don't go ahead of the company's ability to deliver results and also do a thorough analysis of the holders of the company's stock to determine what the investors really want.

Creating value for shareholders operate under three rules, viz.

- Level of profitability has nothing to do with value creation,
- All management teams start on a level playing field for creating value, and
- Different companies face different challenges in creating value.

These three rules are the slippery slope of value creation. No matter how good a company is at creating value, investors give management credit for their performance to date. At the same time this also increases the degree of difficulty in creating future value.

Managing for value is not new, ·yet the practice of managing for value has changed a lot over the last 20 years. In the early 1980s' it consisted largely of performance measures, including profitability metrics, such as "economic profit" and "residual income", which incorporated a "charge" for the capital employed in each business. By explicitly recognising that capital carries with it a cost, these metrics highlighted where capital was being invested unprofitably within a company. While, value-based metrics unlocked enormous value, the system provided little guidance with respect to forward-looking investments, where future earnings and capital requirements are largely unknown—investments such as new product introductions or new market entry. To address these issues, managers needed more than historical measures, they needed an approach that could tie long-term strategic thinking to capital investment planning. That need was filled in the late 1980s with the discipline of value-based management (VBM). VBM joined business strategy and corporate finance, producing an integrated economic framework for analysing business investments. It allowed practitioners to understand and explain the underlying drivers of financial performance and to produce "grounded" financial forecasts. Once they understood the sources and drivers of shareholders value within their business portfolios, firm could identify new and different strategies to create even more value. For instance, Disney discovered that its value-creating stable of cartoon characters could be leveraged in new firm releases and to profitably enter new markets, such as, retail stores and cruise lines. By integrating strategy with finance, VBM allowed these and other firms to identify better investment opportunities and make better strategic choices. In the early 1990s, an organizational perspective was added to value-based management. Indeed early practitioners of VBM found that creating shareholder value year after year required new information and management processes. Strategy development had to be continuous (rather than cycle-driven) and supported by the best available market, competitor and executive compensation processes all needed to be linked to strategy approval to make the strategic planning process truly consequential. Figure 1.4 exhibits these shifting paradigms of value.

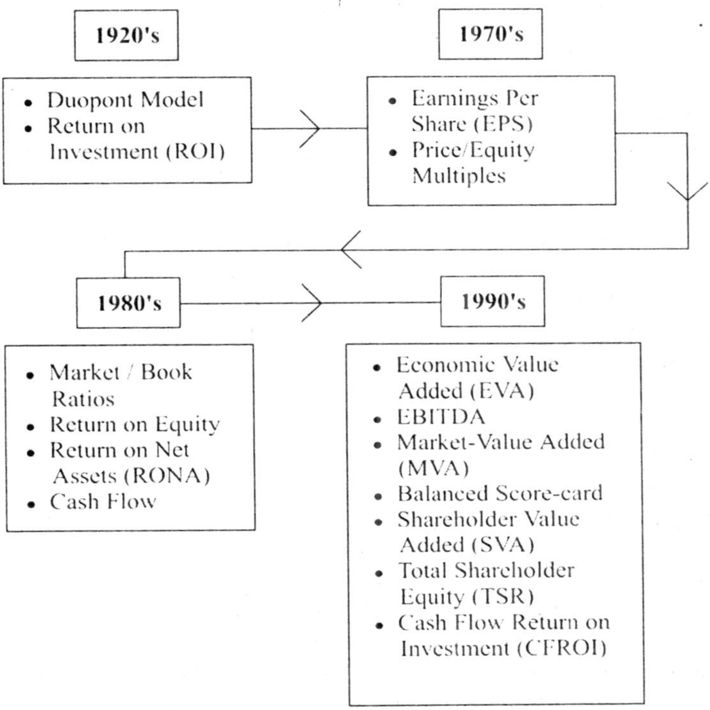

FIG. 1.4
Shifting Paradigms of Value

Once the organisational elements were explicitly incorporated into VBM, it became clear that a company's ability to effectively manage for value could become a source of competitive advantage in and of itself. Over the last few years, value-based management has evolved into an all-encompassing discipline known aptly as "managing for value" (MFV). Whereas value-based management implied a set of tools corporate strategists could apply to high-priority issues, managing for value connotes something every executive should be doing daily.

Interestingly, companies that want to manage for value often follow a path similar to value-based management's evolution. The critical first step is establishing a clear governing objective—to maximise shareholder value and putting in place new, value-based metrics. Next, companies typically adapt their strategic decision-making processes to be more aligned with shareholders' interests. Overtime, the focus shifts towards developing management capabilities and more sophisticated management processes. Eventually, managing for value permeates all aspects of the business, becoming a holistic management framework.

Decision-making has three elements namely, objectives, alternatives and information. The objective of any decision under VBM is to create value, but often, an organization has conflicting objectives that require managers to make trade-offs between objectives, which is difficult to do without a single, overriding objective that provides guidance in making the trade-offs. Managing for value provides a weighing scale to help managers balance different considerations, make trade-offs, and come to decisions that maximise value for the organisation. Managing for value also improves the quality of decision-making by increasing the number of alternatives under consideration. Quality information is the third and most critical element for decision-making. Companies that have better information can use it to gain insight that will enable them to achieve competitive advantages over their rivals. Managing for value focuses managers making, generating a broader set of alternative, and improving the information used to make decisions. Value managed companies focus on value-oriented decision-making in the four key management processes of planning, budgeting, compensation and management reporting. When taken together, the results of value management can help the company build and maintain competitive advantage.

Value management can only be successful in a company if the decision-makers understand what it is and how they can affect value creation through their decisions. To achieve success in value management, the company needs to integrate value-based decision-making throughout the organisation by translating the principles, concepts and practices of value-based decision-making into the language of the business. At the same time managing several critical variables like senior management leadership and commitment where senior management needs to address a combination of issues to ensure successful implementation of value-based decision-making. The management must be aware of the program and acknowledge its importance among company's other priorities. It also needs to demonstrate its commitment by showing interest in the program and ensuring the availability of sufficient resources for the program to be successful.

The program should fit with the management processes and the decision-making environment should reinforce the value-based decisions from all directions and the management processes (planning, budgeting, incentives and reporting) ideally should reinforce the same messages. Establishing clear messages and consistent signals is very important for the success of the value program and for the execution of business strategy. A combination of training and education programs need to be developed so as to build awareness of the value concepts and to integrate them into the day-to-day decisions management makes. To be effective, the education and training programs should be introduced to both line and staff managers, must fulfil the need for baseline as well as technical education, has to be upfronted and ongoing, mandatory for every one and related closely to the business issues facing the company.

Communication is another important variable that is essential for people to understand value creation and discover how the decisions they make influence the amount of value created. A successful communication program requires repeated delivery of messages, their periodic reinforcement, effective translation of the language of value into language of operations and redundancy that helps to enhance the communication effort by increasing the number of times the manager is exposed to value concepts and their applications.

Time horizon and risk sequencing are other important considerations and therefore it is necessary that organisations must choose realistic time horizon and correct sequencing of tasks which could otherwise be the death knell of an implementation program. Because, when the expectations are not met, managers view the program as a failure, which leads to reprioritisation of the implementation program. Finally, the respected managers in the company who carry the torch for the implementation program, referred to as champions are the most critical variables to the success of a value program. They could be content champions and process champions each integral to the success of implementation process. The role of the content champion is to understand the company's business issues and their implications on decision-making, performance measurement and incentive design. It becomes the resource for the company and an internal arbiter regarding the application of value concepts. While the role of a process champion is to manage the implementation process and the focus should be on organisational buy-in and monitor the level of commitment to value in the organisation?

Various value-creating companies have used value-based decision-making and seen the advantages of it for so long, but all of them are not using this approach. This is because many of them have not tried managing for value seriously while the others have failed to implement value-based decision-making. There are various myths that prevent the companies from trying value management.

The first is a belief that the business they are running is different from other business. They believe that the business needs to be managed through their knowledge and expertise and that value management would get in the way of their judgement. The second is an abiding faith in the power of earnings per share and that all management has to do is to take care of earnings, and the value creation will take care of itself. Now looking at the companies that have tried value management and failed we see that they break down into five traps. The first one is "flying by the seat of pants". Those companies that fell into this trap lacked a true commitment to value-based decision-making. The second one relates to "unrealistic expectations" that easily detail the value management program. When the implementation suffers lack of understanding and buy-in by the people at the same time not taking sufficient time to lay the foundation of implementation it runs the risk of dealing. The third reason for failure to implement value-based management into the organisation lies in over-focusing on the measure itself. The most common mistake is to assume the measure of value in the management of value. It makes sense to have a measure that accurately represents the underlying business economics but companies with highly analytical staffs run the risk of allowing the measure to overwhelm the implementation.

The risk of value management program withering from "analysis paralysis" is another trap to which organisations fell as a prey. This is because many-a-times the staff is too concerned about perfecting the measure and analysing potential consequences and not concerned enough about demonstrating the real value of the program. Line managers of an organisation think in terms of operating results not in terms of value creation. This difference in the way operating managers and financial managers think leads to many companies falling in trap assuming that "everyone does speak finance" or try to train a large group of managers in finance or accounting. But a little good planning can go discussion that value management is a powerful tool. When used correctly to focus managers, it will drive dramatic improvements in decision-making. However, like any other tool it can be misused. Therefore, organisations should take time to understand what they are trying to achieve and how their business issues should drive a customised approach to value management. Also they must take adequate time to customise the measures the EVA, CVA, SVA, etc. they use and the way they are integrated into the company.

The number of companies adopting the strategic value-based management tool of EVA to assess corporate's financial performance is increasing day-by-day. A look at the year's 2001 study of India's biggest wealth creators exhibited in Table 1.1 shows that eight of the top ten companies had positive EVA (Economic Value Added), which is the economic profit that remains after deducting the cost of all the capital employed (both debt and equity) in the business to generate the operating profits. In fact, seven of these had actually improved their EVA over the previous year and hence thereby be termed as value generators to shareholders' wealth.

"More profits is not equal to more value add"—has further annoyed a few corporate topline chairmans, for instance, M.S. Banga, Azim H. Premji, N.M. Nilekani etc., as exhibited in Table 1.2 but clearly highlights the superiority and true revelations of company's financial position and that of shareholder's money status through EVA rather than by putting sole reliance on the conventional measures like, PAT, etc.

TABLE 1.1
India's Biggest Wealth Creators

Rank (based on MVA)	*Company's Name*	*Economic Value Added (EVA)*	
		2001 (Rs. Crore)	*2002 (Rs. Crore)*
1.	Hindustan Lever	1,003	765
2.	Wipro	235	111
3.	Infosys Technology	242	224
4.	Reliance Industries	–318	328
5.	ITC	591	420
6.	Ranbaxy Laboratories	–94	–97
7.	Satyam Computer Services	33	160
8.	Dr. Reddy's Laboratories	350	36
9.	Nestle India	100	69
10.	Cipla	71	43

TABLE 1.2
PAT vs. EVA

Company	*PAT'02 (in Rs. Crore)*	*PAT Rank*	*EVA'02 (in Rs. Crore)*	*EVA Rank*
Oil and Natural Gas Corporation	6,198	1	17	42
Reliance Industries	3,243	2	–318	485
Indian Oil Corporation	2,885	3	355	5
Hindustan Lever	1,640	4	1,003	1
Videsh Sanchar Nigam	1,407	5	339	4
Mahanagar Telephone Nigam	1,301	6	–1089	498
ITC	1,190	7	591	2
Gas Authority of India	1,186	8	180	15
Wipro	866	9	235	8
Bharat Petroleum Corporation	850	10	139	9

In recent years shareholder value has become an axiom of contemporary business without which any senior executive walked naked into the boardroom. Value is hot again. A year ago, Graham and Dodd, Modigliani and Miller, and even Warren Buffet were decidedly "unhip". Market commentators deemed their management philosophies outmoded as, at the very least, out of step with the fast-paced "new" economy. That's all changed. Today senior executives are intensely interested in managing their companies to create shareholder value as augmentation of shareholders' value can alone lead to an increase in value to other stakeholders. The primary questions that consume executives' time are—"How is my business doing, and how do I know whether my decisions today will create long-term value?"

Not surprisingly, executives' interest in performance measurement has reached a new peak. Management's obsession with measurement appears to grow unbounded. These days it seems that everyone has a new measurement tool. In fact, executives have at their disposal various new methods of measuring corporate financial performance—activity-based costing, EVA, MVA, SVA, free cash flow analysis, the Balanced Scorecard, Performance Prism, etc. Advances in technology, while increasing measurement capability have added confusion rather than lent clarity. Thus the question remains unanswered—how do we choose the conceptual framework that works best for any company? And thereby for the investors how do we decide which measure to choose?; whether the selected measure is having some correlation with share prices or not?.

In this direction a number of studies have been done for the corporate sector of the developed world and not sufficient research has undertaken with respect to the Indian corporate sector. Thus, a need has been felt to investigate some vital issues regarding one of today's hottest financial idea and a vital measure of total factor productivity, that is, Economic Value Added (EVA) empirically and comprehensively. Through this study, an attempt has been made to explain how effective Indian Inc. has been at creating shareholder value.

1.3 VALUE-BASED PERFORMANCE MEASURES

Every CEO runs the risk of getting caught between two powerful constituencies. On one side, increasingly demanding investors, determined to maximise their returns relative to the risk they take; on the other, the organisation and its managers, largely insulated from shareholders and typically focussed on what's achievable given the constraints of industry, competitive position and corporate culture. The CEO's challenge is to manage the tension between the two: To get the organisation to act in ways that will lead to success in the capital markets. Value management helps CEO in meeting this challenge. By instituting new metrics, like, CVA, SVA, WA, CFROI, etc. that better capture improvements in intrinsic value it focusses a company's executives on improving business fundamentals. And these improvements in intrinsic value will translate automatically into improvements in a company's stock price in an efficient capital market thus rewarding investors. Now, to develop a better understanding of these new performance metrics let's start from the distinction between economic profit and Economic Value Added (EVA).

Economic Profit (EP) *vs.* Economic Value Added (EVA)

In common parlance, both EP and EVA are termed as synonymous to each other and thus can be used interchangeably, but by the very concept the terms are quite distinct from each other that is quite obvious from the methodologies itself as mentioned below: EVA (Economic Value Added) is earning before interest but after taxes less the firm's book value multiplied by the average cost of capital, i.e.,

$$EVA = NOPAT—CE \times WACC$$

whereas,

EP (economic profit) is the book profit less the equity's basic value multiplied by the required return to equity, and hence no consideration of other sources of funds, like, debt, preference shares, etc. whereas for calculating EVA book value of the firm or more specifically capital employed includes capital raised through all possible sources of funds like equity shares, debentures, preference shares, etc. and thus book value of the firm includes book value of equity+book value of debt + book value of preference shares, if any.

Economic Value Added (EVA) *vs.* Value Added Concept of Income

EVA as mentioned above is based on the shareholders' approach[2] i.e., if the interest of a company's shareholders is taken care of and the company is adding value to the wealth provided by them automatically it is taking care of the interest of other stakeholders' group also.

On the other hand, Value Added concept of income is based on the stakeholders approach that is concerned with maximising the wealth of customers, employees, suppliers, society and also the shareholders. In this approach, profit/ wealth maximisation is not the primary goal rather it's the well-being of all stakeholders.

Further, Value Added Income is the sum total of operating profits distributed amongst various stakeholders; whereas EVA is the return spread (NOPAT/CE i.e., ROCE—COCE) times capital—a measure to check whether operating profits are sufficient or not to meet the expectations of shareholders. In today's global business environment where business competitiveness is the crux of market-oriented economies, the only social responsibility of business is to create shareholder value that can be measured by EVA and not by Value Added Income.

Economic Value Added *vs.* Residual Income (RI)

Residual Income (RI) is the profit earned that exceeds an amount "charged" for funds committed to an investment center. The amount charged for funds is equal to a management specified target rate of return multiplied by the assets used by the division.

Residual Income = Income—(Target Rate × Asset Base)

On the other hand, Economic Value Added (EVA) is the excess of operating profits after taxes but before interest over the cost of capital so employed therein to earn these profits, i.e.,

EVA = NOPAT—WACC × CE

where, WACC (Weighted Average Cost of Capital) is the calculated rate not an individual—specified rate.

Other Value-based Performance Metrics

In addition to EVA, several other shareholder—value measures are in vogue. These include:

(i) Market Value Added (MVA)

Market Value Added (MVA) is the difference between the company's market and book value of shares. If the total market value of a company is more than the amount of capital invested in it, the company has managed to create shareholder value; otherwise, the company has destroyed shareholder value.

MVA = Company's total Market Value—Capital Invested

It's the absolute spread between the company's market value and its capital.

With the simplifying assumption that market and book value of debt are equal,

MVA = Market Value of Equity—Book Value of Equity i.e.,
MVA = MVE—BVE
where MVE = MPS × No. of Equity Shares
BVE = All equity equivalent items like reserves, retained provisions.

It represents the stock market's assessment as of a particular time of the net present value of all a company's past and projected capital projects.

MVA, in short, is the external measure of corporate performance.

(ii) Shareholder Value Added (SVA)

SVA is a creation of Dr. Alfred Rappaport[3] of LEK/Alcar Consulting Group. It is based on strategic approach of generating/augmenting return to shareholders i.e., Shareholder Value Approach. Under this approach, SVA is the economic value of an investment estimated by discounting forecasted cash flows by cost of capital. The total economic value of an entity is the sum of the values of its debt and equity. This value of the business is called "corporate value" and the value of the equity portion is called "shareholder value". Corporate value consists of the present value of cash flow from operations, residual value and marketable securities.

(iii) Cash Value Added (CVA)

This concept is quite similar to EVA except that it includes only cash items. Furthermore it keeps the capital costs constant over certain investment period. CVA is the difference between Operating Cash Flow (OCF) and Operating Cash Flow Demand (OCFD) i.e.,

CVA = OCF—OCFD

where, OCF = Earnings before Depreciation, Interest and Tax (EBDIT, adjusted for non-cash charges) + Working capital movement + Non-strategic[4] investments.

OCFD represents the capital costs, i.e., the average capital cost per year (in absolute terms) that meets the investor's financial requirements.

OCFD is constant over the investment period.

(iv) Cash Flow Return on Investment (CFROI)

Developed by Boston Consulting Group, this is somewhat similar to long-term internal rate of return. This is arrived at by computing following two parameters, establishing relationship between the two, and finally translating the same into an internal rate of return by recognising the finite economic life of depreciating assets and the residual value of non-operating assets such as land and working capital.

(a) Inflation—adjusted free cash flows available to investors, and
(b) Inflation—adjusted gross investment made by the owners.

(v) Wealth Added (WA)

It encompasses increase in market value of equity, dividends and share buybacks, net of new equity issuances in excess of investor's expected return (on the market value of a company's equity). To put it as an equation,

Wealth Added (WA) = Change in Market Capitalisation − Required Return + Dividends − New Equity Issues

where, Change in Market Capitalisation
= Market Capitalisation at the end of the period less Market Capitalisation at the beginning of the period.

Required Return = Market Capitalisation at the beginning of the period × cost of equity a long way in avoiding these traps. Thus it is evident from the aforementioned

Notes and References

1. Tejpavan Gandhok and Kumar Subramanian, "Wealth Creators", *Business Today,* April 11, 2004.
2. Mayura R. Jaiswal, "Shareholders' Wealth Maximisation: A Global Perspective", Effective Executive (3), April 2004.
3. Rappaport, Alfred, *Creating Shareholder Value,* The Free Press, U.S., 1998.
4. Non-strategic Investments, are the ones made to Maintain the Value of the Strategic Investment's Created.

CHAPTER

2

EVA and Performance Measurement

2.1 CONCEPTUAL FRAMEWORK OF EVA

Corporate managers now face a period where a new economic framework that better reflect value and profitability must be implemented in their companies. Accounting systems, which been used up until today, are insufficient and will not stand the challenge from the increasing efficient capital markets and owners. The increased efficiency at the capital markets require that capital allocation within companies become more efficient and it is therefore not possible for companies in the future to allocate capital as inefficient as they do today. A new economic framework, a Value Based Management framework that better reflects opportunities and pit is therefore necessary. In my opinion, there are four major frameworks within Value Based Management: Economic Value Added (EVA), Cash Value Added (CVA), Cash Flow Return on Investment (CFROI), and Shareholder Value Added (SVA). Out of these four the study will deal with the hottest one—Economic Value Added (EVA).

2.1.1 The Concept of EVA

The acronym EVA stand for Economic Value Added, a patented word by the New York-based consulting firm, Stern Stewart & Co. and it conveys a new measure of corporate performance. The concept is drawing increasing attention since it has emerged as a critical tool to measure and monitor corporate performance. The concept of EVA has got wide acceptance as a key indicator of performance today since industry is shifting from the product-centric world of the past to a value-centric world of the future.

EVA estimates a particular type of economic profit, which has been part of mainstream economic thinking for more than a century. This concept states that in order to assess whether a company earns genuine profits, it is not only necessary that the company earns sufficient profit to cover the firm's operating costs, but they should also cover the cost of capital, that is, the cost of borrowed money in the business as well as the owner's fund deployed in the business. Only then, the owner of the business can claim to have earned a profit. In other words, EVA is the surplus (or deficit) that remains after levying a charge against after-tax operating profits for the opportunity cost of all capital-equity as well as debt used to generate those profits, i.e.,

$$\begin{aligned} EVA &= NOPAT - WACC \times CE \\ \text{or} &\quad (NOPAT/CE - WACC) \,.\, CE \\ \text{or} &\quad (ROCE - WACC) \,.\, CE \end{aligned}$$

where,

ROCE = Return on Capital Employed.
NOPAT = Net Operating Profit After Taxes
WACC = Weighted Average Cost of Capital
CE = Capital Employed

2.1.2 Computation of EVA

The calculation of EVA begins by putting operating profits on an economic rather than on an accounting basis. This requires some correction of numbers as presented in traditional financial accounting, such as, the immediate expensing of investments in research and development, or provisioning and write-offs of expenses, etc. Specimens of varied accounting practices, across the globe in this context is given in the Table 2.1.

TABLE 2.1

Accounting Treatments Across the Globe

Event or Transaction	*Range of Alternatives*
Asset revaluation	Allowed (Australia, Hong Kong, India, UK); Allowed under some circumstances (France, Italy, Sweden); Not Allowed (Canada, Germany, Japan, US)
Funds statement	Report sources and uses of cash (US, UK, Israel, Korea, India); Report sources and uses of working capital (Mexico, Sweden, Singapore); Not required (France, Germany, Netherlands, Switzerland)
Inflation accounting	Required (Argentina, Brazil, Israel, Mexico); Optional Supplementary Information (Australia, Netherlands, UK, India, US); Not-required (Canada, Indonesia, Japan, Germany, India [but some companies still do], Korea)
Goodwill	Capitalize and write-off against owner's equity (Italy, Singapore, India, South Africa and UK); Capitalise and Write-off through income statement (Australia, US, France, Canada)
R&D costs	Expense (US, Germany, Mexico); Capitalize (Argentina, Korea, Norway, Netherlands); Capitalize Development Costs, Expense Research (UK, Canada, India, Denmark, Israel, Nigeria); Not specified (China, Ireland)
Segment reporting	Sales, profits, assets industry and geographic segment (China, UK, Israel, Italy and Singapore); Sales by industry and geographic segment (France, Germany, Belgium, Netherlands and India); Sales and profits by industry (Korea); Not specified (Indonesia, Norway, Switzerland)
Non-operating leases	Capitalisation required (Belgium, Hong Kong, Israel, US); Capitalisation optional, or allowed under highly specific circumstances (Denmark, Sweden, France, Japan); Expense (India, Italy)
Other post-employment benefits	Accrue expense (Indonesia, Nigeria, India, UK, US); Cash basis (Australia, Germany, Hong Kong, Japan)
Pension plans	Recognise unfunded liability (US, Mexico); Ignore unfunded liability (Canada, Germany, Netherlands, UK); Not specified (Hong Kong, New Zealand, Belgium)

(Taken partly from Leftwitch Richard, 'Obstacles to a Global Accounting Deal', *Financial Times*, July 1998).

Then, the EVA measure deducts a charge for the weighted average cost of all capital from the operating profit arrived at by adding the interest amount with the profit after tax.

For an unlevered firm:

NOPAT = EBIT (I—t)
(without adjustment) = (Sales–COGS—SG and A—D) × (1—t)

For a levered firm:

LNOPAT = NOPAT + t × Interest

The remainder is the rupee amount by which after-tax operating profits in each period exceed or fall short of the cost of capital. Thereby EVA measures the difference between the return on a company's capital and the cost of that capital. A positive EVA indicates that value has been created for shareholders by the company and a negative EVA signifies value has been destroyed by the firm during the period of operation.

2.2 EVA : MEASUREMENT CHALLENGES

The basic EVA formulation is helpful in showing how a value-based metric like EVA differs from a traditional accounting measure of profit such as net income. However, it also introduces the complexity of the economic profit and economic capital calculation in practice. In this context, C.S. First Boston, Goldman Sachs U.S. Equity Research, and Stern Stewart and Co. point out that there are some 160 accounting adjustments that can be made to a firm's financial statements (income and balance sheets) to convert them to a value-based format emphasizing cash operating profit and asset replacement cost considerations. Additionally, there are significant empirical anomalies and academic issues that embroil the weighted average cost of capital, WACC—primarily, the cost of equity. As mentioned before, the firm's EVA is calculated by taking a difference of NOPAT and weighted average cost of capital multiplied by the amount of invested capital in the business. In practice, however, there are numerous accounting items jointly impact the NOPAT, WACC and CE arising from the accounting *versus* economic treatment of depreciation, intangibles (including research and development and goodwill arising from corporate acquisitions), deferred income taxes, inventory costing (LIFO *versus* FIFO), and other equity reserve adjustments. Such EVA measurement issues are important because they impact the analyst's estimate of invested capital and economic profit. We discuss these EVA measurement challenges one-by-one.

NOPAT Adjustments

NOPAT is measured from the Income statement by adding back interest payment and subtracting and adding non-operating income and expenses, respectively to a Net profit figure and after making certain other adjustments which turns accounting profits into economic profits.

NOPAT = Profit After Tax + Non-recurring Expenses + R&D Expenditure + Interest Expense + Provision for Taxes – Non-Recurring Income – R&D amortisation – Cash Operating Taxes

Cash Operating Taxes = (Provision for Taxes + Tax Benefit of Non-Recurring Expenses + Tax Benefit of Interest Expense – Tax on Non-Recurring Income).

So far as the adjustments to accounting profit figure are concerned, Stern-Stewart have identified as many as 164 adjustments subject to the following criteria:

Materiality	Adjustments should make a material difference in EVA.
Manageability	Adjustments should impact future decisions.
Definitiveness	Adjustments should be definitive and objectively determined.
Simplicity	Adjustment should not be too complex.

If an item meet all four of the criteria, it should be considered for adjustments. For example, the impact on EVA is usually minimal for firms having small amounts of operating leases. Under those conditions, it would be reasonable to ignore this item in the calculation of EVA.

Following are the most commonly proposed adjustments out of 164 odd adjustments to have a realistic figure of EVA.

- Research & Development (R&D),
- Deferred taxes,
- Depreciation,
- LIFO reserves,
- Goodwill,
- Restructuring expenses,
- Provisions for warranties and bad debts, and
- Leases.

Research and Development: NOPAT figure calculated from P&L account is adjusted by adding back the after-tax R&D expenditure and capitalising them in the balance-sheet. Only those R&D expenses that have no future value are charged to the income statement. The amount included in the capital is amortised over a period during which benefits of the successful R&D projects will be reaped.

Deferred Taxes: Deferred taxes arise due to the difference in timing of recognition of revenues and expenses for financial reporting *versus* reporting for tax purposes. It is basically the accumulation of the difference between accounting provision of taxes and the amount actually paid under the head 'Reserve for Deferred Taxes'. NOPAT is adjusted for the tax actually paid instead of the accounting provisions. The reserves for deferred taxes are added to the equity.

Depreciation: The straight line depreciation of physical assets work acceptably well in GAAP accounting. But in calculating EVA using straight line depreciation can create a powerful bias against investment in new equipment. That's because the EVA capital charge declines in step with the depreciated carrying value of the assets, so that old assets look much cheaper than new ones. This can make managers reluctant to replace "cheap" old equipment with "expensive" new gear. This distortion can be eliminated by replacing straight-line deprectiation with sinking-fund depreciation. Under sinking fund schedule the annual depreciation charge follows the same pattern as the principal payment in a mortgage, starting out small in the early years and rising rapidly in the last years. The sum of depreciation charge and the EVA capital charge remain constant from year to year, just like a mortgage payment. The switch to sinking fund depreciation, which effectively makes owning an asset look just like leasing, eliminates any bias against new equipment. It also happens to be much closer to economic reality. So long as the depreciation charges are not excessive, the deviations from reality are inconsequential ordinarily that they do not distort decisions, no adjustment is needed. It is only in case of excessive depreciation charge that accounting profit figure need to be adjusted.

LIFO Reserves: For calculating EVA the LIFO system of inventory valuation, adopted by the companies during periods of rising price to save taxes, is changed to FIFO basis which is a better basis for estimating current replacement costs. NOPAT and Equity are adjusted for this change from LIFO to FIFO by adding the difference between the LIFO and FIFO inventory (or LIFO and FIFO cost of goods sold) to the equity and NOPAT. These way tax benefits of LIFO are retained

Goodwill: The annual amortisation is added back for calculation of NOPAT while the accumulated amount of amortisation is added back to equity equivalents. Goodwill amortisation is handled in this manner because by "unamortising" goodwill, the rate of return reflects the true cash-on-yield. In addition, the decision to include the accumulated goodwill in capital improves the real cost of acquiring another firm's assets regardless of the manner in which the acquisition is accounted.

Restructuring Expenses: Restructuring expenses and such other expenses which will benefit the firm in the long-run are capitalised and written-off over period.

Operating Leases: Operating leases are to be capitalised.

Provision for Warranties and Bad Debts: Adding back the provision for warranty claims and bad debts is also made to convert the GAAP profits into economic profits. They are accounted for on the cash basis. While the above adjustments are common in EVA calculations, other items that may require adjustments depend on company-specific activities. For example, when operating leases rather than financing leases are employed, interest expense is not recorded on the income statement, nor is a liability for future lease payments recognised on the balance sheet. Thus, while interest is implict in the yearly lease payments, an attempt is not made to distinguish it as a financing activity under GAAP.

Invested Capital

Capital being used in EVA calculation is not the book capital. It is defined as an approximation of the economic value of all funds invested in going-concern business activities. It is essentially a company's net assets (total assets less non-interest bearing current liabilities), but with three adjustments:

- Marketable securities and construction in progress are subtracted.
- The present value of non-capitalised leases is added to net property, plant and equipment.
- Certain equity equivalent reserves are added to assets:
- Bad debts reserve is added to receivables,
- LIFO reserve is added to inventories,
- The cumulative amortisation of goodwill is added back to goodwill,
- R&D expense is capitalised as a long-term asset and smoothly depreciated over 5 years (a period chosen to approximate the economic life typical of an investment in R & D).
- Cumulative unusual losses (gains) after taxes are considered to be a long-term investment.

Weighted Average Cost of Capital

In the calculation of basic EVA the third major component is Weighted Average Cost of Capital (WACC) that is calculated by the formula given below:

$$\text{WACC} = \frac{K_i \dfrac{B}{V} + K_e \times \dfrac{S}{V} + K_P \times \dfrac{V}{P}}{V}$$

where,

K_i = Effective cost of debt,
K_e = Cost of equity capital,
K_p = Cost of preference capital,
B = Value of debt,
S = Value of equity capital,
P = Value of preference capital, and
V = Total value of the firm.

Cost of debt capital is the discount rate that equates the present value of after-tax-interest-payment cash outflows to the curtent market value of debt capital.

i.e.,

$$k_i = \frac{\text{Total interest expenses (1–Effective Tax Rate)}}{\text{Beginning Total Borrowing}}$$

Cost of preference capital is the discount rate that equates the present value of after tax dividend payment cash outflows to the current market value of preference share capital.

Calculation of cost of equity is little tough as compared to that of cost of debt and cost of preference capital. There are numerous theories to calculate cost of equity capital, out of those, Capital Asset Pricing Model (CAPM) is the most widely used method of calculating the cost of equity capital and the same method has been used in the study also. Under CAPM,

$$K_e = r_f + \beta(r_m - r_f)$$

where,

r_f = Risk – free rate,
$r_m - r_f$ = Equity–Risk Premium
$\beta(r_m - r_f)$ = Specific Risk Premium, and
K_e = Risk–free rate + Specific Risk Premium

While CAPM is a widely used formula for the pricing of investment risk, it does not fully capture risks found to systematically impact the return on stocks. This pricing omission has led to the use of multi-factor risk models that include common factors in addition to market-risk (the only risk considered by the CAPM).

In short, the process of computing EVA can be well explained as consisting of the steps mentioned below:

1. Calculate NOPAT,
2. Identify Company's Capital,
3. Determine a reasonable Capital Cost Rate, and
4. Calculate Company's EVA.

Another point to be noted is that EVA calculated as per the methodology explained is a rupee figure and not a percentage i.e., EVA measures the absolute rupee value of wealth created or destroyed. Hence, it is very clear that measurement of EVA is really a challenge in itself. To help reduce the complexity of the EVA calculation, Benett Stewart offers a practical guide to estimate a firm's net operating profit after tax (NOPAT) and its invested capital. In this context, he shows equivalent "bottom-up and top-down" approaches[1] to estimate a company's net operating profit after taxes along with equivalent "asset and financing" approaches to estimate invested capital. Exhibit 1 shows some of the key accounting adjustments in the equivalent NOPAT approaches recommended by Stewart. (See on Exhibit 2.1)

In the "bottom-up" approach to estimate NOPAT the manager or investor begins with operating profit after depreciation and amortisation. This is just the familiar earning before interest and taxes (EBIT) figure in a company's income statement. To this amount, several value-based accounting adjustments are made to arrive at a closer approximation of the firm's pre-tax cash operating profit. For example, the rise in the LIFO reserve account is added back to operating profit to adjust for the overstatement of cost of goods sold—due to an over statement of product costing—in a period of rising prices, while the net increase in research & development expenditure is added back to operating profit to recognize that R & D investment generates a future stream of benefits.

Likewise, the change in accumulated goodwill amortisation is added back to pre-tax operating profit to reflect

Exhibit 2.1
Calculation of NOPAT from Financial Statement Data

A. Bottom-up approach:

Begin:
Operating profit after depreciation and amortisation

Add:
Implied interest expense on operating leases
Increase in LIFO reserve
Increase in capitalised research and development
Increase in accumulated goodwill amortisation
Increase in cumulative write-offs of special items

Equals:
Adjusted operating profit before taxes

Subtract:
Cash operating taxes

Equals:
NOPAT

B. Top-down approach

Begin:
Sales

Subtract:
Cost of good sold
Selling, general and administrative expenses
Depreciation

Add:
Implied interest expense on operating leases
Increase in equity reserve account
Other operating income

Equals:
Adjusted operating profit before taxes

Subtract:
Cash operating taxes

Equals:
NOPAT

Sources: G. Bennett, Stewart III, The Quest for value, New York, Harper Collins, 1991.

the fact that goodwill is a form of capital investment that needs to earn a cost of capital return just like expenditures on physical capital. In a value-based (economic profit) context, annual corporate restructuring write-offs (a "special item") get added back since they are viewed as a form of restructuring "investment". Also the implied interest expense on operating leases is a form of debt financing. In other words, the implied interest expense on operating leases should be reflected in the firm's cost of debt financing, rather than showing up in its unlevered net operating profit. However, in industries where operating leases are common and similar in financial magnitude, such as in certain segments of retail for example, the manager or investor should use judgement to decide whether the leasing adjustment will materially enhance the accuracy of the economic profit calculation for company comparisons.

From an EVA tax perspective, the rise in a company's deferred tax account (obtained from the balance sheet) should be subtracted from reported income taxes to adjust for the over-statement of actual cash taxes. Also the tax subsidies received of debt financings (including debt equivalents such as operating leases) should be added back to reported income taxes to arrive at a more accurate representation of the cash taxes paid by an unlevered firm. As explained before, tax subsidies received by a company from debt financings show up in the after-tax cost of debt and must therefore be excluded in the estimation of NOPAT. Upon making the "bottom-up" accounting adjustments, the manager or investor arrives at a company's NOPAT by subtracting cash operating taxes from adjusted operating profit before taxes.

In the "top-down" approach to estimate NOPAT, the manager or investor begins with sales or revenue. Usual income statement items such as cost of goods sold, selling, general and administrative expenses, and depreciation are then subtracted from this figure. Next, the EVA items that we mentioned before—including the rise in "equity reserve" accounts (e.g., increase in LIFO reserve and accumulated goodwill amortisation) as well as implied interest expense on operating leases—are added to the EVA income statement to obtain a more accurate measure of the firm's pre-tax cash operating profit. As with the bottom-up approach, cash operating taxes are then subtracted from adjusted operating profit before taxes to arrive at a company's net operating profit after tax (NOPAT).

A look at Exhibit 2.2 reveals the companion EVA accounting adjustments that must be made to arrive at invested capital. Based on the "assets" approach, the manager or investor begins with net short-term operating capital. This reflects

EXHIBIT 2.2

Calculation of Capital using Accounting Financial Statements

A. Asset approach

Begin:

Net short-term operating assets

Add :

Net plant and equipment
Other assets
LIFO reserve
Capitalised research and development
Accumulated good will amortisation
Cumulative write-offs of special items
Present value of operating leases

Equals:

Capital

B. Sources of financing approach

Begin:

Book value of common equity

Add:

Equity equivalents
Preferred stock
Minority interest
Deferred income tax
Equity reserve accounts

Add:

Debt and Debt equivalents
Interest-bearing short-term debt
Long-term debt
Present value of operating leases

Equals:

Capital

moneys tied up in current asset accounts like accounts receivables and inventories as well as a normal amount of cash needed for operations. Current liability accounts such as accounts payable, accrued expenses and taxes payable are netted from the short-term operating asset accounts. Notes payable are excluded from net short-term operating capital because they represent a source of debt financing. Also, their interest cost is reflected in the calculation of a company's rupee cost of capital.

Net plant, property and equipment is then added to capital along with other assets and several equity-based reserve accounts. Some managers or investors may choose to adjust property, plant and equipment to a gross basis by adding back accumulated depreciation in an effort to eliminate differing depreciation policies and to approximate replacement cost of assets. Obviously, the accumulated depreciation adjustment would be made in both asset and financing approaches to calculate capital along with an appropriate annual depreciation 'add-back' to arrive at NOPAT.

As shown in Exhibit 2.2, the equity reserve adjustments to arrive at invested capital include (but are not limited to) the add-back of LIFO reserve, accumulated goodwill amortisation, capitalised research and development and cumulative write-off of special items like restructuring and re-engineering costs. Unfortunately, some companies view a write-off of restructuring costs that result in a reduction of capital as an immediate boost to return on invested capital and then prefers progress in operations. However, unless there is an outright asset disposal, with proceeds received in the sale or liquidation, then this latter adjustment is critical for objective company benchmarking and analysis. Additionally, the present value of operating leases, if any, would be added to the EVA balance sheet to arrive at a company's overall invested capital.

In the sources of "financing" approach, the analysis begins with the book value of common equity. To this, he or she adds several "equity equivalent" accounts including preferred stock, minority interest, deferred income tax reserve, and the equity reserve accounts that were listed in the "assets" approach to invested capital. Debt and debt equivalents are then added to arrive at a value-based figure for invested capital. These debt-related accounts include interest bearing short-term debt, long-term debt, and (as before) the present value of operating leases. Either way—the assets or financing approach—we arrive at invested capital for use in calculation of a firm's economic value added.

2.3 THE USES OF EVA

To judge share performance and to make share selection decisions the EVA tool can be used in four different ways:

(i) Analysing Historical Trends

EVA can measure a company's historical success in creating shareholder wealth. This success depends on two variables:

- Invested capital, a measure of a firm cumulative historical investments adjusted for economic depreciation.
- (ROIC-WACC), the extent to which a firm's return on capital exceeds its costs.

EVA can be calculated in two ways:

EVA = NOPAT – (WACC × Invested Capital), or

EVA = (ROIC – WACC) × Invested Capital

where ROIC = Return on Invested Capital

= NOPAT/Invested Capital

The ideal company not only earns superior returns, as measured by (ROIC- WACC), but also has unlimited investment opportunities. Unfortunately, the universe of companies is small. The more prevalent situation is that either a company's return or its investment opportunities are limited.

Some companies have produced significantly positive EVA by investing in a large number of projects with returns only modestly above the cost of capital. Companies have achieved excellent results by investing in a number of high-return projects. When a company is making an acquisition decision, in order to add value to shareholders, the acquisition target has to have a higher ROIC than the existing operation or have synergy with existing operations which can increase the company's ROIC. By looking behind the EPS numbers, EVA analysis can spot changes in economic profit that point to improving or deteriorating performance. For example, a company can continue to grow earnings per share if it invests in a sufficient number of projects, whether or not these projects exceed the weighted average cost of capital. Investors have demonstrated an ability to spot such situations and eventually penalise value—destroying companies with progressively and lower P/E ratio. In this respect, EVA analysis is particularly useful because it does not depend on one's ability to predict the future but depends on one's ability to analyse facts. To spot emerging trends in a company's performance, the return on invested capital can be measured incrementally from one year to the next. This measure which equals (NOPAT (t) – NOPAT (t–1)/ Invested Capital (t–2), is analogous to a first derivative in calculus. In order to examine the usefulness of this measure, we will see how the incremental capital dropped of a company from 75% in 1995 to a value destroying 15% in 1999, a far sharper drop that is experienced by return on invested capital.

Particulars	*1994*	*1995*	*1996*	*1998*	*1999*
ROI Incremental Capital	8%	75%	35%	20%	15%
ROI Invested Capital	7.7%	10.9%	14.6%	13.8%	12.5%
Average P/E Ratio	98%	68%	57%	50%	45%

The analyst can also use the EVA framework to determine whether companies are creating or destroying shareholder value. A careful analysis can reveal which business or geographic areas are subsiding others in a company.

(ii) Forecasting a Target Share Price

The second use of EVA is to determine whether a share is fairly valued based on a forecast of economic profits. Such a forecast converts discounted EVA into a share price. By discounting future EVA one arrive at 'present value of all future EVA'. The value of a firm resides in:

- Capital invested
- Hidden value of non-consolidated subsidiaries/ associated companies
- NPV of future stream of EVAs
- NPV of terminal EVA

Enterprise value of a firm is defined as follows:

Enterprise value = Invested Capital + Present value of all future EVA.
Also, Enterprise value = Market value of debt + Market value of equity.

As Enterprise value equals value of Debt plus Value of Equity, the share price can be calculated from Enterprise value by backing out debt. If the share is fairly valued, the Present value of all future EVA should equal Market Value Added.

(iii) Quantifying Competitive Advantage Period

Share prices in many cases may reflect a long competitive advantage period. Analysts can use the value driver model to look at their assumptions regarding risk and CAP.

Value of a company's share price = Value of current operations + Value of forward plan
V = NOPAT/WACC+1^AA (ROIC–WACC) x CAP/WACC (1+WACC).
where 1^AA = Annualise new investment in working capital and fixed assets net of depreciation.

By using this model, analysts can see the assumptions the share price is making with regard to any of the variables. The analyst can plug for the ROIC, WACC or the CAP components. The model can also tell analysts when a business should increase debt levels or restructure aggressively.

(iv) Examining Excess Returns and Its Impact on Valuation of a Share

Another way of exploring the explanatory power of the

value drivers in an EVA model is to perform a regression analysis of invested capital (ROIC) minus the weighted average cost of capital (WACC) spread as the independent variable and enterprise value to invest capital as the dependent variable. If the ROIC to WACC spread is the key driver of the Enterprise Value to invested capital multiple, it would appear worthwhile to consider how an analyst might gain a competitive advantage. Dismissing the WACC part of the equation to simplify the analysis, ROIC moves into the spotlight. ROIC, in turn can be broken down into NOPAT divided by invested capital. NOPAT correlates quite well with earnings, and as a result, does not appear to be an area where an analyst can derive a sustainable advantage. Invested capital however tends to get proportionately less attention, and hence may be a better area for analytical focus. The way of gaining an edge as an investor is to understand where the capital is going, how much is going, how much is going there, and with what return that capital will be greeted.

2.3.1 Benefits from using EVA

EVA is more than just performance measurement system. It is also marketed as a motivational, compensation-based management system that facilitates economic activity and accountability at all levels in the firm.

Several benefits claimed for EVA are:

(i) EVA eliminates economic distortions of GAAP to focus decisions on real economic results.

(ii) EVA provides for better assessment of decisions that affect balance sheet and income statement or trade offs between each through the use of the capital charge against NOPAT.

(iii) The motivation to increase EVA made managers more aware of the costs of using capital and the need to manage assets more efficiently and effectively. Thus, EVA acted as a useful guide for both strategic and operational decisions.

(iv) It creates a common language for decision-making, especially long-term decisions. Through its focus on issues that drive value creation, EVA also works as a powerful decision-making tool.

(v) Further, linking performance-related pay to EVA makes it easier to distinguish better performers from weaker ones, encouraged empowerment and a longer term decision perspective, all of which result in the right performance being rewarded in an objective way. Thus, EVA effectively integrates the planning and control functions within an organisation.

Academic researchers have argued for the following additional benefits:

- Goal congruence of managerial and shareholder goals achieved by tying compensation of managers and other employees to EVA measure (*Dierks & Patel, 1997*).
- Better goal congruence than ROI (*Brewer, Chandra & Hock, 1999*).
- Annual performance measured tied to executive compensation.
- Provision of correct incentives for capital allocations (*Booth, 1997*).
- Long-term performance that is not compromised in favour of short-term results (*Booth, 1997*).
- Provision of significant information value beyond traditional accounting measures of EPS, ROA & ROE (*Chen and Dodd, 1997*).

2.3.2 Limitations of EVA

EVA also has its critics inspite of a number of benefits discussed above. Some major criticisms and limitations of this value-based performance metric that have been raised can be mentioned as below:

(i) EVA is biased against new assets. When an investment is made its full cost is taken as capital employed. Depreciation on that reduces profit and EVA remains artificially low. As investment depreciates capital employed and depreciation is reduced thereby increasing profits and EVA.

(ii) EVA is biased in favour of large, low return investments. Large campanies that earn returns only slightly above cost of capital can have bigger EVA than small businesses earning much higher return.
For example, company A has capital employed of Rs. 2000 with NOPAT of 12% whereas WACC is 10%. EVA will be: (2000 × 12%) – (2000 × 10%) = Rs. 40; whereas company B with capital employed of Rs. 200 with NOPAT of 15% with WACC of 10% will have EVA of Rs. 10 (200 × 15%) – (200 × 10%). Thus even though company B has higher rate of return than company A, it has lower EVA as compared to company A.

(iii) As is the case with other financial performance measures, such as return on investment or divisional net income, EVA on its own, is inadequate both for assessing a company's progress in achieving its strategic goals and in measuring divisional performance.

(iv) Using EVA alone to evaluate financial performance may be inappropriate for some firms. For example, for new, high growth companies, such as those in the technology and biotechnology sectors, year-on-year changes in EVA (which may well be negative at times) are unlikely to explain changes in a firm's value, given that value is dependent on future expected cash flows. For these firms, then it is suggested that performance be assessed with reference to both EVA and MVA. Since the latter measure, being market-value based, takes into account future expected cash flow. Thus, using EVA alone to analyse a firm's performance is more suitable for mature companies with substantial assets in place.

(v) EVA cannot be used during times of inflation to estimate actual profitability as EVA based on historic cost accounting is distorted by inflation.

Brewer, Chandra and Hock (1999) cite the following limitations to EVA:

- EVA does not control for size differences across plants or divisions.
- EVA is based on financial accounting method that can be manipulated by managers.
- EVA may focus on immediate results which diminishes innovation.
- EVA provides information that is obvious but offer no solutions in the same way as historical financial statement do.

Also *Chandra (2001)* identifies the following two limitations of EVA:

- Given the emphasis of EVA on improving business unit performance, it does not encourage collaborative relationship between business unit managers.
- EVA although a better measure than EPS, PAT and RONW is still not a perfect measure.

Brewer et. al. (1999) recommend using other performance measures along with EVA and suggest the balanced scorecard system.

Chen Dodd (1997) found that while EVA provides significant information value, other accounting profit measures also provide significant information and should not be discarded in favour of EVA alone.

Biddle, Brown and Wallace (1997) found only marginal information content beyond earnings and suggest a greater association of earnings with returns and firm values than EVA, residual income, or cash flow from operations.

Finally, a key criticism of EVA is that it is simply a retreaded model of residual income and that the large number of "equity adjustments" incorporated in Stern Stewart system may not be necessary *(Barfield, 1998, Chen and Dodd, 1997; O'Hanlon and Peasnell, 1998; Young, 1997).*

Thus, it is very clear that on its own, EVA is not a complete performance measure and will not prevent managers from engaging in dysfunctional behaviour. Like all financial measures, it has also its limitations. However, steps should be taken to minimise these shortcomings by supplementing EVA with other measures, typically non-financial, and by tying incentive pay to group performance. In addition, companies considering implementing EVA must also realise that it is not a cheap, short-term initiative, but one that requires total commitment from top management and a willingness on their part to empower lower level managers and employees.

2.4 EVA *vs.* TRADITIONAL PERFORMANCE MEASURES

Traditional profit-based performance measures have undoubtedly dominated the area of corporate financial performance measurement but so far as the utility of these measures as true indicators of corporate financial performance or as facilitators of shareholders' value creation is concerned, it is very ironical to accept their failure. The list of such measures, e.g., ROI, EPS, NPV, IRR, etc. has proved futile to measure reliably the change in the value of the firm. Many researchers and writers have also recognised the superiority of EVA over traditional performance measures, like, Stern & Stewart, Rappaport, Teitelbaum, Bacidore, Banarjee & Jain, etc. The popularity graph of EVA is touching new heights day-by-day and when compared with the traditional measures it occupies a place of pride on the following grounds:

(i) As a performance measure EVA is most directly linked to the definitive and reliable measure of wealth creation that is Market Value Added (MVA). MVA is in fact the cumulative amount by which a company has enhanced or diminished shareholder wealth. It is the present value of all future EVA. Thus, by increases its EVA, a company increasing its MVA or *vice-versa.*

(ii) ROCE, RONW, ROI, etc. consider only one side of the performance, i.e., the borrowing costs only and not the cost of equity. This leads the decision-makers and financial analyst towards a failure to highlight whether the return is commensurate with the risk of underlying assets that ultimately results into biased and inappropriate decisions regarding rejection of economically profitable project or acceptance of unviable projects. For instance, a company's current ROCE is 20% and it's overall cost of capital is 16%. It receives a new investment opportunity with an estimated ROCE of 18% cost of capital remains the same (i.e., at 16%). To maximise ROCE one will reject the said opportunity. But actually, if accepted it would have added two percent economic surplus to the shareholders' wealth. In another case, the present ROCE of a company is 12% and cost of capital is 16%. It receives a new investment opportunity with an estimated ROCE of 14% with no change in cost of capital. Again, to maximise the absolute return above the cost of capital and not to maximise ROCE the said opportunity will be accepted by the company. But this will destroy shareholders' wealth as shareholders want to maximise percentages. On the contrary, EVA mechanism gives due recognition to the cost of equity in all managerial decisions from board room to the shop floor and thus provides a comprehensive and reliable yardstick to measure the shareholders' value creation (or destruction) by an individual business entity focusing towards maximisation of absolute return above the cost of capital.

(iii) The EVA financial management system eliminates all the inconsistencies among various parameters resulting from the use of different criteria/financial measures for different corporate functions under the typical traditional financial management system, by incorporating all business issues, for instance, reviewing a capital budgeting process, valuing an acquisition, communicating or rewarding management into an integrated criteria of creating value. This would unite all employees in the pursuit of the single goal of creating value. Managers will certainly still have to consider margins, turnover ratios, unit costs and a host of other variables, but the anxiety is always in the context of their impact on EVA. EVA system, thus, covers the full range of managerial decisions against a typical traditional system with inconsistent standards, goals and terminology. The focus on a single measure also simplifies decisions, communication channels get strengthened, decision-making speeded up, team work bolstered and parochial behaviour declined, when every one is putting on the same oar.[2]

(iv) Further, it links the management compensation to the shareholder value in a much refined manner, i.e., with EVA the bonus earned is banked and paid in later years. EVA results that are below target will shrink the banked bonus and *vice-versa*. Thus, EVA-based compensation system ties management's interest with those of shareholders and the value creation notion will permeate the whole organisation.

(v) EVA captures the performance status of corporate system over a broader canvas i.e., to arrive at true profits, cost of borrowed capital as well as cost of equity should be deducted from net operating profits. Further to maximize earnings is not sufficient, at the same time consumption of capital should be minimum/optimum under an EVA-based system.

(vi) The utility of EVA simply does not end by indicating the degree of wealth creation. It goes beyond that, to pinpoint the lacunae in the business performance. A regular monitoring of EVA throws light on the problem areas of a company and thus help managers to take corrective actions.

(vii) EVA does have an extremely important role in strategy formulation. It is used to assess the likely impact of competing strategies on shareholder wealth and thus help the management to select the one that will best serve shareholders. It can be particularly effective in this regard when it is augmented by new tools such as Real Option Analysis, Balanced Score Card, Activity Based costing, etc.

(viii) It also fits well with the concepts of corporate governance and thus is considered to be the best corporate governance system. EVA bonus system does this by giving employees an ownership stake in improvements in the EVA for their divisions or operations. This causes employees to behave like owners and reduces or eliminates the need for outside interferences in decision-making.

(ix) The issue of capital charge compels operating managers to use assets more diligently by focusing directly on the costs associated with inventories, receivables and capital equipment. It enables managers to routinely and automatically consider the cost of capital in every decision and accurately assess the trade-offs between operating costs and capital costs. Combing operating costs and capital costs in a single profit measure that is expressed in rupee rather than a rate of return gives EVA another unique quality. Hence managers could use EVA to guide their future resource allocation decisions and economic income of the firm by any one of the following strategies or a combination of these:

- Improve the return earned on existing capital,
- Invest as long as return exceeds the cost of capital,
- Divest capital when return fail to achieve the cost of capital, and
- Reduce cost of capital by optimising capital structure.

(x) EVA is also ideal technique for companies operating in new-age sectors. The typical knowledge industry is not capital-intensive, and the companies operating in these industries are not faced with too many decisions involving huge amounts of capital. Moreover in such industries return on the capital invested are immediate. As a result, EVA is almost a made-to-order performance metric for the knowledge industries.

Conclusively, EVA is superior to accounting profits as a measure of value creation. It is constructed in such a way that maximizing EVA can be set as a target whereas the traditional measures do not work that way.

2.5 IMPLEMENTATION OF EVA

Implementation of EVA system in an organisation is more than just putting one additional row in income statement, i.e., it does not mean only laying down measurement and computational techniques. It is of course a kind of change process which should be given some management effort. If right actions are taken straight from the beginning then implementing EVA should be one of the easiest change process that a company goes through. The actions might include, e.g.

(i) Gaining the understanding and commitment of all the members of the management group through training and discussing and using this support prominently, during the process.

(ii) Training of other employees, especially all the key persons.

(iii) Adopting EVA in all levels of organisation—it should definitely not be only a tool for the management group.

(iv) Integrating EVA as a bonus base for all employees as it facilitates the process and has favourable effects after the implementation.

Management Commitment Gaining and using EVA

The whole process of opreationlising EVA begins normally with CFO's and CEO's interest in the subject. Thus first step in implementing EVA should be informing the whole management team thoroughly about the subject. "Instead of pouring knowledge into people's heads we need to help them grind a new set of glasses, so they can see the world in a new way". In order to ground EVA as the new way of gauging the financial performance, companies need to avoid setting up "events" where people are simply told about EVA rather it is very important to make sure that everyone understands the concept thoroughly. Just like learning any other skill, there are certain steps and stages that people need to do and learn from before sustainable change occurs, i.e., to implement EVA it is necessary to have managers go through a process of unlearning previous notions about "profitable" behaviours and decision-making processes. They will then need to understand and accept the organisational transformation process that the company will need to undertake using EVA as the vehicle for change. Finally, they will need to understand and accept their role in creating a sustainable future for themselves and the company. After all the managers know exactly what EVA is all about and what differences there are compared to other measures like EPS, RONW, ROCE, ROI and ROA, etc. It is very unlikely that someone is against the concept any longer. After getting the commitment of upper management it is very important to use it. CEO and all the division managers, etc. should signal prominently to their subordinates that they support and believe in the concept.

Employee Training

EVA concept can and often should be told to all employees as the companies that implement EVA eventually realise that the transformational value of using EVA can only be achieved by involving everyone in the companies. Implementing it only at the higher levels of an organisation will have limited, if any, impact on the rest of the organisation. Gone are the days of comment and control management systems where only "management" is expected to make decisions that impact the bottom line. It is the cumulative effect of all of the smaller decisions made throughout the organisation that determine shareholder value. Hence, supervisors should tell about the concept to their subordinates or at least be able to answer most of the questions of their subordinates. Employee training can be done with the help of simplified training material which is produced by some experts, e.g. from financial department.

Taking EVA Downwards

EVA is not even near as powerful as it could be if the concept is not in use at the operating level of the organisation. Often EVA approach helps in opening the eyes of operating employees to see how costly capital is and therefore the working capital can usually be reduced without a similar reduction in revenues. Using EVA in day-to-day operational activities mean that all the actions can be quite easily converted into EVA changes and thus employees would be able to know how to improve EVA.

Bonus Systems for all Employees

Introducing EVA-based bonus systems simultaneously with EVA facilitates the whole change process considerably, since employees are naturally very interested in all that affects their payroll. Bonus systems help also later on in integrating the interest of employees and shareholders and thereby including all the employees to struggle for the common goals. However, in some employee extensive branches it is difficult or impossible to bring EVA-bonus to the level that are stimulating. In that case there is perhaps no sense to introduce any EVA-bonuses for all the employees; but for upper management and key employees EVA-bonuses have almost always favourable and powerful if tailored carefully.

EVA Implementation Process

As a mnemonic device, Stern Stewart has described EVA implementation as a 4-step process also called as 'the 4-M process' and these 4 Ms are:

- Measurement,
- Management system,
- Motivation, and
- Mindset

Measurement: EVA is the most accurate measure of corporate performance over any given period. Any company that wishes to implement EVA should institutionalise the process of measuring the metric regularly. This measurement should be carried out after making the prescribed or otherwise meaningful accounting adjustments using the formula:

$$\text{EVA} = (\text{ROCE}-\text{COCE}) \times \text{Capital Employed}$$

Or

$$\text{EVA} = \text{NOPAT} - \text{WACC} \times \text{Capital Employed}$$

Management System: While simply measuring EVA can give companies a better focus on how they are performing, its true value comes in using it as the foundation for a comprehensive financial management system that encompasses all the policies, procedures, methods and measures that guide operations and strategy. The EVA system covers the full range of managerial decisions including strategic planning, allocating capital, pricing acquisitions or divestitures, setting annual goals even day-to-day operating decisions. In all cases, the goal of increasing EVA is paramount.

Motivation: To instill both the sense of urgency and the long-term perspective of an owner, Stern Stewart advocates the designing of EVA-based bonus system. Basing incentive compensation on improvements in EVA is the source of the greatest power in the EVA system. The only way manager can make more money for themselves is by creating even greater value for shareholders. This makes it possible to have bonus plans with no upside limits. EVA bonus targets are automatically reset each year by formula e.g., next year's bonus will be based on improvement above the new, higher level of EVA. Thus, with an unlimited upside and a bonus that is decoupled from the annual budget, EVA managers are motivated to go for home runs instead of setting for singles, and to make investments with long-run pay-offs.

Mindset: When implemented in its totality, the EVA financial management and incentive compensation system transforms a corporate culture. By putting all financial and operating functions on the same basis, the EVA system effectively provides a common language for employees across all corporate functions. EVA facilitates communication and cooperation among divisions and departments, it links strategic planning with the operating divisions, and it eliminates much of the mistrust that typically exists between operations and finance. The EVA framework is, in effect, a system of internal corporate governance that automatically guides all managers and employees and propels them to work for the best interests of the owners. The EVA system also facilitates decentralised decision-making because it holds managers responsible for and rewards them for delivering value.

Common Mistakes in Implementing EVA

There are a few common mistakes that are often made in implementing or using EVA. Most of them are bound up with either misunderstanding and thus misusing the concept at upper levels or not training all the employees to understand and use EVA.

These common mistakes are:

- Defining capital costs intentionally wrongly,
- Using EVA only at the upper management level, and
- Investing too little in training employees.

Some companies have understood EVA controlling in the same way as ROI controlling; if a unit produces a good return then also capital costs are set at a high level. This kind of procedure is against the whole EVA approach as capital costs are not supposed to set to some kind of target level. The challenges are supposed to build in EVA budgets and not into capital costs because the whole idea is to enable and encourage to make all the investment that offer a return greater than the alternative investments. Also some companies simplify the reporting by building the tax-costs into capital cost rate (so there is no taxes in reporting but capital costs percentage is a little bit higher than the normal one). This is not recommendable due to the following two reasons:

(i) Taxes are calculated wrongly because in this method they depend on capital base and not on the result.
(ii) Capital costs are defined too high and thus in operating activities capital is viewed more expensive than it really is and the optimal inventory, etc. levels are not maintained.

Many companies use and train EVA only at the upper levels of organisation, thereby, a lot of potential at lower levels is lost especially at lower levels in operating activities. Similar 'under capacity situation' is likely if people in organisation are not trained properly and thus employees do not know how to use the concept or are reluctant to use it. Although EVA is a simple concept, it will not be used properly if the advantages and justification of EVA is not told to employees. Now-a-days all the employees are so well educated that they can easily understand and accept EVA if it is properly told to them. The capacity of ordinary employees is usually underestimated and therefore this kind of things are not even tried to explain to all employees. Thus, implementing EVA is and at least should be more than just adding one line in the monthly profit report. EVA affects the way capital is viewed and therefore there might be some kind of change in management's attitude. Of course, this depends on how shareholder value focussed the management and the company has been in the past.

While implementing EVA represents some kind of change in organisation, it should be implemented with care in order to achieve understanding and commitment. It is vital that group level managers gain first thorough understanding from the characteristics of the concept, how these characteristics affect controlling and above all, in what kind of situation the SBUs are currently from the viewpoint of these characteristics. Before implementing EVA to any SBU, the group management ought to access whether the business units are currently cash flow generators in mature businesses or companies in rapidly growing businesses. This assessment should absolutely include careful estimation of the relative age and structure of the assets in order to know whether the current accounting rate of return is over or understating the true rate of return. Only thereafter the concept be properly tailored to the unique situation of each individual business unit. The group level managers ought also to know how to support the strategic goals of a SBU with EVA and how to create value with EVA in this individual SBU.

In fact adopting EVA simply as a performance measurement metric, in the absence of some ideas as to how you are going to create value, isn't going to get us anywhere.

2.6 OUTLINE OF THE STUDY

2.6.1 Objectives and Scope of the Study

The study attempts to examine how the Economic Value Added (EVA)—a measure of corporate performance which is considered to be the best indicator of shareholder value creation is correlated with the firm's performance in terms of other financial measures such as Return On Capital Employed (ROCE), Return On Net Worth (RONW), Earnings Per Share (EPS) on the one hand and the share prices on the other hand.

In the context of the above stated need and scope, the study has been conceived with the following objectives:

1. To examine the relationship between EVA and other financial variables – ROCE, RONW and EPS.
2. To assess the superiority of EVA over traditional measures of corporate financial performance.
3. To examine the relationship of share price with EVA, RONW, ROCE and EPS.
4. To evaluate EVA accounting and reporting practices being followed by Indian companies

To accomplish the objectives of the study, the following null hypotheses have been developed for empirical testing:

Ho 1 There is no significant difference between the financial performance results exhibited by the value-based measure—EVA and the profit-based measures EPS, RONW and ROCE.

Ho 2 There is no significant correlation between share prices and financial variables—EVA, EPS, RONW and ROCE.

Ho 3 EVA disclosures in the published annual reports of Indian companies are not satisfactory.

2.6.2 The Sample

The study began with a universe of 500 companies—the top Indian companies termed as India's biggest wealth creators as per the BT Stern-Stewart ranking, the most accurate report card of India Inc's ability to create (or destroy) wealth.

1. After the first phase of scrutinisation it eliminates the companies for which the requisite financial data is not

available for at least 3 out of 5 financial years covered in the study.

2. Further, it eliminates those companies whose financial year is ending either in the month of September or December but not in the month of March.
3. Additionally, it also eliminates those companies which are not manufacturing.

Hence, the study has used a fairly representative classification of sample companies having uniform accounting year. Out of 154 companies 70 companies have been having data for 5 years, 50 companies for 4 years and 34 companies for 3 years, i.e., availability of data is ensured for at least 3 out of 5 financial years of the study. In all, 154 companies have been finally selected in the study.

2.6.3 Source and Type of Data

The data has been taken for 154 companies having a listing status, either in BSE or in NSE, from a database package PROWESS of CMIE, the Centre for Monitoring Indian Economy, a Bombay-based research firm.

The values of EPS, ROCE and RONW have been taken as given in the database while EVA has been computed using the Stern-Stewart formula, where EVA is the net operating profit after tax, less the charge[3] on economic capital employed. Values of dependent variable—share price has also been taken as given in the PROWESS.

The yearly time series data has been used to examine the relationship between EVA and other measures—EPS, RONW, ROCE on the one hand and between EVA and share prices on the other.

2.6.4 Time Frame for the Study

The data has been taken for the period 1998 to 2002, i.e., 5 years, on an yearly basis for both accounting and economic variables of the companies selected for the study. The share prices of the sample companies have been taken as the average of high, low, opening and closing values of that financial year.

2.6.5 Identification of Study Variables

For the purpose of statistical analysis of the relationship between share prices and EVA, the market price of shares has been taken as the dependent variable and the independent variables have been classified into two categories, i.e., Accounting variables and Economic (value-based) variable. The set of accounting variables include variables like earnings per share, profitability (as measured by Return On Net Worth, Return On Capital Employed). The set of economic variables includes Economic Value Added (EVA)—the true measure of shareholders' wealth.

2.6.6 Method of Investigation and Analysis

To analyse the data various statistical tools have been used. Mean, Standard Deviation, Correlation Coefficient, Coefficient of Determination have been employed to have an idea of the general profile of the variables. To examine the relationship between EVA and the selected accounting variables—RONW, ROCE and EPS, Karl Pearson's coefficient of correlation has been used. Regression Analysis has been used to examine the relationship between EVA, EPS, ROCE and RONW with share prices. The data has been computer analysed using SPSS package and MS-Excel. To determine the proportion of explained variation in the share prices the coefficient of determination (R^2) has been worked out. The significance of R^2 has been tested with the help of F-value. To find out the percentage contribution of each independent variable in explaining the variation in share prices, Multiple Regression has been used.

Notes and References

1. James, L. Grant and James, A. Abate, Focus on Value: A Corporate and Investor Guide to Wealth Creation, John Wiley & Sons, New York, 2001.
2. Chakrabarti, Ahindra (2000), "Economic Value Added (EVA): Performance Metric to Sustain Competitiveness," *Global Business Review*, 1:2, pp. 279-99.
3. Capital charge has been applied on the ending economic capital.

CHAPTER

3

EVA as a Corporate Philosophy

3.1 OVERVIEW

Economic Value Added, if adopted as a corporate philosophy, can be very useful in improving productivity of a firm—measured in terms of creation of shareholders' wealth. An appropriate corporate philosophy should result in goal congruence and should channelise all efforts of the management and employees towards a common goal. Over the years management experts and consultants have proposed many tools and techniques for improving productivity. Some of the most notable of these are:

- Management Information System (MIS),
- Business Process Reengineering (BPR), and
- Enterprise Resource Planning (ERP) etc.

Almost all these tools and techniques are used to improve productivity in physical terms. BPR by simplifying existing processes and eliminating non-value added activities, MIS by improving the quality and flow of information and ERP by ensuring efficient allocation and utilisation of enterprise resources and ignore the value concept, i.e., these tools fail to distinguish between value-creating and value-destroying activities because they do not measure economic surplus being generated by different activities. Moreover, successful implementation of these tools and techniques across the firm is a long drawn process and possibility of success is not very high. In contrast, EVA when used as a corporate philosophy improves business literacy because of easy understandability and conceptual clarity. Business literacy is the effort of management to convey to all the employees the fact that for any activity to be value enhancing, the return should be greater than the cost of capital employed for that activity. This small shift in the outlook of employees immediately raises the threshold limit of the acceptable returns. The one component consideration of the cost of capital, sets EVA apart from other tools and techniques. Further, when used as a corporate philosophy it does not come in the way of building the EVA culture in an organisation. Compensation methods based on EVA work better in achieving the objective of goal congruence and minimise the agency cost. It also helps employees in conducting self-examination of every action taken by them rather than being controlled by managers explicitly and induces managers towards value creation activities. Use of EVA improves financial corporate governance in the sense that it motivates a manager to get rid of value destructing activities, and to invest only in those projects that are expected to enhance shareholder value. Hence, it may be concluded that EVA should be used as a corporate philosophy, to improve the internal governance of a firm.

3.2 EVA IN BONUS SYSTEMS

With the increasing emphasis on corporate performance and of shareholders' value, newer value-based metrics like EVA have evolved to identify corporate winner and losers. In order to win the battle for creating a sustained market advantage, committed executives are required. It is evident that when we talk of executives their compensation and a method that links compensation to corporate performance occupies prominence. Unless a well defined method of evaluation, where performance is rewarded and non-performance is discouraged, is made clear to executives, sustained corporate performance could be in limbo. One such desired bonus system is surely the EVA bonus system. The bonus plan under EVA-based system is devised following three tenets. Managers are rewarded for increasing EVA related to target and they are penalised for falling short. These three tenets act as guides in their decision-making. The rules are : (1) to improve operating profits without tying up any more capital, (2) to draw down more capital on the line of credit as long as the additional profits are more than the cost of capital, (3) to free up capital and pay down the line of credit so long as any earnings below cost of capital. With EVA bonus system the target performance level becomes objective. Bonus can be paid according to some percentage of possible EVA or according to some percentage of improved (positive) EVA. Traditionally, bonuses are often subjective, because they are based on the negotiated budgets. The managers negotiating their potential performance level. This is because revealing the real potential would mean smaller bonus. With objective and unlimited bonus level, the managers have an incentive to maximise performance and value instead of sandbagging their potential and wasting time and effort in managing earning and the expectations of corporate office. Tying incentive compensation to EVA rather than to budget helped streamline the budgeting and planning processes. No more fussing around in the fall for months, messing around with a huge planning documents and worrying about sandbagging and things like that. It is gone. Interest of having budgets drive bonuses, the bonus system ought to drive the budgets, and, here the EVA bonus system suits the most, management's bonuses linked with the objective target performance level proves beneficial both to management and shareholders. Performance level is likely to rise often introducing such bonus system (EVA-based) and so as the bonuses paid to management, the better it is for shareholder, as EVA bonus is far from a cost to shareholders—it is often a share in the discretionary value created.

EVA bonus systems are also good in decreasing agency problems. Management of a subsidiary wants usually to invest in their business as much as headquarters allow. Not many management teams conclude voluntarily that they do not have enough good investment projects and thus it is better to give the period's free cash flow out as dividends. Even if there would not be enough good investment projects, the subsidiaries would like to keep the excess capital in their balance-sheet as liquid assets (or invest it in not so-good projects). With enough motivating and rewarding EVA-based bonus system the management aimed to avoid this kind of behaviour. That is because all capital producing a return less than WACC decreases their bonuses, i.e., if the incentives tied to the change of EVA, excess capital in current assets or over investments in mature business can do a lot of harm to bonuses, EVA-based bonus system unite the interest of management and shareholders because EVA measure the ultimate aim of any company.

With EVA-based bonus system it becomes possible to pay managers for performance. Private entrepreneurs, the managers of their own firm got paid just as they make money. Some successful entrepreneurs got rich and there is no set limit to their income level. Corporate managers can have large amount of capital under management. However they are not paid accordingly, i.e., with the line of the shareholder wealth increases. Even a little improvement in capital might imply a big improvement in shareholder wealth in absolute measure. Some of this kind of big improvement should be paid out of managers in order to pay according to performance. In practice that would mean paying more than currently to good performers and less to bad performers. Further EVA-based bonus system can be well explained to be a method to link the growth of productivity to payroll with line workers. If part of the positive EVA is always handed over to employees by paying them according to the change in productivity, they might be able to realise the connection between company's productivity (profitability) and their own payroll. EVA bonuses could also bring some elasticity in the payroll of workers. When the state of the market is good the employees get bonuses and when the state of the market is not so good there are no bonuses since there are positive EVA. Good bonuses could prevent, if negotiated that way, some oversized wage increase demands. On the other hand, if wage increases go over the growth of productivity it is not possible to reach positive EVA and then there would be no bonus. In that sense, the rise of the EVA-based bonuses follows quite well the increase in company's productivity.

Feasible EVA-based bonus system must possess the under-mentioned characteristics to be enough motivating and rewarding to the management:

(i) The bonuses for corporate managers should always be tied to long-run EVA. The long-run can be incorporated into EVA-based bonuses by "banking" the bonuses. This implies that when EVA is good the managers earn a certain percentage of it, but the bonus should not be paid out to them entirely e.g., only one-third of the bonus should be paid out to managers and the rest, two-thirds should be put in a bonus bank. In the following years managers earn again a certain bonus and this bonus is also put in the bank and then managers are paid one-third of the bonuses in the bank. Each year the earned bonuses increase the balance in the bank and managers are paid one-third (or whatever the percentage is) of the accumulated bonuses. If the periodic EVA-based bonus is negative, then the bonus put in the bank is negative and it decreases the balance already earned. This exposes the managers partly to the risk the shareholders are used to bear. At the same time it gives golden handcuffs to the good performers (with big positive balance in the bank) and encourages the bad performers (with negative balance in the bank) to leave the company.

(ii) EVA-based bonuses should be consistent from year to year. If management earns big bonuses along with outstanding results, the bonus system should not be altered in order to reduce these bonuses in the future.

(iii) To have desirable effects bonuses ought to be motivating. Positive EVA, if reached, can and should be truly rewarding, i.e., top performers get big bonuses. If a business unit operates already at positive EVA, the hurdle should be raised and bonus would follow only after the target EVA is exceeded. Other possibility is again to tie bonuses to the change of EVA.

(iv) The bonuses should not be capped, nor should they have diminishing marginal return. It would certainly not motivate the managers to reach for stars if the bonus is limited to certain amount of money; rather the bonuses should follow the movement in EVA figure. Thus, EVA-based bonus systems neither have limits, nor would it be wise to make the bonuses raise with decreasing rate if certain EVA-target is exceeded. It should deviate from linear only if it has increasing marginal return.

(v) Management rewards, i.e., bonuses should be tied to year-to-year change in EVA instead of absolute values. A bonus system based on change in EVA emphasises the focus on continuous improvement.

(vi) EVA-based bonuses should always be tied to the current situation of the business unit in question. Some business units might have mature line of business with strong positive periodic EVA and thus imminent danger of wasting the ample free cash flow via over-investments in mature business. Other business units in turn might have plenty of profitable investment opportunities and good prospects of profitable investment opportunities and good prospects of long term EVA although weak current EVA. The bonus system ought to be formulated so that it does not fight against strategic goals. If EVA do not fit in the business unit's current situation it should be left out.

3.2.1 A Few Possible EVA-based Bonus Patterns

Depending on the nature and kind of a particular business unit following may be the positive EVA-based bonus patterns:

Example 1:

Amount of bonus earned for each year

$$= \text{Absolute EVA} \times Z\% + \text{Periodic change in EVA} \times 5\% \times Z\%.$$

Amount of bonus will be put in bonus bank every year. The bonus paid is 1/3 of the current balance in the bank.

Change of EVA will increase bonus only if the EVA is positive. Improving negative EVA does not bring any bonus unless EVA increases above zero.

Example 2:
Annual bonus earned = Change in EVA x Y%

The amount of bonus will be put in bonus bank every year. The bonus paid is 1/4 of the current balance in the bank.

Example 3:
Amount of bonus earned for each year
= (EVA – Target EVA) x Z% + Change in EVA x 5 x Z%.

The amount of bonus will be put in bonus bank every year. The bonus paid is 1/3 of the current balance in the bank. "Target-EVA" can be e.g., current EVA or Current EVA plus something or some other EVA level determined by group managers.

3.3 EVA AND OTHER COST MANAGEMENT TECHNIQUES

ABC, the Balanced Scorecard and EVA are modern tools for performance measurement and management that are being used by many companies across the world. In this section we will first discuss ABC and Balanced Scorecard in brief and then find out whether the ABC, Balanced Scorecard and EVA frameworks are mutually exclusive or interrelated with each other and can be used together in the same organisation or not.

Activity-based Costing: ABC is a cost measurement system that provides a cost for each product, service or customer by analysing each activity needed to produce a product or service a customer. This costing system address the drawback in the traditional cost accounting systems. The traditional cost systems are based on a few cost drivers, usually direct labour or direct machine hours and do not accommodate the recent changes in business environment. As an organisation's product and customer mix becomes more diverse, the assignment of overhead expenses becomes grossly misleading, distorting the costs of individual products/services. As a result, many manufacturing organisations have cost systems, which can support financial reporting, but provide distorted information about the individual products. This sends the wrong signal to decision-makers. In such a scenario, ABC provides useful insights for decision-making. ABC can be used in any type of organisation. It is most useful, though when an organisation has complex transfer pricing issues, high indirect costs and shared processing stations. Procter and Gamble makes use of ABC technologies to identify per case of inefficient industry practices, and the amounts that can be saved by improving those practices. Process reengineering programs often follow an ABC analysis, with streamlined processes, reduced cost and higher quality pursued.

The difference from traditional methods is illustrated in Figure 3.1. For example, a product that has a short processing cycle may use a disproportionate amount of inventory space or time on the receiving dock. When indirect costs are allocated to products based on the wrong cost driver product will appear less or more expensive than they actually are. ABC is used to identify all activities, direct and indirect, and allocate the costs associated with these activities more precisely.

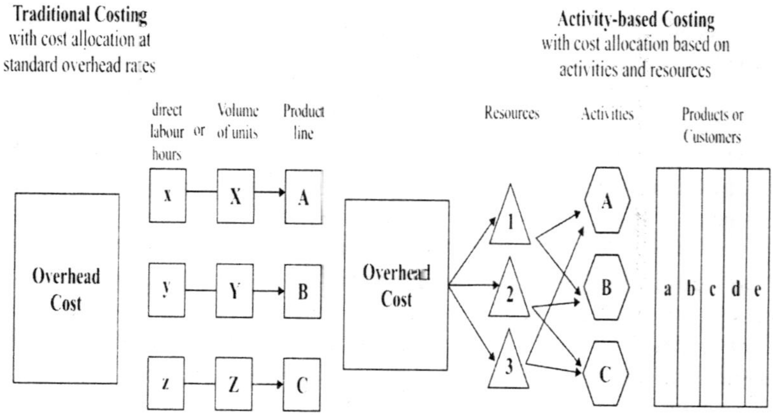

FIG. 3.1
A Comparison of Traditional and Activity-based Costing System

Many ABC systems are designed to capture costs that appear on the P & L statement only. One may agree that this approach is flawed because it provides incomplete information. One must also capture the cost of capital employed to produce a certain product or serve a certain customer. For example, if a customer insists on extended terms of payment, the additional carrying cost of Accounts Receivable associated with this customer must be captured in the ABC system. Managers must focus on cost and capital. But even when a typical ABC system is upgraded to include the cost of capital, it still provides an incomplete picture. While the cost aspect is vital, managers need to understand the impact on revenues, volumes, customer satisfaction, market position, employee morale and many other factors. Therefore, cost information alone, regardless of how accurate it is, is insufficient to maximise value. Managers need to understand how costs interact with other performance indicators before they can improve the performance of their business units. This ties into the Balanced Scorecard.

The Balanced Scorecard

The Balanced Scorecard was created by Robert Kaplan and David Norton to translate vision and strategy into objectives. It provides a broader view of the business and recognises the need to identify and track a number of financial and non-financial measures to provide a broader view of the business. For this purpose, an organisation is not limited to accounting data. A company may select indicators of process efficiency, safety, customer satisfaction or employee morale. This can capture information about current performance and emphasise leading indicators of future success. The objective is to produce a set of measures matched to the business so that performance can be monitored and valuated. The Balanced Scorecard is meant to help managers keep their finger on the pulse of the business. Each organisation will emphasise different measures depending on their strategy. Management, is, in effect, translating their strategy into objective that can be measured.

The scorecard is a collection of data that helps a manager to understand performance. The measures help managers balance their focus in-between current and future performance.

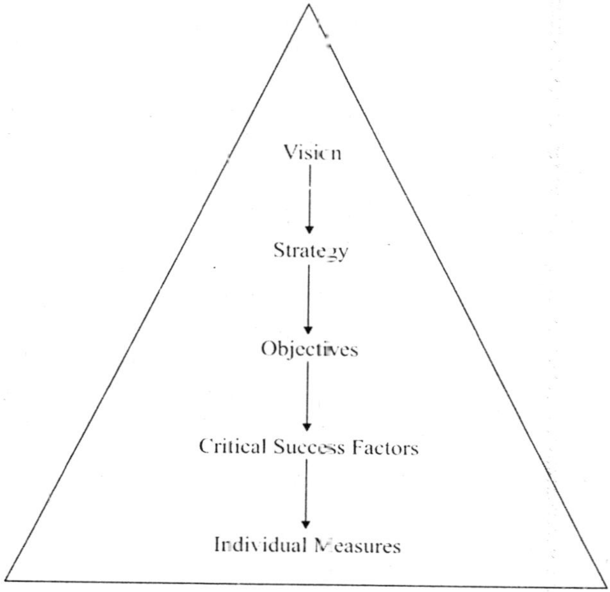

FIG. 3.2
The Balanced Scorecard Links Strategy to Measures

Leading variables are future performance indicators, and lagging variables are historic results. Financial measurements are typically lagging variables, telling managers how well they have done. On the other hand, an example of a leading indicator is training costs, which influences customer satisfaction and repeat business. Some variables exhibit both lagging and leading characteristics, such as on time deliveries (a lagging measure of operational performance and a leading indicator of customer satisfaction). The balanced scorecard usually has four broad categories, such as financial performance, customers, internal processes and learning and growth. Typically, each category will have two to five measures. If the business strategy is to increase market share and reduce operating costs, the measures may include market share and cost per unit. Another business may choose financial indicators that focus on price and margin, willingly foregoing market share for a higher-priced niche product. These measures should be set after the strategy is in place. A list of objectives, targets, measurements and initiatives with each variable are as shown in Figure 3.3. The saying "we manage what we measure" holds true. One reason the balanced scorecard works is because it raises awareness.

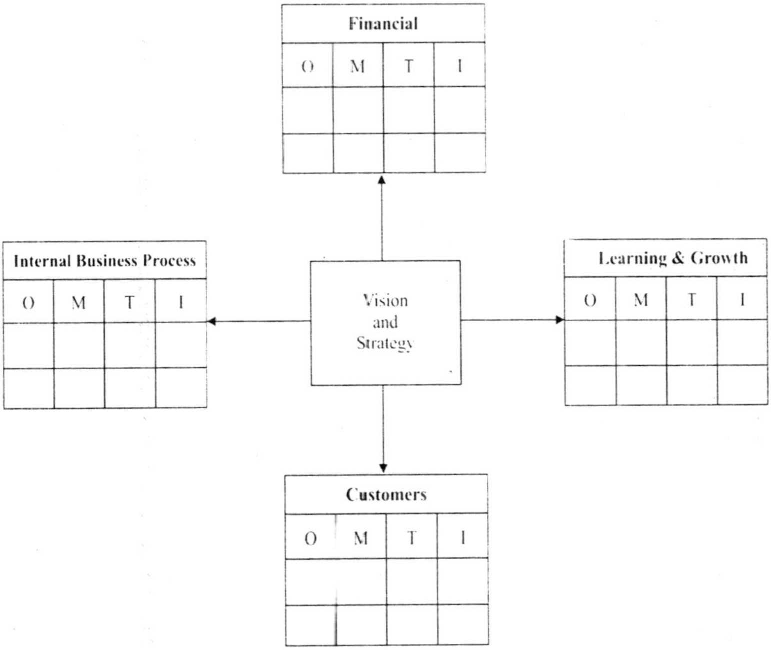

O = Objectives
M = Measures
T = Targets
I = Initiatives

FIG. 3.3
The Balanced Scorecard Translating Vision and Strategy : Four Perspectives

The balanced scorecard, if properly implemented, is an excellent management framework that can help managers to track the many factors that influence performance. But it lacks a single focus for accountability. Management needs one overriding goal to summarise the interaction between the variables and, ultimately, determine success. EVA tells us whether managers have balanced the scorecard measures "right" and as Kaplan says, "Creating EVA is the ideal outcome of a successful strategy, and that's what we are trying to do".

ABC, BS and EVA: The Balanced Scorecard and EVA are useful tools that can help a company to achieve greater success in the current dynamic and competitive business environment. These three frameworks are quite complementary. ABC can help managers understand the cost and capital impact of their decision. The Balanced Scorecard broadens the view of performance to include financial and non-financial indicators of both a leading and lagging nature. EVA provides a link between decisions, performance measures and rewards, which focuses managers on performing better. Managers perform best when they have the information, decision frameworks, performance measures and rewards that motivate them to behave like owners. Regardless of whether one of these tools has been implemented, the other two should be considered. In business, a manager must manage many inputs, and both ABC and the Balanced Scorecard help managers to make decisions. But EVA is needed to determine whether we win or lose. By using EVA for decisions, performance measures and rewards, managers are motivated and use the information at hand to act as owners and create value.

3.4 CONCLUSION

Economic value added measures corporate performance in terms of change in value. It measures whether the operating profit is enough compared to the total cost of capital employed inclusive of the cost of equity. It is calculated as the surplus of Net Operating Profit After Taxes (NOPAT) after adjusting for capital cost. Certain adjustments are to be made to a company's accounting profits and capital so as to reveal the true economic position of that company. Accounting for principles gives a lot of flexibility to corporate in accounting for certain matters like valuation of inventory, R & D expenses, depreciation, etc. Hence, accounting profits may not reveal the true economic position of a company. The proponents of this concept have identified 164 adjustments to accounting figures for a realistic estimate of EVA subject to the significance of amount, ready availability of required information and understandability by non-finance professionals as well. This adds complications to EVA calculations as most enterprises do not maintain indepth data required for these adjustment and even if it is maintained it is not easily accessible to outsiders. Even for insiders having access to the data, hiring of a consultant becomes essential that involves incurrence of additional costs. Thus, to keep the matters simple and to reduce their complexity these 164 odd adjustments have to be scaled down to around 10 to 15 adjustments based on the relevance and incremental information that they offer, like R&D, Depreciation, Goodwill, LIFO reserves, restructuring expenses, operating leases, provisions for warranties and bad debts, etc. The mechanism of EVA is very simple. It shows the rupee amount of wealth a business has created or destroyed in each accounting period. Positive EVA implies that the firm has created value over the period of question and if EVA is negative, it indicates that the firm was a value destroyer. A company having consistently high EVA implies that it has been successful in creating value for the business. On the other hand, a company having oscillating EVA or consistently negative EVA indicates that there is something wrong with the company.

The number of companies adopting EVA is increasing rapidly worldwide. Even in the academic world it is topic of the hour for the researchers. Studies have been conducted specially abroad on some aspects. The subsequent chapters endeavour to empirically analyse this relationship in context of the Indian Corporate sector during the period 1998-99 to 2002-03.

CHAPTER 4

Studies on Economic Value Added

4.1 OVERVIEW

Economic Value Added (EVA), a patented word by the NewYork-based consulting firm, Stern Stewart and Co. is drawing increasing attention everywhere. In India also it has emerged as a critical tool to measure and monitor corporate performance. The word value has existed from time immemorial in trade, industry and commerce. Over the years as trade, industry and commerce have developed from subsistence level to higher value creation level, the term 'value' has emerged as a consistent measurement tool for economic entities. The concept of EVA has got wide acceptance as a key indicator of performance today since industry is shifting from the product-centric world of the past to a value-centric world of the future. Hundreds of companies worldwide now use EVA, and evidence shows that most of them significantly outperform other companies in their industries.

The academic world outside India has come up with various empirical studies on EVA and related issues, like, supporting the superiority of EVA over the traditional performance measures, narrating the relationship between EVA and share prices or explaining the features of an EVA-based bonus system or even criticising and questioning the claim of its proponents. However, there is not much research available on this topic relevant to the Indian conditions since it is a phenomenon that has gained popularity only during the last decade. An extensive review of literature has been carried out in this chapter to enhance the present level of understanding of the concept and to formulate the problem for further research in this area. Broadly, the literature review has been done on empirical studies in books, journals, published papers, etc. In Section 4.2, the studies conducted outside India have been reviewed and summarised and in Section 4.3, literature though limited has been reviewed on studies conducted in India. The final Section 4.4 gives the conclusion of the chapter.

4.2 STUDIES CONDUCTED ABROAD

The ensuing research work in literature roughly falls into the following three categories:

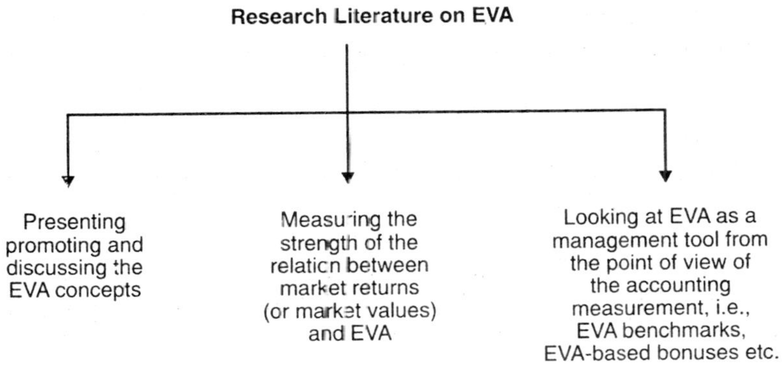

FIG. 4.1

4.2.1 EVA Concepts

Anderson Anne M., Bey Rogu P. and Weaver Samuel C. have conducted a study addressing the consistency, sensitivity and validity of EVA as a measure of economic value. A major consideration in the application of EVA is the adjustment of a large number of accounting variables but unfortunately there is no economic theory to guide the selection of the most relevant variables. The relevant set of variables is dependent on the financial structure and nature of the given firm. The objectives of this study are: (1) to determine whether accounting adjustments significantly impact EVA; (2) to determine the sensitivity of EVA to accounting adjustments and to identify which adjustments are most critical; and (3) to determine the impact of accounting adjustments on the explanatory power of EVA.

Four hundred and eighty companies with complete data in Compustat and the Stern Stewart 1000 listing in *the Journal of Applied Corporate Finance* for the period of 1988-97 were studied. For each year and each company, the EVA (with and without adjustments) and MVA were calculated in accordance with G. Benett, Stewart III. The results of the study indicate that EVA adjustments are very unstable both on an individual basis and on when aggregated. The instability makes it difficult to apply EVA in a consistent manner either over time within a given company or across companies. EVAs lack of an economic basis or comparison standard prevents carrying out any tests concerning the economic significance of the adjustments. Also, the strong relationship between adjusted and unadjusted EVAs questions the need or significance of even attempting to identify and/or apply EVA adjustments. The need to select and tinker with the accounting adjustments may lead to the application of the golden rule, that is "He/She who has the gold, makes the rules." In this case he/she who makes the adjustments may collect the gold. The potential for EVA agency costs exists and the economic significance of accounting adjustments is unanswered.

Bacidore, et al. (1997)[1] observed the refined economic value added (REVA) provides an analytical framework for evaluating operating performance in the context of shareholder value creation. EVA performs quite well in terms of its correlation with shareholder value creation, but REVA is a theoretically superior measure for assessing whether a firm's operating performance is adequate from the standpoint of compensating the firm's financers for the risk to their capital. A comprehensive statistical analysis of both REVA and EVA is used to promote their correlation with and their ability to predict shareholder value creation. REVA statistically outperforms EVA in this regard.

H. Fred Walker[2] presented a new and evolving method for capital equipment cost justification of Advanced Manufacturing Technology (AMT)—"Economic Value Added Analysis" (EVA). The key distinguishing feature of EVA is that it does account for the value of equity stakeholders have in such projects. Accordingly, EVA promises to help professionals from many functional backgrounds (i.e., Finance, Accounting, Production, Engineering, etc.) recalibrate the methods they use in the allocation of financial resources. After describing in detail the concept of EVA and the (AMT, both of the common financial tools are reviewed, an analysis equating EVA to Present Worth (PW) and Annual Worth (AW) is made, a case applying EVA in an actual cost justification of AMT is discussed. It is observed that the most common financial tools used throughout industry today for capital equipment cost justification (i.e., PW and AW) are not inconsistent with the EVA analysis. Rather the analysis produce equivalent results when calculated at the same interest rate. What EVA does offer, however, is a more realistic picture of the true cost of using capital—whether that capital is borrowed or is available within an organisation. As ITs continue to work in dynamic environments, the methods used to conduct business and remain competitive change. EVA represents a means to ensure that capital is allocated in the most efficient and effective manner possible. And since it is frequently called upon to justify the cost of capital equipment and/or AMT, updating the tools they will be able to bring to bear in the industrial environment must remain a priority.

Narcyz Roztocki and Kim Lascola Needy presents a cost and management performance measurement system that integrates the Activity-Based Costing (ABC) method with the Economic Value Added value-based financial performance measure. This system is an engineering management tool that helps to successfully manage cost and capital. It allows enterprise leaders to create shareholder value through cost structure improvement. In this ABC-and-EVA system, the cost of activities does not only include the rate of consumption of resources, as it does in a traditional ABC system, but also capital demand. To implement this system following steps have been given:

- Review the company's financial information through obtaining its income statement and balance-sheet,
- Identify the main activities describing the manufacturing and business processes of the company that consume operating resources or are responsible for capital investments,
- Determine operating cost for each activity,
- Determine capital charge for each activity using Activity Capital Dependence Analysis,
- Select cost drivers, and
- Calculate product costs inclusive of operating costs and capital costs.

Nicholas A. Wood[3] observed that EVA is more than just an internal business performance measure or a basis for determining incentive pay. If implemented fully, it represents a comprehensive financial management system that integrates planning and control activities and provides a common language for decision-making. With its emphasis on value creation, it closely aligns the goals of management and shareholders and provides an objective means for instituting performance-related pay. In the South African context, this latter benefit will assume greater importance as the call for transparency in directors' remuneration increases. Like all financial measures, EVA has its limitations. On its own, it is not a complete performance measure and will not prevent managers from engaging in dysfunctional behaviour. However, steps can be taken to minimise these shortcomings by supplementing EVA with other measures, typically, non-financial and by tying incentive pay to group performance. In addition, companies considering implementing EVA must also realise that it is not a cheap, short-term initiative, but one that requires total commitment from top management and a willingness on their part to empower lower level managers and employees.

Salmi, Timo and Ilkka Virtanen[4] evaluated and compared EVA with traditional profitability measures within a controlled simulation framework. It is observed that EVA is very sensitive to its cost of equity component, but it is unexpectedly insensitive to its cost of debt component under regular conditions. EVA and its variability are observed to be strongly affected by the firm's growth policies because of leverage effects. EVA is observed to be much more unstable than the traditional return on investment and directly related to the return on equity measure. Traditional financial ratios are commonly used for distress prediction. It is observed that EVA does not have incremental value in the predicting.

Stern (1990)[5] observed that EVA is the financial performance measure that comes closer than any other to capture the true economic profit of an enterprise. It is the performance measure most directly linked to the creation of shareholder wealth over time. EVA-based financial management and incentive compensation system gives manager superior information and superior motivation to make decisions that will create the greatest shareholder private enterprise.

Tully (1983)[6] observed that there is nothing fancy or complicated about how to make EVA go up. It is a fundamental measure of return on capital, and there are just three ways to increase it: earn more profit without using more capital, use less capital and invest capital in high return projects. Rewarded by knockout results, managers and investors are peering into heart of what makes business valuable by using a tool called EVA.

Mayfield (1997)[7] observed that shareholder value is enhanced by investing in all those projects which give a positive NPV and by harvesting all those existing products and projects whose return on capital is less than encouraging management and employees to create long-term value. While the accountants are familiar with the concept of residual value, its application in Economic Value Measurement (EVM) as a means of evaluating underlying business performance is nothing short of an overhaul of traditional accounting concepts. When effectively applied and implemented it provides an excellent tool for strategy planning, investment appraisal, pricing decision and a basis for incentive compensation.

Booth (1997)[8] observed that economic profit should be a part of company's performance measurement framework. Value-based management and shareholder value analysis are well known concepts—responses to shareholder activism in the 1980s—but there is now a renewed interest in them and also newer related concepts such as EVA. In the past, many corporate strategies have been criticised for destroying shareholder value. One way to reduce the risk of this is to build an analysis of shareholder value into selection of corporate strategy.

Putnam (1997) observed that to understand why investors were right to be bullish on US equities in 1995 and 1996, and why 1997 may be much more volatile year, one can examine the equity market essentially if it were a single big company. To do that, a framework of analysis, such as, EVA is extremely useful. EVA focuses on five key factors to analyse how shareholders' value is created: net operating profit after tax and before financing costs, the weighted average cost of capital, investments in the business, the rate of return on investments and the competitive advantage period.

Teitelbaum (1999)[9] observed that EVA has moved from a buzzword to financial phenomenon. As a performance measure, as an analytic tool and as a management discipline, EVA is cropping up all over. Community hospitals harness EVA to improve efficiency. Lots of many managers use it to pick stocks. Even the US Postal Service employs EVA to help run its operations.

4.2.2 Relationship between EVA and MVA

This section reviews the literature to highlight the correlation between EVA and MVA to see the strength of the relation between market-returns (or market value) and EVA compared to the relation between market returns and the traditional income measures.

O'Byrne (1996) concludes that EVA, unlike NOPAT (net operating profit after taxes) or other earnings measures like net income or earnings per share, is systematically linked to market value. He capitalised EVA as independent variable in a regression where market value divided by capital is the dependent variable. He finds that the level of EVA explains 31% of the variance in market value, whereas the level of net operating profit after taxes explain only 17%. When looking at changes in EVA and market value O'Byrne finds that changes in EVA explain 55% of variations in changes in market value. Changes in NOPAT explain only 33%. It should provide a better predictor of market value than other measures of operating performance.

Chen and Dodd (1997)[10] conclude that EVA measures provide relatively more information than the traditional measures of accounting in terms of the stock return association. In their study ROA explained stock returns best with R-squared of 24.5%. The R-squared for other metrics are: EVA 20.2%. Residual income 19.4% and EPS, ROE approximately 5-7% but that EVA should not entirely replace the traditional measures since measures such as P/E, ROA and ROE have incremental value in monitoring firm performance. They also observe that there is no significant difference between EVA and the traditional RI in terms of the association with stock returns. The study is based on 566 U.S. companies from 1983-92.

Milunovich and Tsuei (1996) review the correlation between MVA and several conventional performance measures in the computer industry. They find EVA to correlate somewhat better with MVA than the other measures. R-squared is for EVA 0.42, for EPS growth 0.34 and for ROE and EPS 0.29.

Grant (1996)[11] calculates regression statistics between the MVA-to-Capital and EVA-to-Capital ratios from the data of 983 firms. He finds explanatory levels (R-squared) of 32% with statistical significance. Regressing MVA-to-Capital and the spread between return and cost of capital reveals R-squared of 37%.

Luber (1996)[12] observed that MVA tends to move in tandem with the market. So it's no surprise that vast majority of the companies on the list, buoyed by one of the longest bull markets in history, have done quite well. For second year in row, Coca Cola ranks as the top wealth creator, cumulatively generating source $87.8 billion for its shareholders. General Electric, again in the second spot, has generated $80.8 billion. Motorola plummeted from the tenth spot to 21st destroying $3.4 billion of shareholder wealth in the process. Studies have shown that a company rates up positive EVA year after year will see it's MVA soar, while negative EVA will drag down MVA as the market loses faith that company will ever provide a decent return on invested capital. The top five wealth creators on the list—Coke, GE, Microsoft, Merck and Philip Morris, all of whom have strong EVAs will continue to do well in the years to come.

Lehn and Makhija (1996)[13] study EVA and MVA as performance measures and signals for strategic change. Their data consists of 241 U.S. companies and cover years 1987, 1988, 1992 and 1993. The researchers first find out that both measures correlate positively with stock returns and that the correlation is slightly better than with traditional performance measures like return on assets (ROA), return on equity (ROE) and return on sales (ROS). Additionally they study how companies' performance, as measured in terms of EVA and MVA, affect on the CEO firings. Finally they examine the relationship between EVA/MVA and corporate focus. Lehn and Makhija find an inverse relation between EVA/MVA and abnormal CEO turnover. They also find that firms with greater focus on their business activities have significantly higher MVA than their less focussed counterpart. They conclude that their results suggest EVA and MVA to be effective performance measures that contain information about the quality of strategic decisions and serve as signals of strategic change.

Uyemura, Kantor and Pettit (1996)[14] from Stern Stewart and Co. present findings on the relationship between EVA and MVA with 100 bank holding companies. They calculate regressions to 5 performance measures including EPS, Net-Income, ROE, ROA and EVA. According to their study, the correlations between these performance measures and MVA are: EVA 40%, ROA 13%, ROE 10%, Net Income 8% and EPS 6%. The data is from the ten-year period 1986 through 1995.

Biddle, Bowen and Wallace (1996)[15] present evidence on the relative and incremental information content of EVA, residual income, earnings and operating cash flow. According to the abstract of the study, the writers conclude that "residual income and/or EVA add incremental information in some settings, but that, on average, neither dominates earnings as a performance measure."

Stewart (1990)[16] has also studied the relationship between EVA and MVA with market data of 618 U.S. companies. He states that EVA and MVA correspond each other in reality quite well among U.S. companies (the data was from late 1980's).

Only the relationship between negative EVA and negative MVA does not hold very well. According to Stewart, this is because the potential of liquidation, recovery, recapitalisation, or takeover sets a floor on a company's market value. For example, with companies which have a lot of fixed assets this is quite easy to understand. Market value will always reflect the value of assets even though the company has very low or negative rate of return (and so theoretically it should sell a lot below book value). That is because the company can always be liquidated; the owners have an option to liquidate the assets if the return looks weak also in the future. On the other hand markets do not believe that the weak returns can go on forever. Markets are expecting a change, an improvement, in the long run. If EVA is positive, the relationship is more direct. Then the market valuation happens on the basis of return and growth potential and not on the basis of liquidation or recovery value. Stewart finds also that MVA and EVA correspond each other best when we talk about changes in EVA and MVA and not the absolute levels. Changes in EVA and MVA are not affected so much by accounting distortions and inflation than the absolute values.

4.2.3 EVA in Management Bonus Plans

Keith Kefgen and Rosemary Mahoney (1996) identified EVA as a new performance measure for linking pay and performance. EVA is a measurement tool that determines if a business is earning more than its true cost of capital. This measurement tool should be used in determining incentive pay as it motivates managers to think like shareholders and the performance always improves when employers have a vested interest in the ownership of the business. Furthermore, rewards are more clearly based on true performance of the business. So far as the implementation of an EVA-based incentive plan is concerned it can be done like any other incentive plan. Sufficient time should be taken while benchmarking EVA criteria, create formulas that are easy to comprehend and then train your employers to remove resistance for its adoption.

Myers (1997)[17] showed that when Quaker Oats Co. made a disastrous $1.7 billion purchase of snapple Beverages Co. in late

1994, it used a discounted cash flow model to evaluate its acquisition, using EVA, a value-based performance metric, as an incentive compensation tool, when evaluating the deal. Using HOLT Value Associates LP's CFROI (Cash Flow Return on Investment) methodology, the suggested price for snapple was $5.55 per share more than Quaker actually paid.

Wallace[18] has examined the effects of adopting management bonus plans based on residual income measures. The sample in the study consists of 40 firms that have some residual income measure mainly EVA, as bonus base. This sample is compared to sample of same size consisting of similar companies where the bonus is tied to accounting based measures. Wallace tests with various methods the management actions in these sample groups and interprets the results as being consistent with a residual income-based performance measure providing incentives for managers to act more like owners, thus mitigating the inherent conflict between manager and shareholders. Wallace's test support the adage, "you get what you measure", with significant increases noted in residual income for the firms adopting residual income-based compensation relative to the comparison group. The firms that adopted residual income-based compensation outperformed the market over the 24 month period by over 4% points in cumulative terms.

4.3 STUDIES CONDUCTED IN INDIA

Ashok Banarjee and S.C. Jain[19] have examined the relationship between shareholder wealth and certain financial variables such as earnings per share, Adjusted Return On Net Worth (ARONW), capital productivity, labour productivity, EVA and MVA. A statistical analysis of the drugs and pharmaceutical industry between 1990-91 and 1997-98 reveals that in every year except 1991-92 and 1997-98, EVA was the most significant variable. During the two years when EVA was not found to be a significant variable, none of the select variables was significant. It has also been established in the study that traditional accounting measures like EPS, ARONW have significant relationship with shareholder wealth.

Niranjan Swain, C.S. Misra, K.R. Jayasimha and S. Vijaylakshmi[20] examined how the Market Value Added (MVA)—a measure of external performance which is considered to be the best indicator of shareholder value creation is correlated with the firm's performance in terms of financial measures of the company such as Economic Value Added (EVA), Net Operating Profit After Tax (NOPAT), Return on Capital Employed (ROCE), Return on Net Worth (RONW), Earnings Per Share (EPS) on the one hand and the purely economic factors of the company such as labour productivity, capital productivity, total factor productivity, sales and R&D expenditure on the other hand. A sample of 28 companies has been taken from pharmaceutical industry during the period spanning 1992-93 to 2000-01. Linear regression analysis has been used to find out the relationship between MVA and different financial and economic measures. The time-series regression has been performed company-wise to explain the variations in MVA. Finally, the regression has been performed over the sample in the long-run. The study concludes that EVA, NOPAT and sales outperform other financial and economic measures in predicting MVA in most of the companies in Indian pharmaceutical industry. However, in the long-run, no evidence is being found to support the above findings for the industry as a whole.

Asish K. Bhattacharyya and B.V. Phani[21] examined whether EVA is a superior performance measure both for corporate reporting in U.S.A. and other advanced economies. It concludes that though EVA does not provide additional information to investors, it can be adapted as a corporate philosophy for motivating and educating employees to differentiate between value creating and value destroying activities. This would lead to direct all efforts in creating shareholder value. They also bring to attention the dangerous trend of reporting EVA casually that might mislead investors.

Dr. A. Vinay Kumar and Dr. Mohinder N. Kaur[22] conducted a study aims to understand the relationship between Indian corporate performance and the present compensation system. It aims to explore the need to connect compensation system to wealth creation. A sample of fifty companies, which form part of popular stock indexes such as NSE Sensex and NSE Nifty were considered. At a basic level, it was studied whether there is any relationship between executive compensation and reported accounting earnings along with stock returns. Then it was studied whether the present executive compensation system is related to dynamic value added parameters like EVA and MVA. The study brings out that executive compensation is related to mundane accounting profits but is not related to dynamic value added parameters like EVA and MVA. Therefore, it stress the need to switch to an EVA method of compensation and attempts to throw open the subject for further inquire.

Manoj Anand[23] surveys 81 CFOs of India to find out about their corporate finance practices *vis-a-vis* capital budgeting decisions, cost of capital, capital structure and dividend policy decisions. The respondents were asked to indicate the relative importance of different objectives of management decision-making in corporate finance in their organisation. While 85.10 percent of the respondents consider the objective to maximise earnings before interest and tax (EBIT) and earnings per share (EPS) as very important/important, 75.90 percent of the respondents consider the objective to maximise the spread between return on assets (ROA) and WACC, i.e., EVA objective as very important/important. Nearly 54 percent of the respondents consider the objective to maximise the spread between cash flow return on investment (CFROI) and the WACC, i.e., CVA objective as very important/important. Approximately 53 percent of the respondents consider the objective to maximise the market value added (MVA) of the firm very important/important. Interestingly, public sector is more likely to follow maximisation of MVA as a corporate objective than private sector (rating of 4.30 *versus* 3.19). Surprisingly, the objective to reduce side costs in the form of conflicts amongst various stakeholders of the firm is not a very popular objective in corporate India. Only 33 percent of the respondents consider it as an important objective.

Capital Budgeting: The firms use DCF methodology for capital budgeting decisions today more than in the pervious times. Most respondents select IRR and NPV as their most frequently used capital budgeting techniques. 85% of the respondents consider IRR as a very important/important project choice criterion. About 65% of the respondents always or almost always use NPV. The payback period method is also popular. There is no difference in the technique used by EVA and non-EVA firms, high WACC and low WACC firms and highly levered and low debt firms. Public sector firms are more likely to use profitability index than the private sector firms.

Cost of Capital: The results indicate that CAPM is the most popular method (54.32%) of estimating cost of equity capital. The second and third most popular methods are Gordon's dividend discount model (52.1%) and earnings yield (34.2%) respectively. Very few firms (7%) use multifactor model to estimate the cost of equity. Further, industry average beta is the most popular measure of the systematic risk being presently used by corporate India. The average market risk premium of 9 to 10% is most widely used by corporate India. The practice of capturing tax advantage of interest on debt in the cost of debt computation is widely prevalent amongst corporate India. Corporate India uses all possible weights in the computation of WACC.

Capital Structure: Retained earnings are the most favoured source of finance amongst the CFOs. Nearly 89% of the respondents consider it very important/important source of finance. Loans from financial institutions and private placement of debt are the next most widely used sources of finance (59% and 32.9% respectively). Equity capital as a source of finance is not preferred by the CFO respondents (16.9%).

Dividend Policy: The results of the survey indicates that 81.50% of the respondents strongly agree/agree that their firm has a long-run target dividend payout ratio. Nearly 85% of the respondents strongly agree/agree that dividend changes in their organisation follow shift in long-run sustainable earnings. Only 46.95% of the respondents agree that the dividend policy is a residual decision after meeting desired investment needs.

Dyal Bhatnagar and Chandra Shekhar[24] have examined whether the findings of previous research studies regarding superiority of EVA hold true in various industries or not? For the purpose of this research, a total sample of 56 companies listed on BSE was drawn and they were classified into five industrial categories. The data pertains to ten years viz. 1988-89 to 1997-98. The multiple regression model was used to explore as to which of the independent variables viz. EVA, EPS, ROCE,

NPV, Kp and Lp was more capable of explaining movements in share prices in each industry. The analysis revealed that EVA was the most significantly related variable with MVA in case of 'Chemical and Pharmaceutical Industry', 'Consumer Goods Industry' and 'General Engineering Industry'. In case of 'Infrastructure Industry', capital productivity (kp) was most significantly related to MVA. The analysis with regard to 'Miscellaneous Industry' revealed that both EPS and EVA were significant variables which explained movements in MVA.

4.4 CONCLUSION

Although there is a plethora of research literature on Economic Value Added (EVA), most of the studies have been done for the corporate world of the developed countries especially U.S.A. In India, very limited research has been done on this hottest financial idea. Very few books are available in context of Indian corporate sector. None of the few studies conducted in India have explored the significance of EVA in predicting share price movements, especially in terms of the relationship between EVA and share prices. The present study makes an attempt to fill these voids and aims to investigate the financial performance of Indian companies during 1998-2002, especially in terms of their capacity to add value to shareholders' wealth. The subsequent chapters are devoted to the achievement of these objectives.

NOTES AND REFERENCES

1. Bacidore, J.M. Boquist, J.A. Milbourn, T.T. Thakor, A.V. (1997), "The Search for the Best Financial Performance Measure", *Financial Analysts Journal*, May/June, 1997, pp. 11-20.
2. H. Fred Walker, 'Cost Justification of Capital Equipment using Economic Value Added Analysis", *Journal of Industrial Technology*, Volume 15, Number 2—February to April, 1999.
3. Nicholas, A. Wood, "Economic Value Added (EVA): Uses, benefits and limitations—A South African Perspective, *Southern African Business Review*, pp. 1-12.
4. Salmi, Timo and Ilkka Virtanen, "Economic Value Added, A Simulation Analysis of the Trendy Owner-Oriented Management—Tool", ACTA WASAENSIA, No. 90, Business Administration 35, Accounting and Finance, 2001.
5. Stern, M. Joel, "EVA is Working", *Business Today*, Sept. 22-Oct. 6, 1997.

6. Tully, Shawn, "The Real Key to Creating Wealth", *Fortune*, Sept. 20, 1993.
7. Mayfield, John (1997), "Economic Value Management", *Management Accounting*, Sept., pp. 32-33.
8. Booth, Rupert (1997), "EVA as a Management Incentive", *Management Accounting*, Oct., Vol. 75(9), p. 48.
9. Teitelbaum, Richard (1997), "America's Greatest Wealth Creators", *Fortune*, Nov. 10, pp. 265-76.
10. Dodd, James L; Chen, Shimin (1996), "EVA: A New Panacea?" *Business and Economic Review*, Vol. 42; July-Sept. 1996, pp. 26-28.
11. Grant, J.L. (1996), "Foundations of EVA for Investment Managers", *The Journal of Portfolio Management*, Vol. 23, Fall 1996.
12. Luber, R.B. (1996), "Who are the Real Wealth Creators?" *Fortune*, December 9.
13. Lehn, K. and Makhija, A.K. (1996), "EVA and MVA: As Performance Measures and Signals for Strategic Change", *Strategy & Leadership*, Vol. 24, May/June, 1996, pp. 34-38.
14. Uyemura, Kantor and Pettit, Justin, "EVA for Bank Value Creation, Risk Management and Profitability Measurement", *Journal of Applied Corporate Finance*, Vol. 9, No. 2, Summer, p. 94.
15. Biddle, G., Bowen, R.M., Wallace, J.S. (1996), "Abstract of Evidence on Relative and Incremental Information Content of EVA, Residual Income, Earnings and Operating Cash Flow", University of Washington, Seattle, WA.
16. Stewart, G. Bennett, "EVATM: Fact and Fantasy", *Journal of Applied Corporate Finance*, pp. 6-19.
17. Myers, Randy (1997), "Metrics Wars", CFO, Vol. 12, Oct. 1997, pp. 41-50.
18. Wallace, J.S. (1997), "Adopting Residual Income-Based Compensation Plans: Evidence of Effects on Management Actions", Working Paper, University of California, Irvine, CA.
19. Banarjee, Ashok and Jain, S.C., "Financial Variables: Measuring Performance", *The Chartered Accountant*, February, 1999.
20. Swain, N., Mishra, C.S., Kumar, M. and Vijayalakshmi, S., "Shareholder Wealth Maximization in Indian Pharmaceutical Industry: An Econometric Analysis", *ICFAI Journal of Applied Finance*, November, 2002.
21. Bhattacharyya, K. Ashish and B.V. Phani, "Economic Value Added: In Search of Relevance, *Decision*, Vol. 27, No. 2, July-December, 2000.
22. Kumar, A. Vinay and Kaur, N. Mohinder, "Executive Compensation and Corporate Performance: An EVA Approach", *South Asian Journal of Management*, Vol. 9, Issue 3, pp. 12-20.
23. Manoj, Anand, "Corporate Finance Practices in India: A Survey", *Vikalpa*, Vol. 27, No. 4, October-December, 2002.
24. Dyal, Bhatnagar and Chandra Shekhar, "In Search of A Potent Measure of Financial Performance Among Indian Industries", www.jimsindia.org.

CHAPTER

5

Economic Value Added vs. Traditional Performance Measures

Shareholders' value creation and maximisation has become the hallmark of corporate parlance. It has emerged as the current and strongest demand of the investors' group. Removal of government protection, stringent legislative control on stock market to take care of investors' interest, increase in competition due to coming up of foreign companies, etc. have compelled the corporate enterprises to direct all their decisions towards shareholders' value maximisation. A sea change has come up in the organisational goals, that is, a shift from the earlier socio-economic issues to newly-minted shareholders' value. The corporate mission statements of companies in India now-a-days have phrases like "enhancing shareholder value", "big is no longer beautiful". Hence the success or failure of a company would be driven by how much value it has created for its' shareholders. The present chapter, therefore makes an attempt to examine the superiority of EVA over the traditional performance measures, to check whether EVA can be finally substituted for EPS, RONW, ROCE, etc. or not in terms of the relationship of all these variables with share prices.

Accordingly, the following null hypotheses have been tested:

Ho 1 : EVA cannot be substituted in place of EPS, RONW, ROCE

Ho 2 : No correlation exists between share price and the financial and economic variables—EVA, EPS, RONW and ROCE

5.1 METHOD OF INVESTIGATION AND ANALYSIS

The study began with the universe of all 500 companies—the top Indian companies termed as India's biggest wealth creators as per the BT Stern-Stewart listing, the most accurate report card of India Inc's ability to create (or destroy) wealth.

After the first phase of scrutinisation it eliminates the companies for which the requisite financial data is not available for at least 3 out of 5 financial years covered in the study.

Further, it eliminates those companies whose financial year is ending either in the month of December or June but not in the month of March. Additionally, it also eliminates the companies falling in the category of non-manufacturing industry.

Thus, an attempt has been made to take up a fairly representative sample group of Indian corporate sector having uniform accounting year. Availability of data is ensured for at least 3 out of 5 financial years of the study. In all, 154 companies have been covered in the study. The list of companies has been given in Appendix V(A) at the end of this thesis.

The requisite financial data used for this analysis has been collected from the CMIE's Prowess database. It is considered as an authentic source of information and has the advantage of easy accessibility, wide coverage and consistency of data. Apart from this, the published annual reports of companies have been used, wherever felt necessary.

Empirical analysis of sample companies has been done for five financial years, i.e., 1998-99 to 2002-03, on an yearly basis as well as over the total period for both accounting and economic variables. The share price is taken as the dependent variable and independent variables have been classified into two categories—accounting variables: EPS, ROCE and RONW; economic variable—EVA.

Shareholder value addition/destruction can be measured in the following two broad ways:

1. Broad value-based performance measure, namely, economic value added (EVA),
2. Traditional profit-based measures, namely, Return on Net Worth (RONW), Return on Capital Employed (ROCE) and Earning Per Share (EPS).

I. Economic Value Added (EVA)

EVA is the quantum of economic value generated by a company in excess of its cost of capital (both debt and equity). It measures whether the operating profit is sufficient enough to cover the cost of capital invested in an enterprise or not. To the extent income after charging for the cost of capital is positive, the firm is adding value to its shareholders but if this income is negative, the firm is destroying value.

EVA=NOPAT – Cost of Capital x Economic Capital

where,

NOPAT = Net Operating Profit after Taxes

These items have been computed in the following way for the purpose of this analysis:

(i) NOPAT = (Profits after Tax + Non-Recurring Expenses + Revenue Expenditure on R&D + Interest Expense + Goodwill Written-off + Provision for Taxes) – Non-recurring Income – R&D Amortization – Cash Operating Taxes.

(ii) Cash Operating Taxes = (Provision for Taxes + Tax Benefit of Non-Recurring Expenses + Tax Benefit of Interest – Tax on Non-Recurring Income).

(iii) Economic Capital = Net Fixed Assets + Investments + Current Assets – (NIBCLs + Miscellaneous Expenditure Not Written-off + Intangible Assets) – (Cumulative Non-Recurring Losses + Capitalised Expenditure on R&D + Gross Goodwill) – Revaluation Reserve – Cumulative Non-Recurring Gains.

(iv) Information on the risk-free rates was obtained from the RBI's annual reports.

(v) Cost of capital is determined by the prevailing interest-rates in the country i.e., the prime lending rates of commercial banks and financial institutions.

(vi) Following adjustments were made to convert book profits and book capital to operating profits and economic capital:

- non-recurring income and expenditure,
- research and development,
- goodwill,
- interest,
- non-interest bearing current liabilities (NIBCLs),
- investments in marketable securities,
- investments in subsidiary companies.

2. Return on Net Worth (RONW)

Return on Net Worth (RONW) is a relatively narrow measure of shareholder value creation. It is profit before interest and taxes divided by net worth i.e.,

$$\text{Return on Net Worth} = \frac{\text{Profit before Interest and Tax}}{\text{Net Worth}}$$

where,

Net Worth = Equity Capital Plus Free Reserves and Surplus

3. Return on Capital Employed (ROCE)

It is another measure of shareholder wealth which is based on the narrow criterion of absolute profits only. ROCE is profits before interest and taxes divided by the capital employed i.e.,

$$ROCE = \frac{PBIT}{CE}$$

where,

PBIT = Profit before Interest and Taxes
CE = Total Capital Employed by a Company

4. Earning Per Share (EPS)

$$EPS = \frac{\text{Net Profit available to Equity Holders}}{\text{Number of Ordinary Shares Outstanding}}$$

where,

Net Profit available to Equity Holders = Earnings before Interest and Taxes – Interest – Tax Liability – Preference Shareholders' Dividend

The accounting and other information recorded for each company for these measures have been given in Appendix V(B).

5. Share Price (SP)

The share price of the 154 companies has been taken as the average of high, low, opening and closing values of that financial year. Since no huge transitions had occurred in the trends of share prices over the period considered, the fluctuations are not far-off from the obtained average value.

To make the data comparable absolute EVA figures have been converted into relative figure by applying the following formula:

$$EVACE = \frac{EVA}{CE} \times 100$$

where,

EVACE = Economic Value Added as Percentage of Capital Employed
EVA = Economic Value Added
CE = Capital Employed

The following analysis has been carried out for the sample companies for five years using the value added metric – EVA and the traditional metrics – RONW, ROCE, EPS and the share prices:

1. Intra-firm comparison over the study period to see if shareholder value has improved over five financial years.
2. Inter-firm comparison for average five years period to see who are the winners/losers in terms of shareholder value creation/destruction.
3. Establish relationship between traditional performance measures – RONW, ROCE, EPS and the new economic performance metric – EVA with the help of Pearson's correlation coefficient. Further, the superiority of EVA over ROCE, RONW and EPS is examined using coefficient of determination.
4. Establish relationship, if any, between the financial and economic variables – EPS, ROCE, RONW, EVA and the share prices. For this purpose, regression analysis has been used.

5.2 EMPIRICAL RESULTS

5.2.1 Value-Added Performance Results

This section presents the results of value-added performance of sample companies using the performance metrics namely, EVA, ROCE, RONW, and EPS. These detailed empirical results are given in Appendix V(C). First, the value of these metrics has been computed for each firm for the five years. Then the analysis is extended to cover inter-firm comparison as well.

(i) Intra-firm Comparison with EVA, RONW, ROCE and EPS

An examination of financial performance of one hundred and fifty-four sample companies reveals, on an average, negative value is created in term of economic performance (EVA) and positive value in terms of accounting profitability

(RONW, ROCE) as shown in Table 5.1. This table gives the computed values of EVA, RONW, ROCE and EPS for these firms for five cross-sectional financial years.

The variations across these five years in terms of all the four performance metrics, namely, EVA, ROCE, RONW and EPS has been examined by employing the statistical technique of clusture analysis. The firms, as per this technique, are classified on the basis of particular characteristic into groups or clusters/ so that items within the group are fairly and sufficiently more homogenous than across different clusters. The technique, in this case has been applied by categorizing the firms into following three groups for each performance metric separately.

Group I: Companies with Value Addition/Increased Profitability

This group consists of firms where trend of increasing value addition/profitability across five years period has been observed. This indicates the improvement in financial performance of firms in terms of shareholder value addition.

Group II: Companies with Value Erosion/Decreased Profitability

This group includes firms where trend of decreasing value addition/profitability across the study period has been observed.

Group III: Companies with no relation to Value Addition/Erosion or Increased/Decreased Profitability

Companies which do not show any clear-cut (i.e. either of increasing value addition/profitability or of decreasing value addition/profitability) trend in five years are categorised in this group.

Observations from Table 5.1

1. EVA and Intra-firm Comparison

EVA has been computed for all sample firms for five financial years to see whether shareholder value has improved

TABLE 5.1
Intra-firm Analysis with Economic and Accounting Variables

A. Intra-firm Analysis with EVACE

Company Name	*EVACE*					*Average*
	Year 1	*Year 2*	*Year 3*	*Year 4*	*Year 5*	
(1)	*(2)*	*(3)*	*(4)*	*(5)*	*(6)*	*(7)*
Aarti Drugs Ltd.	0	-2.92	-7.09	-3.79	-160.64	-34.888
Aban Loyd Chiles Offshore Ltd.	0	0	-6.62	-3.87	-4.17	-2.932
Advani-Oerlikon Ltd.	-3.5	0	0	-5.58	-4.52	-2.72
Ambalal Sarabhai Enterprises Ltd.	-38.74	0	-29.41	-31.71	-20.94	-24.16
Amtek Auto Ltd.	0	0	-6.02	-0.56	1.1	-1.096
Apollo Tyres Ltd.	-8.38	5.99	-3.45	-8.76	-6.64	-4.248
Asian Paints (India) Ltd.	-4.53	-1.21	2.61	0.92	6.31	0.82
Asian Star Co. Ltd.	0	0	-18.99	-18.83	-15.03	-10.57
Associated Cement Cos. Ltd.	0	-16.01	-21.09	-13.39	-7.69	-11.636
Aurobindo Pharma Ltd.	14.59	8.56	12.15	5.42	1.3	8.404
B A S F India Ltd.	-14.82	-8.12	-8.17	-5.71	-3.13	-7.99
B S E L Information Systems Ltd.	0	23.76	24.06	-2.33	-23.17	4.464

(Contd.)

TABLE 5.1 (*Contd.*)

(1)	(2)	(3)	(4)	(5)	(6)	(7)
B S E S Ltd.	-9.98	-6.58	-6.42	-5.05	-1.96	-5.998
B S L Ltd.	0	0	-8.62	-3.82	-14.05	-5.298
Bajaj Auto Ltd.	-16.28	-5.14	-7.03	-10.07	-4.7	-8.644
Bajaj Tempo Ltd.	-21.77	-37.77	0	-30.87	-8.75	-19.832
Balkrishna Industries Ltd.	0	0	0	-12	-6.28	-3.656
Balmer Lawrie & Co. Ltd.	0	0	-9.56	-6.14	-7.41	-4.622
Berger Paints India Ltd.	-2.01	-3.87	-4.12	-1.25	3.45	-1.56
Bharat Electronics Ltd.	0	-0.93	0	5.64	5.11	1.964
Bharat Forge Ltd.	-10.96	-18.12	-9.19	-4.06	-4.25	-9.316
Bharat Heavy Electricals Ltd.	0	-14.06	-16.39	-30.28	-6.9	-13.526
Bharat Petroleum Corpn. Ltd.	0	-1.36	-2.28	-2.35	2.47	-0.704
Birla Corporation Ltd.	-25.58	-30.07	-21.87	-15.53	-10.93	-20.796
Birla Ericsson Optical Ltd.	-4.41	-4.46	-12.42	-8.54	-10.59	-8.084
Blue Star Ltd.	-8.31	-7.08	-5.39	-0.87	7.3	-2.87
Bongaigaon Refinery & Petrochemicals Ltd.	0	-12.35	-11.5	-26.45	-93.5	-28.76
Britannia Industries Ltd.	-8.2	-2.13	1.78	0.62	10.21	0.456
C M C Ltd.	0	-11.75	-9.19	-26.84	-14.42	-12.44
Cadila Healthcare Ltd.	0	2.08	0	-3.21	-4.2	-1.066

Carrier Aircon Ltd.	4.18	8.13	-15.23	-18.93	-28.25	-10.02
Ciba Specialty Chemicals (India) Ltd.	-16.93	-6.37	-8.31	-5	1.67	-6.988
Cipla Ltd.	-3.07	1.65	2.11	5.98	8.03	2.94
Clariant (India) Ltd.	0.72	7.28	6.1	5.44	8.27	5.562
Colgate-Palmolive (India) Ltd.	-9.22	0.42	-8.8	-1.59	7.79	-2.28
Colour-Chem Ltd.	-7.16	-6.43	-3.83	-11.72	-9.57	-7.742
Cosmo Films Ltd.	0	0	-12.35	-2.97	2.7	-2.524
Crompton Greaves Ltd.	-16.52	-12.3	-36.99	-37.01	-9.03	-22.37
Cummins India Ltd.	-2.33	-6.85	0.39	0.34	-3.18	-2.326
Dabur India Ltd.	-7.47	-4.27	-6.29	1.18	1.96	-2.978
Dr. Reddy's Laboratories Ltd.	-11.53	-7.69	-9.2	6.09	23.79	0.292
Duphar-Interfran Ltd.	-5.16	-0.1	0	-15.01	-4.61	-4.976
Eicher Motors Ltd.	-32.27	-0.19	0	5.13	7.64	-3.938
Eimco Elecon (India) Ltd.	-7.85	0	0	-2.64	0	-2.098
Electrosteel Castings Ltd.	0	7.29	10.28	-0.42	1.94	3.818
Elgi Equipments Ltd.	-10.85	-9.61	-13.93	-13.2	-6.52	-10.822
Essel Propack Ltd.	0	0	-1.33	-2.56	-7.85	-2.348
F D C Ltd.	-6.62	0	4.92	4.23	9.5	2.406
Floatglass India Ltd.	-27.68	0	-95.3	-38.21	-19.18	-36.074
Gabriel India Ltd.	-14.09	0	-12.15	-7.73	-5.84	-7.962
George Williamson (Assam) Ltd.	0	-11.68	-16.2	-7.45	-8.07	-8.68

(Contd.)

TABLE 5.1 (Contd.)

(1)	(2)	(3)	(4)	(5)	(6)	(7)
German Remedies Ltd.	0.73	7.47	9.16	0	1.33	3.738
Godavari Fertilisers & Chemicals Ltd.	-5.03	0	-17.59	0	-12.59	-7.042
Godfrey Phillips India Ltd.	1.57	0.69	4.52	5.33	3.2	3.062
Goodlass Nerolac Paints Ltd.	-6.4	-6.38	-4.02	-5.99	-4.23	-5.404
Gujarat Sidhee Cement Ltd.	-27.28	-68.89	0	-119.26	-67.14	-56.514
Hero Honda Motors Ltd.	11.83	13.06	20.82	17.17	39.27	20.43
Hi-Tech Gears Ltd.	0	-6.28	0	0	8.53	0.45
Hlkal Ltd.	0	0	4.17	-1.6	0.54	0.622
Hindustan Inks & Resins Ltd.	16.08	11.79	-3.68	-5.87	-2.52	3.16
Hindustan Motors Ltd.	-21.37	-20.55	-25.92	-24.24	-18.72	-22.16
Hindustan Petroleum Corpn. Ltd.	0	-7.82	-2.88	-0.6	-1.24	-2.508
Hindustan Powerplus Ltd.	-13.94	-8.82	-10.95	-10.26	-11.13	-11.02
I C I India Ltd.	-7.09	-7.87	-3.36	0	0	-3.664
I P Rings Ltd.	0	0	0	-7.21	-10.79	-3.6
I T C Ltd.	-3.1	-3.08	9.6	10.71	12.85	5.396
I T W Signode India Ltd.	-22.82	-36.83	0	-3.49	0	-12.628
Ind-Swift Ltd.	0	-6.71	-3.99	0	5.06	-1.128
India Glycols Ltd.	-5.81	0	-6.02	-4.29	-8.71	-4.966

India Gypsum Ltd.	2.87	3.2	0	-8.48	-5.58	-1.598
Indo National Ltd.	2.67	2.53	2.53	-6.12	4.53	1.228
Indo Rama Synthetics (India) Ltd.	-20.34	0	-15.09	-5.6	-3.04	-8.814
Infosys Technologies Ltd.	-11.29	3.26	2.64	16.12	11.63	4.472
Infotech Enterprises Ltd.	0	17.11	-10.92	-5.05	-2.36	-0.244
Ingersoll-Rand (India) Ltd.	3.61	9.32	3.92	-5.17	0.73	2.482
Ipca Laboratories Ltd.	-7.22	-7.19	-7.52	-5.88	0	-5.562
J B Chemicals & Pharmaceuticals Ltd.	-11.25	-4.26	-2.03	2.34	8	-1.44
J K Synthetics Ltd.	0	0	-398.38	105.18	47.12	-49.216
Jayant Agro Organics Ltd.	0	0	8.03	24.94	16.85	9.964
Jubilant Organosys Ltd.	0	0	-12.51	-4.13	-3.97	-4.122
Jupiter Bioscience Ltd.	0	0	-4.46	3.74	4.18	0.692
Kalyani Brakes Ltd.	-15.63	0	-7.45	-5.92	-0.94	-5.988
Krebs Biochemicals Ltd.	11	1.2	-2.16	1.07	4.18	3.058
Lakhani India Ltd.	-14.8	-15.64	-18.34	-16.57	-15.11	-16.092
Lakshmi Auto Components Ltd.	0.63	0	1.22	1.2	5.43	1.696
Larsen & Toubro Ltd.	-12.2	-9.54	-10.36	-8.63	-6.92	-9.53
Lumax Industries Ltd.	0	0	-11.56	-16.06	-7.24	-6.972
Madras Cements Ltd.	-8.13	0	-9.79	-7.34	-6.84	-6.42
Mangalore Refinery & Petrochemicals Ltd.	-24.22	-13.37	-19.66	-17.58	-17.05	-18.376

(Contd.)

TABLE 5.1 (Contd.)

(1)	(2)	(3)	(4)	(5)	(6)	(7)
Medicorp Technologies India Ltd.	0	0	-9.35	-16.65	-21.67	-9.534
Mirc Electronics Ltd.	-11.01	-7.77	-2.51	-6.14	-1.49	-5.784
Mirza Tanners Ltd.	6.18	7.9	0	-4.88	-0.96	1.648
Monsanto India Ltd.	0	6.44	13.98	-6.44	0.83	2.962
Moser Baer India Ltd.	-7.24	-2.23	-10.82	-5.12	-5.61	-6.204
Motherson Sumi Systems Ltd.	-4.44	-4.32	0	0	3.89	-0.974
Munjal Showa Ltd.	-3.42	0.76	-1.34	0	9.61	1.122
N R B Bearings Ltd.	-0.84	-7.67	-6.67	-7.12	-1.94	-4.848
Narmada Cement Co. Ltd.	-21.51	00.77	0	-35.23	-29.6	-24.022
Narmada Chematur Petrochemicals Ltd.	0	-17.04	-16.95	-4.51	-5.21	-8.742
Nava Bharat Ferro Alloys Ltd.	0	0	0	-4.51	-1.22	-1.146
Nicholas Piramal India Ltd.	-5.44	1.4	-5.42	-0.19	9.83	0.036
Nirma Ltd.	-4.75	-0.86	-4.47	-2.54	1.83	-2.158
Novartis India Ltd.	7.77	6.78	10.91	5.93	7.08	7.694
Orient Information Technology Ltd.	1.12	6.93	-13.24	-9.01	-28.22	-8.484
Orient Paper & Inds. Ltd.	-30.27	-28.14	-25.1	-9.41	-6.63	-19.91
P C S Industries Ltd.	0	-14.57	-25.71	-18.75	-24.82	-16.77
Panacea Biotec Ltd.	0	-5.52	6.07	0	3.55	0.82

Parke-Davis (India) Ltd. [Merged]	-15.27	0	6.3	31.51	8.49	6.206
Pidilite Industries Ltd.	3.71	7.06	5.42	4.06	8.22	5.694
Polaris Software Lab Ltd.	0	21.89	-2.9	3.64	0.41	4.608
Premer Instruments & Controls Ltd.	-12.89	-10.24	-4.76	-1.11	-7.76	-7.352
Priyadarshini Cement Ltd.	-10.71	-18.89	-17.59	-5.14	-13.43	-13.152
Punjab Tractors Ltd.	22.46	19.31	17.16	8.27	1.54	13.748
Rallis India Ltd.	-7.47	-8.08	-3.77	-14.12	-12.54	-9.196
Ramco Industries Ltd.	0	-12.13	-36.47	-7.69	-8.34	-12.926
Reliance Industries Ltd.	-11.9	-7.27	-2.20	1.51	-0.76	-4.136
Rico Auto Inds. Ltd.	-4.93	-12.81	0	1	12.74	-0.8
Salora International Ltd.	0	-12.81	-5.23	-11.2	-10.76	-8
Satyam Computer Services Ltd.	-4.78	0.19	-5.4	16.83	1.7	1.708
Shasun Chemicals & Drugs Ltd.	0	0	7.83	-0.92	2.02	1.786
Sona Koyo Steering Systems Ltd.	-13.65	-7.69	-4.88	-10.69	-6.26	-8.634
Sonata Software Ltd.	-3.85	-1.99	7.86	9.87	-8.03	0.77
Sri Vishnu Cement Ltd.	-10.58	-9.33	-23.72	-7.48	-13.74	-12.97
Sundram Fasteners Ltd.	-5.01	-2.18	0	-2.47	2.67	-1.398
Swaraj Engines Ltd.	14.72	17.36	15.93	15.22	19.44	16.534
Swaraj Mazda Ltd.	-10.38	-7.36	-7.2	-4.89	1.75	-5.616
Tamilnadu Telecommunications Ltd.	0	-29.67	-19.18	-11.28	-21.85	-16.396

(Contd.)

TABLE 5.1 (Contd.)

(1)	(2)	(3)	(4)	(5)	(6)	(7)
Tata Elxsi Ltd.	-13.39	-21.09	-14.3	-4.94	6.83	-9.378
Tata Engineering & Locomotive Co. Ltd.	-20.84	-23.11	0	-27.53	-12.64	-16.824
Tata Honeywell Ltd.	-13.67	-5.89	3.85	-5.99	0	-4.34
Tata Infomedia Ltd.	0	-9.47	-6.27	-6.92	-13.15	-7.162
Tata Infotech Ltd.	-0.07	-4.75	-27.84	-19.32	-20.4	-14.476
Tata Metaliks Ltd.	0	0	-5.66	11.89	16.51	4.548
Tata Sponge Iron Ltd.	0	0	-2.08	-2.19	-1.14	-1.082
Tata Telecom Ltd.	-43.27	-43.48	-25.69	-8.83	-3.07	-24.868
Thirumalai Chemicals Ltd.	-13.84	-11.63	-9.35	-12.62	-6.53	-10.704
Timex Watches Ltd.	-19.33	-34.49	-36.06	-1616.77	-225.19	-386.368
Timken India Ltd.	0	-10.08	0	-4.87	-16.1	-6.21
Titan Industries Ltd.	-12.18	-9.13	-12.97	-9.03	-9.24	-10.51
Torrent Gujarat Biotech Ltd.	0	-49.19	0	-24.4	-17.92	-18.302
Torrent Pharmaceuticals Ltd.	-10.91	-10.73	-1.32	1.06	5.96	-3.188
Ucal Fuel Systems Ltd.	-7.21	-5.64	-6.07	0	5.66	-2.652
Unichem Laboratories Ltd.	-7.67	-0.84	-2.86	1.63	10.25	0.102
V I P Industries Ltd.	-13.93	-10.97	0	-10.27	-13.95	-9.824
V S T Industries Ltd.	-15.85	0	0.94	4.92	19.01	1.804

Vikrant Tyres Ltd.	-5.4	-5.31	0	-15.59	-10.82	-7.424
Visualsoft Technologies Ltd.	6	43.67	-1.13	16.56	-7.81	11.458
Voltas Ltd.	-14	-17.28	-14.19	-24.97	-24.07	-18.902
West Coast Paper Mills Ltd.	0	0	-6.82	1.15	0.88	-0.958
Wimco Ltd.	-30.04	0	-69.97	-70.7	-18.8	-37.902
Wipro Ltd.	-1.11	8.65	7.42	5.84	9.26	6.012
Wyeth Ltd.	0	-2.93	1.57	1.98	5.99	1.322
Yokogawa Blue Star Ltd.	0	-5.21	-10.43	-17.38	-16.24	-9.852
Zandu Pharmaceutical Works Ltd.	-12.81	-3.76	-6.2	-2.05	4.92	-3.98

(*Contd.*)

TABLE 5.1 (Contd.)

B. intra-firm Analysis with RONW

Company Name	RONW					Average
	Year 1	Year 2	Year 3	Year 4	Year 5	
(1)	(2)	(3)	(4)	(5)	(6)	(7)
Aarti Drugs Ltd.	14.25	12.74	21.48	17.99	21.03	17.50
Aban Loyd Chiles Offshore Ltd.	-20.56	6.12	-29.5	1.38	14.81	-5.55
Advani-Oerlikon Ltd.	16.45	14.34	7.62	5.14	10.21	10.75
Ambalal Sarabhai Enterprises Ltd.	-41.14	-45.05	-47.18	-44.01	-26.4	-40.76
Amtek Auto Ltd.	19.38	15.84	16.22	19.32	12.19	16.59
Apollo Tyres Ltd.	21.54	15.22	19.17	5.83	1.47	12.65
Asian Paints (India) Ltd.	24.5	24.12	29.35	27.77	27.98	26.74
Asian Star Co. Ltd.	16.32	17.98	30.84	23.67	15.45	20.85
Associated Cement Cos. Ltd.	-1.67	-1.23	-7.84	6.35	12.52	1.63
Aurobindo Pharma Ltd.	40.9	51.74	43.3	27.27	18.8	36.40
B A S F India Ltd.	10.04	10.28	11.07	9.56	13.97	10.98
B S E L Information Systems Ltd.	0.19	58.2	77.76	33.13	-0.15	33.83
B S E S Ltd.	14.9	13.1	13.07	13.13	13.54	13.55
B S L Ltd.	1.92	7.8	9.84	10.39	1.85	6.36

Bajaj Auto Ltd.	20.57	19.98	15.58	10.26	13.79	16.04
Bajaj Tempo Ltd.	1.46	-17.89	-11.91	-14.64	1.35	-8.33
Balkrishna Industries Ltd.	16.29	10.08	9.41	3.04	9.78	9.72
Balmer Lawrie & Co. Ltd.	10.83	-4.44	11.65	6.11	2.67	5.36
Berger Paints India Ltd.	25.28	22.01	20.61	21.4	22.22	22.30
Bharat Electronics Ltd.	15.7	14.15	22.82	26.52	25.89	21.02
Bharat Forge Ltd.	11.68	8.73	15.08	8.83	11.99	11.26
Bharat Heavy Electricals Ltd.	17.5	8.87	7.91	-14.28	3.42	4.68
Bharat Petroleum Corpn. Ltd.	23.44	24.62	22	20.67	22.55	22.66
Birla Corporation Ltd.	-24.77	-35.25	-25.61	-12.07	-5.85	-20.71
Birla Ericsson Optical Ltd.	1.63	16.53	14.67	16.76	8	11.52
Blue Star Ltd.	14.7	15.59	20.64	20.26	20.98	18.43
Bongaigaon Refinery & Petrochemicals Ltd.	12.67	5.47	5.14	-11.25	-72.44	-12.08
Britannia Industries Ltd.	25.08	24.29	26.78	23.11	15.12	22.88
C M C Ltd.	13.21	10.75	20.12	33.75	36.07	22.78
Cadila Healthcare Ltd.	29.77	42.51	13.47	12.27	12.06	22.02
Carrier Aircon Ltd.	38.87	30.66	9.64	2.67	-5.14	15.34
Ciba Specialty Chemicals (India) Ltd.	10.32	6.33	17.23	7.67	11.54	10.62
Cipla Ltd.	34.16	28.41	25.89	27.06	28.51	28.81
Clariant (India) Ltd.	27.51	31.54	25.91	23.46	25.6	26.80
Colgate-Palmolive (India) Ltd.	30.23	14.7	18.09	21.64	26.08	22.15

(Contd.)

TABLE 5.1 (Contd.)

(1)	(2)	(3)	(4)	(5)	(6)	(7)
Colour-Chem Ltd.	-4.48	23.25	17.47	5.78	6.81	9.77
Cosmo Films Ltd.	-9.21	-3.84	5.37	14.88	21.62	5.76
Crompton Greaves Ltd.	3.49	3.94	-34.33	-65.11	-8.62	-20.13
Cummins India Ltd.	24.75	18.97	21.19	19.59	12.92	19.48
Dabur India Ltd.	22.27	17.63	19.22	24.01	16.22	19.87
Dr. Reddy'S Laboratories Ltd.	20.51	16.19	16.76	34.62	57.3	29.08
Duphar-Interfran Ltd.	6.19	12.59	19.39	6.49	8.55	10.64
Eicher Motors Ltd.	6.36	14.11	27.08	32.16	23.96	20.73
Eimco Elecon (India) Ltd.	13.75	15.6	15.68	14.1	13.65	14.56
Electrosteel Castings Ltd.	35.07	40.77	41.97	21.51	21.54	32.17
Elgi Equipments Ltd.	8.47	10.54	7.89	4.68	11.15	8.55
Essel Propack Ltd.	12.82	17.16	18.61	7.78	7.82	12.84
F D C Ltd.	17.75	26.84	25.99	22.87	29.38	24.57
Floatglass India Ltd.	-215.49	-109.43	-165.98	-69.72	12.39	-109.65
Gabriel India Ltd.	7.86	-2.39	3.25	5.49	5.33	3.91
George Williamson (Assam) Ltd.	35.88	36.08	27.65	13.93	9	24.51
German Remedies Ltd.	33.76	33.67	32.08	25.52	16.82	28.37
Godavari Fertilisers & Chemicals Ltd.	37.28	22.62	8.98	-14.85	-1.02	10.60

Godfrey Phillips India Ltd.	34.07	29.39	30.5	24.01	21.42	27.88
Goodlass Nerolac Paints Ltd.	22.99	17.9	17.26	11.98	11.74	16.37
Gujarat Sidhee Cement Ltd.	-289.02	196.45	60.33	40.02	16.42	4.84
Hero Honda Motors Ltd.	45.61	48.49	50.09	47.52	68.82	52.11
Hi-Tech Gears Ltd.	12.46	18.51	34.8	25.6	30.28	24.33
Hikal Ltd.	4.67	-11.49	61.59	48.12	40.3	28.64
Hindustan Inks & Resins Ltd.	23.48	43.44	27.57	19.01	15.96	25.89
Hindustan Motors Ltd.	13.39	-14.05	-30.99	-62.18	-31.86	-25.14
Hindustan Petroleum Corpn. Ltd.	16.21	17.84	19.57	16.89	12.84	16.67
Hindustan Powerplus Ltd.	15.66	7.55	7.31	8.14	6.65	9.06
I C I India Ltd.	18.51	9.35	13.14	5.2	5.39	10.32
I P Rings Ltd.	11.85	7.82	9.59	8.26	4.92	8.49
I T C Ltd.	38.16	31.63	29.77	30.38	29.77	31.94
I T W Signode India Ltd.	8.54	-26.27	2.81	12.19	12.93	2.04
Ind-Swift Ltd.	21.24	23.08	31.15	31.14	26.4	26.60
India Glycols Ltd.	14.09	7.29	11.09	11.9	7.8	10.43
India Gypsum Ltd.	25.97	23.98	5.13	2.76	1.51	11.87
Indo National Ltd.	29.24	26.66	21.57	11.26	19.81	21.71
Indo Rama Synthetics (India) Ltd.	-17.05	-40.26	-4.11	6.08	9.83	-9.10
Infosys Technologies Ltd.	43.29	38.58	40.66	57.58	46.57	45.34
Infotech Enterprises Ltd.	32.49	44.44	39.11	35.01	27.97	35.80

(Contd.)

TABLE 5.1 (Contd.)

(1)	(2)	(3)	(4)	(5)	(6)	(7)
Ingersoll-Rand (India) Ltd.	32.11	28.81	22.93	5.67	15.26	20.96
Ipca Laboratories Ltd.	15.51	18.72	14.28	12.76	22.8	16.81
J B Chemicals & Pharmaceuticals Ltd.	29.23	13.04	17.61	21.81	23.92	21.12
J K Synthetics Ltd.	119.05	37.12	22.71	18.73	8	41.12
Jayant Agro Organics Ltd.	15.1	10.41	33.58	42.5	31.11	26.54
Jubilant Organosys Ltd.	29.2	19.7	-0.17	10.48	17.26	15.29
Jupiter Bioscience Ltd.	19.84	19.32	14.46	26.66	27.58	21.57
Kalyani Brakes Ltd.	13.49	3.38	16.22	15.06	19.67	13.56
Krebs Biochemicals Ltd.	60.92	37.79	26.6	20	19.47	32.96
Lakhani India Ltd.	10.03	1.2	2.17	1.9	2.04	3.47
Lakshmi Auto Components Ltd.	34.46	37.71	27.49	19.79	19.21	27.73
Larsen & Toubro Ltd.	13.17	11.04	6.85	5.5	8.34	8.98
Lumax Industries Ltd.	13.35	6.13	5.46	-7.54	1.65	3.81
Madras Cements Ltd.	10.78	11.95	11.12	12.3	7.69	10.77
Mangalore Refinery & Petrochemicals Ltd.	5.52	-1.12	-29	-34.14	-164.03	-44.55
Medicorp Technologies India Ltd.	-17.36	6.53	19.69	-13.23	-38.75	-8.62
Mirc Electronics Ltd.	23.62	25.77	34.68	20.3	20.92	25.06
Mirza Tanners Ltd.	29.06	30.95	25.01	16.14	16.35	23.50

Monsanto India Ltd.	40.81	35.19	30.49	13.3	14.01	26.76
Moser Baer India Ltd.	31.34	29.99	31.71	31.87	26.91	30.36
Motherson Sumi Systems Ltd.	22.58	19.06	30.5	31.04	24.16	25.47
Munjal Showa Ltd.	34.94	23.35	19.58	19.21	30.81	25.58
N R B Bearings Ltd.	17.7	10.75	14.91	9.63	10.27	12.65
Narmada Cement Co. Ltd.	-8.92	-72.94	-139.44	-491.39	1027.88	63.04
Narmada Chematur Petrochemicals Ltd.	2.65	-10.36	-9.3	17.84	9.79	2.12
Nava Bharat Ferro Alloys Ltd.	3.83	-11.3	-3.82	6.07	17.32	2.42
Nicholas Piramal India Ltd.	19.6	14.4	15.94	17.69	27.14	18.95
Nirma Ltd.	36.99	30.62	31.47	23.02	14.56	27.33
Novartis India Ltd.	18.21	27.45	29.39	14.28	23.45	22.56
Orient Information Technology Ltd.	42.24	41.61	23.85	22.51	5.63	27.17
Orient Paper & Inds. Ltd.	-11.22	-61.29	-115.25	-71.4	-111.92	-74.22
P C S Industries Ltd.	1.71	2.45	1.61	2.16	-9.44	-0.30
Panacea Biotec Ltd.	26.96	26.69	44.99	30.15	28.89	31.54
Parke-Davis (India) Ltd. [Merged]	28.86	46.07	23.22	13.33	11.18	24.53
Pidilite Industries Ltd.	28.4	30.61	29.91	23.41	22.2	26.91
Polaris Software Lab Ltd.	34.58	50.84	42.62	36.37	27.44	38.37
Premier Instruments & Controls Ltd.	18.24	8.91	17	17.52	9.16	14.17
Priyadarshini Cement Ltd.	26.99	10.78	-16.86	5.61	-41.12	-2.92
Punjab Tractors Ltd.	49.66	47.71	39.56	28.58	22.58	37.62

(*Contd.*)

TABLE 5.1 (Contd.)

(1)	(2)	(3)	(4)	(5)	(6)	(7)
Rallis India Ltd.	15.5	20.6	19.4	-21.18	-63.96	-5.93
Ramco Industries Ltd.	14.31	12.58	15.46	14.61	11.57	13.71
Reliance Industries Ltd.	17.81	17.31	22.6	22.66	15.02	19.08
Rico Auto Inds. Ltd.	18.9	22.23	37.78	31.73	40.92	30.31
Salora International Ltd.	9.6	12.87	14.85	4.63	5.85	9.56
Satyam Computer Services Ltd.	26.65	54.08	52.1	54.59	35.78	44.64
Shasun Chemicals & Drugs Ltd.	7.95	19.1	42.84	17.36	19.41	21.33
Sona Koyo Steering Systems Ltd.	20.49	8.93	13.02	2.43	2.58	9.49
Sonata Software Ltd.	41.82	31.9	42.54	43.16	14.9	34.86
Sri Vishnu Cement Ltd.	47.03	2.87	-63	45.8	-4.03	5.73
Sundram Fasteners Ltd.	21.86	21.29	26.92	18.22	16.76	21.01
Swaraj Engines Ltd.	48.36	54.62	52.52	37.22	35.24	45.59
Swaraj Mazda Ltd.	78.94	16.95	17.65	22.02	35.12	34.14
Tamilnadu Telecommunications Ltd.	-0.54	10.16	10.26	20.41	1.45	8.35
Tata Elxsi Ltd.	7.32	8.94	20.98	38.45	41.86	23.51
Tata Engineering & Locomotive Co. Ltd.	9.12	-2.58	-6.62	-19.01	-7.72	-5.36
Tata Honeywell Ltd.	18.46	42.86	54.58	30.17	19.97	33.21
Tata Infomedia Ltd.	11.96	12.02	14.79	13.1	9.62	12.30
Tata Infotech Ltd.	28.41	32.17	4.03	14.42	3.85	16.58

Tata Metaliks Ltd.	10.87	0.6	11.23	45.82	34.26	20.56
Tata Sponge Iron Ltd.	16.04	12.19	21	16.02	13.75	15.80
Tata Telecom Ltd.	2.97	-43.75	-14.17	5.76	21.63	-5.51
Thirumalai Chemicals Ltd.	11.33	5.55	10.2	-3.92	4.51	5.53
Timex Watches Ltd.	-3.57	-50.11	-52.85	-402.67	-375.3	-176.90
Timken India Ltd.	19.45	8.8	17.64	18.91	-0.95	12.77
Titan Industries Ltd.	7.55	8.66	4.51	6.9	6.63	6.85
Torrent Gujarat Biotech Ltd.	-126.83	846.1	24.54	10.68	8.56	152.61
Torrent Pharmaceuticals Ltd.	24.82	18.83	28.4	17.44	20.29	21.96
Ucal Fuel Systems Ltd.	35.18	20.27	18.65	22.21	23.81	21.09
Unichem Laboratories Ltd.	31.66	24.57	24.93	24.96	33.28	27.88
V I P Industries Ltd.	9.47	9.51	13.42	5.33	3.38	8.22
V S T Industries Ltd.	6.75	5.88	56.25	52.4	51.12	34.48
Vikrant Tyres Ltd.	28.39	17.62	11.54	-9.88	-18.31	5.87
Visualsoft Technologies Ltd.	38.22	83.14	54.93	54.72	16.33	49.47
Voltas Ltd.	-7.93	-9.66	2.88	-10.69	-13.94	-7.87
West Coast Paper Mills Ltd.	10.07	15	17.43	30.82	27.83	20.23
Wimco Ltd.	-19.41	-42.67	-83.08	-52.11	16.27	-36.20
Wipro Ltd.	38.75	42.97	54.71	50.16	38.29	44.98
Wyeth Ltd.	28.88	26.58	23.28	21.36	23.49	24.72
Yokogawa Blue Star Ltd.	25.71	7.35	14.89	2.74	-3.5	9.44
Zandu Pharmaceutical Works Ltd.	20.5	20.9	7.78	15.31	18.94	16.69

(Contd.)

TABLE 5.1 (Contd.)

C. Intra-firm Analysis with ROCE

Company Name	ROCE					Average
	Year 1	Year 2	Year 3	Year 4	Year 5	
(1)	(2)	(3)	(4)	(5)	(6)	(7)
Aarti Drugs Ltd.	26.91	26.96	30.58	22.78	25.33	26.51
Aban Loyd Chiles Offshore Ltd.	16.93	30.44	20.86	27.09	38.76	26.82
Advani-Oerlikon Ltd.	24.54	22.71	16.65	18.62	20.16	20.54
Ambalal Sarabhai Enterprises Ltd.	-13.04	-23.84	-22.36	-22.69	-10.16	-18.42
Amtek Auto Ltd.	19.31	16.08	15.95	20.74	19.25	18.27
Apollo Tyres Ltd.	32.43	25.14	23.51	14.95	16.32	22.47
Asian Paints (India) Ltd.	33.29	27.69	35.55	35.23	36.95	33.74
Asian Star Co. Ltd.	40.29	38.93	55.78	52.82	41.46	45.86
Associated Cement Cos. Ltd.	5.84	8.43	4.31	11.77	15.03	9.08
Aurobindo Pharma Ltd.	45.08	51.42	45.16	37.37	27.26	41.26
B A S F India Ltd.	13.9	15.5	18.93	16.65	21.36	17.27
B S E L Information Systems Ltd.	0.19	60.91	78.73	32.03	0.86	34.54
B S E S Ltd.	14.68	15.39	16.11	13.35	14.25	14.76
B S L Ltd.	16.89	17.17	18.72	19.63	15.2	17.52

Bajaj Auto Ltd.	29.21	26.21	20.42	9.98	17.3	20.62
Bajaj Tempo Ltd.	12.28	-6.18	1.76	2.55	9.73	4.03
Balkrishna Industries Ltd.	20.07	14.79	12.87	7.48	14.66	13.97
Balmer Lawrie & Co. Ltd.	15.59	7.06	12.47	11.58	9.38	11.22
Berger Paints India Ltd.	39.61	30.3	25.95	27.4	26.36	29.92
Bharat Electronics Ltd.	33.31	28.42	34.59	36.94	38.77	34.41
Bharat Forge Ltd.	13.16	10.93	15.94	14.16	16.06	14.05
Bharat Heavy Electricals Ltd.	30.22	21.76	17.83	-12.79	11.27	13.66
Bharat Petroleum Corpn. Ltd.	26.06	30.1	26.42	25.25	29.55	27.48
Birla Corporation Ltd.	-1.32	-0.63	2.55	4.7	6.48	2.36
Birla Ericsson Optical Ltd.	10.03	18.28	16.94	20.58	10.35	15.24
Blue Star Ltd.	19.39	19.81	22.35	25.19	26.55	22.66
Bongaigaon Refinery & Petrochemicals Ltd.	14.61	6.5	6.47	-9.14	-63.51	-9.01
Britannia Industries Ltd.	33.25	33.89	36.22	37.22	29.33	33.98
C M C Ltd.	26.81	24.4	33.78	46.48	51.51	36.60
Cadila Healthcare Ltd.	33.73	31.24	15.08	13.05	14.16	21.45
Carrier Aircon Ltd.	50.53	39.92	15.4	8.9	-0.08	22.93
Ciba Specialty Chemicals (India) Ltd.	21.05	18.85	27.82	20.78	20.69	21.84
Cipla Ltd.	43.29	38.34	33.74	36.33	38.08	37.96
Clariant (India) Ltd.	41.54	47.58	42.29	39.92	39.71	42.21
Colgate-Palmolive (India) Ltd.	47.6	24.68	30.45	36.71	44.89	36.87

(Contd.)

TABLE 5.1 (Contd.)

(1)	(2)	(3)	(4)	(5)	(6)	(7)
Colour-Chem Ltd.	10.32	20.84	22.3	11.47	14.6	15.91
Cosmo Films Ltd.	3.19	6.69	12.05	18.56	24.72	13.04
Crompton Greaves Ltd.	14.89	14.55	-3.19	-14.9	9.32	4.13
Cummins India Ltd.	34.89	27.41	29.7	25.96	17.47	27.09
Dabur India Ltd.	21.06	18.74	19.83	24.97	19.37	20.79
Dr. Reddy's Laboratories Ltd.	24.53	20.74	20.8	43.81	58.48	33.67
Duphar-Interfran Ltd.	10.33	20.62	28.5	9.99	12.8	16.45
Eicher Motors Ltd.	14.51	17.64	24.82	27.57	31.74	23.26
Elmco Elecon (India) Ltd.	26.14	28.31	26.02	23.97	20.29	24.95
Electrosteel Castings Ltd.	32.48	40.91	43.49	24.77	23.37	33.00
Elgi Equipments Ltd.	18.62	16.61	13.72	9.77	19.16	15.58
Essel Propack Ltd.	16.95	23.61	23.14	13.17	12.72	17.92
F D C Ltd.	20.84	34.89	35.5	27.41	33.11	30.35
Floatglass India Ltd.	-2.07	-1.35	-22.67	-19.78	49.3	0.69
Gabriel India Ltd.	13.5	8.84	11.14	11.91	13	11.68
George Williamson (Assam) Ltd.	40.75	40.66	36.23	24.22	15.19	31.41
German Remedies Ltd.	39.96	42.86	38.46	32.4	23.77	35.49
Godavari Fertilisers & Chemicals Ltd.	28.82	34.35	21.52	8.95	19.4	22.61

Godfrey Phillips India Ltd.	54.4	44.6	44.53	36.92	32.55	42.60
Goodlass Nerolac Paints Ltd.	30.6	23.46	24.34	17.95	16.46	22.56
Gujarat Sidhee Cement Ltd.	3.14	-31.64	-48.97	-48.58	-8.32	-26.87
Hero Honda Motors Ltd.	53.99	61.7	71.98	70.98	96.27	70.98
Hi-Tech Gears Ltd.	20.23	24.8	40.39	35.34	41.59	32.47
Hikal Ltd.	2.75	4.02	17.77	15.54	14.94	11.00
Hindustan Inks & Resins Ltd.	35.46	48.87	30.74	20.9	23.13	31.82
Hindustan Motors Ltd.	18.24	7.75	7.04	-3.12	0.91	6.16
Hindustan Petroleum Corpn. Ltd.	20.87	24.58	22.72	21.4	19.01	21.72
Hindustan Powerplus Ltd.	22.57	18.97	21.04	19.98	14.88	19.49
I C I India Ltd.	28.46	19.21	15.32	11.38	13.21	17.52
I P Rings Ltd.	13.02	9.06	11.11	10.6	7.7	10.30
I T C Ltd.	42.54	36.81	43.39	47.33	43.29	42.67
I T W Signode India Ltd.	20.15	-17.46	5.93	22.81	23.43	10.97
Ind-Swift Ltd.	26.91	29.77	34.38	36.9	36.27	32.85
India Glycols Ltd.	18.54	11.09	14.54	13.59	9.47	13.45
India Gypsum Ltd.	27.65	26.91	8.26	11.42	12.82	17.41
Indo National Ltd.	38.1	36.65	32.4	18.22	30.09	31.09
Indo Rama Synthetics (India) Ltd.	4.41	1.55	10.9	13.05	12.21	8.42
Infosys Technologies Ltd.	46.29	43.66	46.33	64.19	54.69	51.03
Infotech Enterprises Ltd.	32.18	42.52	31.24	26.86	31.02	32.76

(*Contd.*)

TABLE 5.1 (Contd.)

(1)	(2)	(3)	(4)	(5)	(6)	(7)
Ingersoll-Rand (India) Ltd.	48.36	42.07	33.97	14.66	22.49	32.31
Ipca Laboratories Ltd.	21.45	24.04	19.44	17.69	26.06	21.74
J B Chemicals & Pharmaceuticals Ltd.	30.71	15.13	17.85	26.24	29.48	23.88
J K Synthetics Ltd.	-34.67	-30.39	-47.34	73.21	-6.36	-9.11
Jayant Agro Organics Ltd.	16.53	12.72	37.71	47.13	33	29.42
Jubilant Organosys Ltd.	27.74	20.2	13	18.05	20.59	19.92
Jupiter Bioscience Ltd.	14.52	15.92	18.68	28	28.03	21.03
Kalyani Brakes Ltd.	12.65	4.8	13.27	11.68	17.67	12.01
Krebs Biochemicals Ltd.	43.97	27.32	28.04	21.99	23.99	29.06
Lakhani India Ltd.	19.05	9.68	9.52	8.39	8.8	11.09
Lakshmi Auto Components Ltd.	44.01	31.66	25.44	25.02	27.04	30.63
Larsen & Toubro Ltd.	13.16	12.67	12.32	11.74	12.84	12.55
Lumax Industries Ltd.	18.05	11.7	12.74	3.96	8.61	11.01
Madras Cements Ltd.	15.86	15.37	13.59	12.86	11.59	13.85
Mangalore Refinery & Petrochemicals Ltd.	14.8	8.51	-0.02	-0.65	-2.54	4.02
Medicorp Technologies India Ltd.	-2.43	9.52	18.78	1.88	-0.11	5.53
Mirc Electronics Ltd.	26.78	26.36	27.23	19.37	20.91	24.13
Mirza Tanners Ltd.	43.39	46.4	33.02	25.29	29.2	35.46

Monsanto India Ltd.	59.83	47.74	36.89	15.69	16.83	35.40
Moser Baer India Ltd.	20.56	23.15	18.97	25.07	21.68	21.89
Motherson Sumi Systems Ltd.	31.8	28.07	34.06	42.86	35.13	34.38
Munjal Showa Ltd.	45.14	30.89	25.47	27.02	44.49	34.60
N R B Bearings Ltd.	27.67	16.2	21.19	17.48	17.81	20.07
Narmada Cement Co. Ltd.	-0.44	-15.81	-3.38	-2.83	2.66	-3.96
Narmada Chematur Petrochemicals Ltd.	2.6	4.51	7.86	18.37	16.68	10.00
Nava Bharat Ferro Alloys Ltd.	17.82	11.82	12.58	16.96	20.24	15.88
Nicholas Piramal India Ltd.	17.73	17.65	20.82	20.97	39.57	23.35
Nirma Ltd.	29.28	24.65	21.08	17.93	19.38	22.46
Novartis India Ltd.	33.31	44.99	48.9	26.23	34.51	37.59
Orient Information Technology Ltd.	39.39	40.64	24.97	23.72	6.06	26.96
Orient Paper & Inds. Ltd.	5.02	-4.7	-1.21	13.45	12.93	5.10
P C S Industries Ltd.	13.64	15.43	16.74	17.13	9.18	14.42
Panacea Biotec Ltd.	31.64	28.72	44.35	42.39	43.52	38.12
Parke-Davis (India) Ltd. [Merged]	29.01	33.34	44.25	37.25	22.42	33.25
Pidilite Industries Ltd.	34.15	44.09	47.16	36.01	34.07	39.10
Polaris Software Lab Ltd.	35.87	50.47	47.93	36.77	29.2	40.05
Premier Instruments & Controls Ltd.	25.86	15.55	21.69	22.68	16.53	20.46
Priyadarshini Cement Ltd.	42.49	25.55	17.69	22.82	8.21	23.35
Punjab Tractors Ltd.	66.58	66.28	56	42.32	28.1	51.86

(Contd.)

TABLE 5.1 (Contd.)

(1)	(2)	(3)	(4)	(5)	(6)	(7)
Rallis India Ltd.	33.95	30.5	26.27	11.08	-1.27	20.11
Ramco Industries Ltd.	15.22	14.38	13.99	16.35	15.18	15.02
Reliance Industries Ltd.	13.39	12.88	16.29	18.43	18.38	15.87
Rico Auto Inds. Ltd.	22.95	21.62	23.98	24.68	40.45	26.74
Salora International Ltd.	15.93	18.7	25	10.91	11.85	16.48
Satyam Computer Services Ltd.	25.1	34.06	38.95	49.8	36.78	36.94
Shasun Chemicals & Drugs Ltd.	21.32	26.49	40.94	22.39	23.22	26.87
Sona Koyo Steering Systems Ltd.	23.78	13.57	19.01	9	10.61	15.19
Sonata Software Ltd.	45.29	35.29	42.28	44.45	15.58	36.58
Sri Vishnu Cement Ltd.	24.31	14.79	2.21	18.88	13.01	14.64
Sundram Fasteners Ltd.	24.57	23.94	27.89	23.25	26.78	25.29
Swaraj Engines Ltd.	42.74	54.87	64.46	54.77	59.62	55.29
Swaraj Mazda Ltd.	29.93	19.34	17.76	28.86	32.62	25.70
Tamilnadu Telecommunications Ltd.	8.7	11.28	12.53	30.61	13.87	15.40
Tata Elxsi Ltd.	18.48	22.12	38.5	58.11	58.5	39.14
Tata Engineering & Locomotive Co. Ltd.	15.1	6.88	6.12	-0.05	5.89	6.79
Tata Honeywell Ltd.	27.85	45.68	54.88	38.68	25.43	38.50
Tata Infomedia Ltd.	17.11	17.98	20.76	21.74	15.02	18.52
Tata Infotech Ltd.	47.69	47.64	6.27	21.76	5.92	25.86

Tata Metaliks Ltd.	18.87	12.96	15.3	36.27	43.54	25.39
Tata Sponge Iron Ltd.	12.71	11.78	18.52	15.79	16.8	15.12
Tata Telecom Ltd.	21.39	-2.41	10.68	19.96	32.27	16.38
Thirumalai Chemicals Ltd.	12.55	11.54	13.99	7.15	12.39	11.52
Timex Watches Ltd.	7.37	-5.56	-1.64	-102.08	-215.16	-63.41
Timken India Ltd.	26.91	15.35	26.87	26.38	2.74	19.65
Titan Industries Ltd.	15.85	17.01	15.3	15.95	16.77	16.18
Torrent Gujarat Biotech Ltd.	-11.59	-7.24	-0.73	-2.52	0.23	-4.37
Torrent Pharmaceuticals Ltd.	25.55	21.71	29.64	24.15	27.94	25.80
Ucal Fuel Systems Ltd.	28.68	19.5	17.73	20.19	24.91	22.20
Unichem Laboratories Ltd.	28.43	25.5	22	23.87	33.31	26.62
V I P Industries Ltd.	15.81	14.89	15.53	12.76	12.31	14.26
V S T Industries Ltd.	17.68	17.77	32.11	34.76	59.47	32.36
Vikrant Tyres Ltd.	32.3	20.78	11.83	2.35	5.89	14.63
Visualsoft Technologies Ltd.	37.2	82.7	56.34	55.33	17.19	49.75
Voltas Ltd.	12.42	10.17	13.23	3.24	-1.01	7.61
West Coast Paper Mills Ltd.	23.62	26.84	27.67	41.41	30.56	30.02
Wimco Ltd.	8.81	7.97	-13.02	-22.99	121.03	20.36
Wipro Ltd.	36.93	41.66	61.01	58.03	43.03	48.13
Wyeth Ltd.	42.48	37.95	37.54	35.66	36.1	37.95
Yokogawa Blue Star Ltd.	32.86	14.05	18.16	7.82	2.48	15.07
Zandu Pharmaceutical Works Ltd.	25.97	25.97	16.28	24.74	31.46	24.88

during the period. The year-wise analysis has been summarized as follows:

Group I (Companies with Value Addition)

The set of forty seven companies belonging to this group show an increasing trend of shareholder value addition during the study period i.e., performance of such companies indicates improvement from first year to second year to third year to fourth year to the fifth year. However, very few companies like Asian Paints (India) Ltd., Cipla Ltd., Cosmo Films Ltd., Eicher Motors Ltd., Hi-Tech Gears Ltd., JB Chemicals & Pharmaceuticals Ltd., Swaraj Mazda Ltd., Tata Metaliks Ltd., VST Industries Ltd., Wyeth Ltd., have resulted in positive value addition to shareholders in the study period which has improved thereafter in subsequent two or three years. Other companies like Asian Star Co. Ltd., BASF India Ltd., BSES Ltd., Balkrishna Ltd., Industries Ltd., Orient Paper and Inds. Ltd., Tata Telcom Ltd., have revealed decreased value erosion from first financial year to the fifth indicating an improvement in value addition in subsequent years.

Group II (Companies with Value Erosion)

This group of companies indicating decrease in value addition from first financial year to the fifth has twenty seven companies in it. Most of the companies in this group show value erosion in the initial financial years which has increased in the subsequent years. Companies belonging to this group include Aarti Drugs Ltd., Bongaigaon Refinery and Petrochemicals Ltd., Essel Propack Ltd., Gujarat Sidhee Cement Ltd., IP Rings Ltd., Lakhani India Ltd., Medicorp Technologies India Ltd., Narmada Cement Co. Ltd., PCS Industries Ltd., Tata Infotech Ltd., Timex Watches Ltd., Voltas Ltd., Yokogawa Blue Star Ltd. Then there are companies like Aurobindo Pharma Ltd., Cadila Healthcare Ltd., Carrier Aircon Ltd., German Remedies Ltd., Hikal Ltd., Hindustan Inks and Resins Ltd., India Gypsum Ltd., Infotech Enterprises Ltd., Mirza Tanners Ltd., which showed positive shareholder value addition in the initial years(s) which subsequently reduced to value erosion in the subsequent years.

Group III (Companies with no Relation to Value Addition/Erosion)

Sample companies in this group indicates neither value addition nor value erosion categorically rather indicate both in a phased manner. This group has the maximum number of companies (80) belonging to it. Companies such as BSEL Information Systems Ltd., Electrosteel Castings Ltd., Polaris Software Lab Ltd., Visual Soft Technologies Ltd., all showed marked increase in shareholder value addition in the initial two to three years which was lost in the subsequent fourth/fifth year. Then, there are companies like Aban Loyd Chiles Offshore Ltd., Amtek Auto Ltd., Associated Cement Co. Ltd., Bajaj Tempo Ltd., Dabur India Ltd., Bharat Electronics Ltd., Ciba Speciality Chemicals (India) Ltd., Munjal Showa Ltd., Panacea Biotec Ltd., Satyam Computer Service Ltd., Wimco Ltd., which have shown significant deterioration in the initial two to three years with improvement in the fourth/fifth year(s).

2. RONW and Intra-firm Comparison

The technique of cluster analysis has been followed for the next measure of value addition, RONW for different group of companies.

Group I (Companies with Increased Profitability)

Only nine companies out of the total sample of one hundred and fifty-four have shown improvement in profitability in terms of RONW in the five financial years. The companies which have shown marked improvement include CMC Ltd., Cosmo Films Ltd., Eicher Motors Ltd., Floatglass India Ltd., Rico Auto Inds. Ltd., and Tata Elxsi Ltd. There are other companies which have shown an increasing trend, though not very significant. These include Blue Star Ltd., FDC Ltd., and Hero Honda Motors Ltd.

Group II (Companies with Decreased Profitability)

Thirteen companies get categorized in this group showing decrease in profits according to the traditional measure of value addition in the five financial years. Companies like Bajaj Auto Ltd., German Remedies Ltd., Goodlass Nerolac Paints Ltd., Wyeth Ltd., have shown decrease in profitability like Bongaigaon Refinery and Petrochemicals Ltd., Orient Information Technology Ltd., Vikrant Tyres Ltd., have shown significant deterioration in profitability in the study period.

Group III (Companies with neither Increased nor Decreased Profitability)

A majority of one hundred and thirty-two companies belong to this group indicate neither the increasing trend nor the decreasing trend during the study period. Same companies have shown marked improvement in profitability in the initial years which gets lost in the subsequent years. To name a few companies, Asian Star Co. Ltd., Aurobindo Pharma Ltd., BASF India Ltd., BSEL Information Systems Ltd., Bharat Petroleum Corpn. Ltd., Cadila Healthcare Ltd., Clariant (India) Ltd., Duphar-Interfran Ltd., Eimco Elecon (India) Ltd., Electresteel Casting Ltd., Hindustan Inks and Resins Ltd., Infotech Enterprises Ltd., Lakshmi Auto Components Ltd., Mirc Electronics Ltd., Novartis India Ltd., Salora International Ltd., Shashun Chemicals and Drugs Ltd., Tata Honeywell Ltd., VIP Industries Ltd., Wipro Ltd., all belong to this category.

Further, there are few companies like Aarti Drugs Ltd., Aban Loyd Chiles Offshore Ltd., Bharat Forge Ltd., Birla Ericsson Optical Ltd., Colour-Chem. Ltd., Gabriel India Ltd., ICI India Ltd., Ipca Laboratories Ltd., Kalyani Brakes Ltd., Motherson Sumi Systems Ltd., Premier Instruments and Control Ltd., Tata Infotech Ltd., Yokogawa Blue Star Ltd., which have shown no trend in the study period w.r.t. their profitability position.

3. ROCE and Intra-firm Comparison

The observation with this measure of profitability are given below:

Group I (Companies with Increased Profitability)

Very few companies (twenty) indicate an increased

profitability in but increase in most cases is very significant. Companies like Blue Star Ltd., CMC Ltd., Cosmo Films Ltd., Eicher Motors Ltd., Hero Honda Motors Ltd., Hi-Tech Gears Ltd., Satyam Computer Services Ltd., Tata Elxsi Ltd., VST Industries Ltd., all add positive profits to shareholders which has increased subsequently.

For companies like Torrent Gujarat Biotech Ltd., Birla Corporation Ltd., Medicorp Technologies Ltd., profits in first year is negative but has decreased each year indicating an improvement in profitability.

Group II (Companies with Decreased Profitability)

This group has nineteen companies again exhibiting the same trend. Few companies started with positive value in the first year which reduced subsequently. Illustrative instances include Bongaigaon Refinery and Petrochemicals Ltd., George Williamson (Assam) Ltd., Godfrey Philips India Ltd., Goodlass Nerolac Paints Ltd., Lakhani India Ltd., Madras Cements Ltd., Manglore Refinery and Petrochemicals Ltd., Punjab Tractors Ltd., Rallis India Ltd., and VIF Industries Ltd.

Some companies started with negative value which increased in subsequent years. Examples include Ambalal Sarabhai Enterprises Ltd., Floatglass India Ltd., Synthetics Ltd., and Timex Watches Ltd.

Group III (Companies with neither Increased nor Decreased Profitability)

The last group with maximum number of companies at one hundred and twelve indicates no effect on the profitability of companies over the five year period thus not showing any increasing or even decreasing trend in the study period. The companies included in this list are Aarti Drugs Ltd., Advani-Oerlikon Ltd., BSES Ltd., Bajaj Auto Ltd., Cipla Ltd., Colour-Chem Ltd., FDC Ltd., Hindustan Inks and Resins Ltd., Indo National Ltd., Infosys Technology Ltd., Ipca Laboratories Ltd., Larsen and Toubro Ltd., Mirc Electronics Ltd., Moser Baer India Ltd., Novartis India Ltd., Panacea Biotec Ltd., Sona Koyo

Steering Systems Ltd., Sonata Software Ltd., Tata Info-media Ltd., Tata Sponge Iron Ltd., Timken India Ltd., Vishal Soft Technologies Ltd., Wimco Ltd., and Wipro Ltd.

The above mentioned observations are summarised in Table 5.2.

(ii) Inter-Firm Analysis with EVA, RONW and ROCE

After a thorough assessment of value addition with firms, an investigation has been conducted to measure variations across firms for all the three performance metrics for the whole study period. In this case also, technique of cluster analysis has been applied by:

1. ranking the firm by all three performance metrics separately in descending order,
2. classifying firms with similar values into broad clusters or groups, and
3. examining these groups and explaining them.

Table 5.3 gives the average performance results in the study period by all three performance metrics, namely EVA, RONW and ROCE along with their respective rankings. A perusal of the ranking in the Table 5.3 reveals the following groups:

Group I: Companies with Value Addition/Positive Returns in Five Years

This group consists of companies with positive values/ returns indicating that such firms have added to shareholders value in the study period.

Group II: Companies with Value Erosion/Negative Returns in Five Years

This group consists of companies with negative values/ returns indicating that these firms have eroded value in the study period.

TABLE 5.2

Intra-firm Analysis with EVA, RONW AND ROCE: Summary of Results

Group	EVA		RONW		ROCE	
	No. of Companies	Percentage	No. of Companies	Percentage	No. of Companies	Percentage
(1)	(2)	(3)	(4)	(5)	(6)	(7)
Group I	47	31	9	6	20	13
Group II	27	17	13	8	22	14
Group III	80	52	132	86	112	73
Total	154	100	154	100	154	100

*Group I : Companies with Value Addition/Increased Profitability.
Group II : Companies with Value Erosion/Decreased Profitability.
Group III : Companies with no relation to Value Addition/Erosion or Increased/Decreased Profitability.

TABLE 5.3
Inter-firm Analysis with EVA, RONW and ROCE

(Rs. In Crores)

Company Name	Average EVACE	Rank	Average RONW	Rank	Average ROCE	Rank
(1)	(2)	(3)	(4)	(5)	(6)	(7)
Aarti Drugs Ltd.	-34.88	149	17.5	76	26.51	57
Aban Loyd Chiles Offshore Ltd.	-2.93	69	-5.55	139	26.82	85
Advani-Oerlikon Ltd.	-2.72	67	10.75	102	20.54	85
Ambalal Sarabhai Enterprises Ltd.	-24.16	146	-40.76	150	-18.42	152
Amtek Auto Ltd.	-1.10	52	16.59	80	18.27	94
Apollo Tyres Ltd.	-4.25	79	12.65	94	22.47	74
Asian Paints (India) Ltd.	0.82	35	26.74	37	33.74	32
Asian Star Co. Ltd.	-10.57	121	20.85	67	45.86	7
Associated Cement Cos. Ltd.	-11.64	125	1.63	134	9.08	136
Aurobindo Pharma Ltd.	8.40	6	36.4	12	41.26	11
B A S F India Ltd.	-7.99	103	10.98	100	17.27	99
B S E L Information Systems Ltd.	4.46	16	33.83	17	34.54	28
B S E S Ltd.	-6.00	91	13.55	91	14.76	114
B S L Ltd.	-5.30	85	6.36	120	17.52	96
Bajaj Auto Ltd.	-8.64	108	16.04	83	20.62	84

Bajaj Tempo Ltd.	-19.83	140	-8.33	142	4.03	144
Balkrishna Industries Ltd.	-3.66	73	9.72	109	13.97	120
Balmer Lawrie & Co. Ltd.	-4.62	81	5.36	125	11.22	129
Berger Paints India Ltd.	-1.56	57	22.3	56	29.92	47
Bharat Electronics Ltd.	1.96	26	21.02	64	34.41	29
Bharat Forge Ltd.	-9.32	113	11.26	99	14.05	119
Bharat Heavy Electricals Ltd.	-13.53	131	4.68	127	13.66	122
Bharat Petroleum Corpn. Ltd.	-0.70	46	22.66	54	27.48	50
Birla Corporation Ltd.	-20.80	142	-20.71	147	2.36	146
Birla Ericsson Optical Ltd.	-8.08	105	11.52	98	15.24	109
Blue Star Ltd.	-2.87	68	18.43	75	22.66	71
Bongaigaon Refinery & Petrochemicals Ltd.	-28.76	148	-12.08	145	-9.01	150
Britannia Industries Ltd.	0.46	40	22.88	52	33.98	31
C M C Ltd.	-12.44	126	22.78	53	36.6	22
Cadila Healthcare Ltd.	-1.07	50	22.02	58	21.45	81
Carrier Aircon Ltd.	-10.02	119	15.34	85	22.93	70
Ciba Specialty Chemicals (India) Ltd.	-6.99	96	10.62	104	21.84	78
Cipla Ltd.	2.94	23	28.81	26	37.96	17
Clariant (India) Ltd.	5.56	11	26.8	35	42.21	10
Colgate-Palmolive (India) Ltd.	-2.28	61	22.15	57	36.87	21
Colour-Chem Ltd.	-7.74	101	9.77	108	15.91	104

(Contd.)

TABLE 5.3 (Contd.)

(1)	(2)	(3)	(4)	(5)	(6)	(7)
Cosmo Films Ltd.	-2.52	65	5.76	122	13.04	124
Crompton Greaves Ltd.	-22.37	144	-20.13	146	4.13	143
Cummins India Ltd.	-2.33	62	19.48	72	27.09	51
Dabur India Ltd.	-2.98	70	19.87	71	20.79	83
Dr. Reddy's Laboratories Ltd.	0.29	42	29.08	25	33.67	33
Duphar-Interfran Ltd.	-4.98	84	10.64	103	16.45	101
Eicher Motors Ltd.	-3.94	75	20.73	68	23.26	69
Eimco Elecon (India) Ltd.	-2.10	50	14.66	87	24.95	63
Electrosteel Castings Ltd.	3.82	17	32.17	20	33	35
Elgi Equipments Ltd.	-10.82	123	8.55	115	15.58	107
Essel Propack Ltd.	-2.35	63	12.84	92	17.92	95
F D C Ltd.	2.41	25	24.57	45	30.35	45
Floatglass India Ltd.	-36.07	150	-109.65	153	0.69	147
Gabriel India Ltd.	-7.96	102	3.91	128	11.68	127
George Williamson (Assam) Ltd.	-8.68	109	24.51	47	31.41	42
German Remedies Ltd.	3.74	18	28.37	28	35.49	24
Godavari Fertilisers & Chemicals Ltd.	-7.04	97	10.6	105	22.61	72
Godfrey Phillips India Ltd.	3.06	20	27.88	29	42.6	9

Goodlass Nerolac Paints Ltd.	-5.40	86	16.37	82	22.56	73
Gujarat Sidhee Cement Ltd.	-56.51	153	4.84	126	-26.87	153
Hero Honda Motors Ltd.	20.43	1	52.11	3	70.98	1
Hi-Tech Gears Ltd.	0.45	41	24.33	48	32.47	38
Hikal Ltd.	0.62	39	28.64	27	11	132
Hindustan Inks & Resins Ltd.	3.16	19	25.89	40	31.82	41
Hindustan Motors Ltd.	-22.16	143	-25.14	148	6.16	140
Hindustan Petroleum Corpn. Ltd.	-2.51	64	16.67	79	21.72	80
Hindustan Powerplus Ltd.	-11.02	124	9.06	113	19.49	92
I C I India Ltd.	-3.66	74	10.32	107	17.52	96
I P Rings Ltd.	-3.60	72	8.49	116	10.3	134
I T C Ltd.	5.40	12	31.94	21	42.67	8
I T W Signode India Ltd.	-12.63	127	2.04	133	10.97	133
Ind-Swift Ltd.	-1.13	53	26.6	38	32.85	36
India Glycols Ltd.	-4.97	83	10.43	106	13.45	123
India Gypsum Ltd.	-1.60	58	11.87	97	17.41	98
Indo National Ltd.	1.23	33	21.71	60	31.09	43
Indo Rama Synthetics (India) Ltd.	-8.81	111	-9.1	144	8.42	137
Infosys Technologies Ltd.	4.47	15	45.34	6	51.03	4
Infotech Enterprises Ltd.	-0.24	45	35.8	13	32.76	37
Ingersoll-Rand (India) Ltd.	2.48	24	20.96	66	32.31	40

(Contd.)

TABLE 5.3 (Contd.)

(1)	(2)	(3)	(4)	(5)	(6)	(7)
Ipca Laboratories Ltd.	-5.56	87	16.81	77	21.74	79
J B Chemicals & Pharmaceuticals Ltd.	-1.44	56	21.12	63	23.88	66
J K Synthetics Ltd.	-49.22	152	41.12	9	-9.11	151
Jayant Agro Organics Ltd.	9.96	5	26.54	39	29.42	48
Jubilant Organosys Ltd.	-4.12	77	15.29	86	19.92	90
Jupiter Bioscience Ltd.	0.69	38	21.57	61	21.03	82
Kalyani Brakes Ltd.	-5.99	90	13.56	90	12.01	126
Krebs Biochemicals Ltd.	3.06	21	32.96	19	29.06	49
Lakhani India Ltd.	-16.09	133	3.47	130	11.09	130
Lakshmi Auto Components Ltd.	1.70	30	27.73	31	30.63	44
Larsen & Toubro Ltd.	-9.53	115	8.98	114	12.55	125
Lumax Industries Ltd.	-6.97	95	3.81	129	11.01	131
Madras Cements Ltd.	-6.42	94	10.77	101	13.85	121
Mangalore Refinery & Petrochemicals Ltd.	-18.38	138	-44.55	151	4.02	145
Medicorp Technologies India Ltd.	-9.53	116	-8.62	143	5.53	141
Mirc Electronics Ltd.	-5.78	89	25.06	43	24.13	65
Mirza Tanners Ltd.	1.65	31	23.5	51	35.46	25
Monsanto India Ltd.	2.96	22	26.76	36	35.4	26

Moser Baer India Ltd.	-6.20	92	30.36	23	21.89	77
Motherson Sumi Systems Ltd.	-0.97	49	25.47	42	34.38	30
Munjal Showa Ltd.	1.12	34	25.58	41	34.6	27
N R B Bearings Ltd.	-4.85	82	12.65	94	20.07	89
Narmada Cement Co. Ltd.	-24.02	145	63.04	2	-3.96	148
Narmada Chematur Petrochemicals Ltd.	-8.74	110	2.12	132	10	135
Nava Bharat Ferro Alloys Ltd.	-1.15	54	2.42	131	15.88	105
Nicholas Piramal India Ltd.	0.04	44	18.95	74	23.35	67
Nirma Ltd.	-2.16	60	27.33	32	22.46	75
Novartis India Ltd.	7.69	7	22.56	55	37.59	19
Orient Information Technology Ltd.	-8.48	106	27.17	33	26.96	52
Orient Paper & Inds. Ltd.	-19.91	141	-74.22	152	5.1	142
P C S Industries Ltd.	-16.77	135	-0.3	135	14.42	117
Panacea Biotec Ltd.	0.82	35	31.54	22	38.12	16
Parke-Davis (India) Ltd. [Merged]	6.21	8	24.53	46	33.25	34
Pidilite Industries Ltd.	5.69	10	26.91	34	39.1	14
Polaris Software Lab Ltd.	4.61	13	38.37	10	40.05	12
Premier Instruments & Controls Ltd.	-7.35	99	14.17	88	20.46	86
Priyadarshini Cement Ltd.	-13.15	130	-2.92	136	23.35	67
Punjab Tractors Ltd.	13.75	3	37.62	11	51.86	3
Rallis India Ltd.	-9.20	112	-5.93	140	20.11	88

(*Contd.*)

TABLE 5.3 (Contd.)

(1)	(2)	(3)	(4)	(5)	(6)	(7)
Ramco Industries Ltd.	-12.93	128	13.71	89	15.02	113
Reliance Industries Ltd.	-4.14	78	19.08	73	15.87	106
Rico Auto Inds. Ltd.	-0.80	47	30.31	24	26.74	55
Salora International Ltd.	-8.00	104	9.56	110	16.48	100
Satyam Computer Services Ltd.	1.71	29	44.64	8	36.94	20
Shasun Chemicals & Drugs Ltd.	1.79	28	21.33	62	26.87	53
Sona Koyo Steering Systems Ltd.	-8.63	107	9.49	111	15.19	110
Sonata Software Ltd.	0.77	37	34.86	14	36.58	23
Sri Vishnu Cement Ltd.	-12.97	129	5.73	123	14.64	115
Sundram Fasteners Ltd.	-1.40	55	21.01	65	25.29	62
Swaraj Engines Ltd.	16.53	2	45.59	5	55.29	2
Swaraj Mazda Ltd.	-5.62	88	34.14	16	25.7	60
Tamilnadu Telecommunications Ltd.	-16.40	134	8.35	117	15.4	108
Tata Elxsi Ltd.	-9.38	114	23.51	50	39.14	13
Tata Engineering & Locomotive Co. Ltd.	-16.82	136	-5.36	137	6.79	139
Tata Honeywell Ltd.	-4.34	80	33.21	18	38.5	15
Tata Infomedia Ltd.	-7.16	98	12.3	96	18.52	93
Tata Infotech Ltd.	-14.48	132	16.58	81	25.86	58

Tata Metaliks Ltd.	4.55	14	20.56	69	25.39	61
Tata Sponge Iron Ltd.	-1.08	51	15.8	84	15.12	111
Tata Telecom Ltd.	-24.87	147	-5.51	138	16.38	102
Thirumalai Chemicals Ltd.	-10.79	122	5.53	124	11.52	128
Timex Watches Ltd.	-386.37	154	-176.9	154	-63.41	154
Timken India Ltd.	-6.21	93	12.77	93	19.65	91
Titan Industries Ltd.	-10.51	120	6.85	119	16.18	103
Torrent Gujarat Biotech Ltd.	-18.30	137	152.61	1	-4.37	149
Torrent Pharmaceuticals Ltd.	-3.19	71	21.96	59	25.8	59
Ucal Fuel Systems Ltd.	-2.65	66	24.09	49	22.2	76
Unichem Laboratories Ltd.	0.10	43	27.88	29	26.62	56
V I P Industries Ltd.	-9.82	117	8.22	118	14.26	118
V S T Industries Ltd.	1.80	27	34.48	15	32.36	39
Vikrant Tyres Ltd.	-7.42	100	5.87	121	14.63	116
Visualsoft Technologies Ltd.	11.46	4	49.47	4	49.75	5
Voltas Ltd.	-18.90	139	-7.87	141	7.61	138
West Coast Paper Mills Ltd.	-0.96	48	20.23	70	30.02	46
Wimco Ltd.	-37.90	151	-36.2	149	20.36	87
Wipro Ltd.	6.01	9	44.98	7	48.13	6
Wyeth Ltd.	1.32	32	24.72	44	37.95	18
Yokogawa Blue Star Ltd.	-9.85	118	9.44	112	15.07	112
Zandu Pharmaceutical Works Ltd.	-3.98	76	16.69	78	24.88	64

I. EVA and Inter-Firm Comparison

Average economic value added (EVA) has been computed for the study period for all sample firms to see which firms have added value for their shareholders and which have destroyed it. Following classifications have been done based on empirical results.

Group I (Companies with Value Addition)

This group consists of forty four companies (rank 1-44) only out of the sample of one hundred and fifty four companies which have revealed positive value addition in terms of EVA. The shareholder value addition has been in the range of 20.43 crores (by Hero Honda Motors Ltd. which got the 1st rank) to 0.04 crores (by Nicholas Piramal Ltd. which got 44th rank. In-between, there were big business houses like Punjab Tractors Ltd., Asian Paints (India) Ltd., Aurobindo Pharma Ltd., BSEL Information Systems Ltd., Britannia Industries Ltd., Clariant (India) Ltd., Godfrey Phillips India Ltd., Hindustan Inks and Resins Ltd., ITC Ltd., Infosys Technologies Ltd., Jayant Agro Organics Ltd., Munjal Showa Ltd., Novartis India Ltd., Pidilite Industries Ltd., Polaris Software Lab Ltd., Satyam Computer Services Ltd., Tata Metasliks Ltd., Wipro Ltd. etc.

Group II (Companies with Value Erosion)

All the rest of the companies from rank 45th to 154th (i.e. in total 110 companies) belong to this group with negative value addition in the study period. The range of value erosion has been from -0.24 crores (by Infotech Enterprises Ltd.) to the tune of -386.37 crores (by Timex Watches Ltd.). In-between, there are companies like Aarti Drugs Ltd., Associated Cement Cos. Ltd., Bajaj Tempo Ltd., Bharat Heavy Electrical Ltd., Birla Corporation Ltd., CMC Ltd., Carrier Aircon Ltd., Crompton Greaves Ltd., Duphar Interfran Ltd., Eicher Motors Ltd., Elgi Equipments Ltd., Floatglass India Ltd., Gujarat Sidhee Cement Ltd., Hindustan Motors Ltd., Hindustan Powerplus Ltd., ITW Signode India Ltd., JK Synthetics Ltd., Lakhani India Ltd., Mangalore Refinery and Petrochemicals Ltd., Narmada Cement

Co. Ltd., PCS Industries Ltd., Ramco Industries Ltd., Tata Telecom Ltd., Titan Industries Ltd., VIP Industries Ltd., Wimco Ltd., Yokogawa Blue Star Ltd. etc. which have resulted in value erosion over the study period.

2. *RONW and Inter-Firm Comparison*

The empirical analysis has been carried out with this traditional measure of profitability and the following observations are made:

Group I (Companies with Positive Returns)

Grouping companies according to traditional measure of performance (RONW) resulted in one hundred and thirty-four companies (rank 1-134) falling in the first group with the range of the 152.61 crores (by Torrent Gujarat Biotech Ltd. which got the 1st rank) to 1.63 crores (by Associated Cement Cos. Ltd. with 134th rank). In-between, again there were big industrial houses like Aarti Drugs Ltd., Amtek Auto Ltd., Asian Paints (India) Ltd., Bharat Petroleum Corpn. Ltd., Dr. Reddy's Laboratories Ltd., Eicher Motors Ltd., Hero Honda Motors Ltd., ITC Ltd., Infosys Technologies Ltd., JK Synthetics Ltd., Krebs Biochemical Ltd., Moser Baer India Ltd., Narmada Cement Co. Ltd., Polaris Software Lab Ltd., Rico Auto Indus. Ltd., Swaraj Mazda Ltd., Tata Infotech Ltd., Visualsoft Technologies Ltd., Wyeth Ltd., Wipro Ltd., etc. all showed positive returns to shareholders.

Group II (Companies with Negative Returns)

Twenty companies (from rank 135th to 154th) belonged to this group which revealed negative value for average study period ranging from -0.3 (PCS Industries Ltd.) to -176.9 (by Timex Watches Ltd.). In-between, there were companies like, Ambalal Sarabhai Enterprises Ltd., Bajaj Tempo Ltd., Birla Corporation Ltd., Crompton Greaves Ltd., Floatglass India Ltd., Hindustan Motors Ltd., Indo Rama Synthetics (India) Ltd., Mangalore Refinery and Petrochemicals Ltd., Medicorp Technologies India Ltd., Tata Engineering and Locomotive Co.

Ltd., Tata Telecom Ltd., Voltas Ltd., all of which have resulted in losses for their shareholders in the study period.

3. ROCE and Inter-Firm Comparison

This measure of profitability in the study period has again grouped sample companies into following two categories:

Group I (Companies with Positive Returns)

One hundred and forty-seven companies, from rank first to one hundred and forty-seven, belong to this group with positive ROCE ranging from 70.98 crores (by Hero Honda Motors Ltd., getting the 1st rank) to 0.69 crores (by Float Glass India Ltd.). Few other companies which have revealed positive returns over the study period include Aarti Drugs Ltd., Advani Oerlikon Ltd., Apollo Tyres Ltd., Britannia Industries Ltd., Clariant (India) Ltd., Dr. Reddy's Laboratories Ltd., Electrosteel Castings Ltd., FDC Ltd., George Williamson (Assam) Ltd., German Remedies Ltd., Hi-Tech Gears Ltd., Hindustan Inks and Resins Ltd., ITC Ltd., Infosys Technologies Ltd., Lakshmi Auto Components Ltd., Mirza Tanners Ltd., Novartis India Ltd., Polaris Software Lab Ltd., Punjab Tractors Ltd., Tata Elxsi Ltd., Wipro Ltd. etc.

Group II (Companies with Negative Returns)

From rank 148-154, only seven companies fall in this category of negative returns over the study period. The values range from -3.96 crores (by Narmada Cement Co. Ltd.) to -63.41 crores (by Timex Watches Ltd.). Other companies in this category include Ambalal Sarabhai Enterprises Ltd., Gujarat Sidhee Cement, J.K. Synthetics Ltd., Torrent Gujarat Biotech Ltd., Bongaigaon Refinery and Petrochemicals Ltd. The summary of results of inter-firm analysis with the performance metrics—EVA, RONW and ROCE is presented below in Table 5.4.

TABLE 5.4

Inter-firm Analysis with EVA, RONW and ROCE: Summary of Results

Group	EVA			RONW			ROCE		
	Ranks	*No. of Companies*	*%*	*Ranks*	*No. of Companies*	*%*	*Ranks*	*No. of Companies*	*%*
(1)	*(2)*	*(3)*	*(4)*	*(5)*	*(6)*	*(7)*	*(8)*	*(9)*	*(10)*
I	1-44	44	29	1-134	134	87	1-147	147	95
II	45-154	110	71	135-154	20	13	148-154	07	5
Total		154	100		154	100		154	100

Group I : Companies with Value Addition/Positive Returns.
Group II: Companies with Value Erosion/Negative Returns.

5.2.2 Relationship between EVA, RONW, ROCE and EPS: Correlation Results

Relationship between EVA—the broad measure of value creation and traditional performance measures—RONW, ROCE and EPS has been established with the help of Karl Pearson's coefficient of correlation. The results are given in Table 5.5.

Correlating EVA using Pearsonian correlation coefficient with the traditional measure of performance RONW, ROCE and EPS shows that the relationship is positive and low with EPS and highly positive with RONW and ROCE except the year 1999-2000 in which it is negative and low with RONW. The co-efficient of determination (R^2) indicates that EPS explains the total variation in shareholder wealth only to the extent of 5%; RONW upto the extent of 43% and ROCE upto the extent of 53% approximately. This proves that as compared with the traditional performance measures, EVA is the real key to create shareholders' wealth and the true indicator of the financial performance of a company. The empirical results indicate that not even a single traditional performance measure can be relied upon and used to measure the variation in shareholder value in totality. Traditional performance measures do not reflect the real wealth of shareholders. Hence it should be measured through EVA.

5.2.3 Relationship between Share Price and Other Economic and Financial Variables—EVA, RONW, ROCE and EPS: Regression Results

The relationship of share price with EVA, RONW, ROCE and EPS is examined by using regression analysis. The regression analysis is done on both yearly and on an average basis over the study period.

The detailed regression results for the year 1998-99, 1999-2000, 2000-01, 2001-02, 2002-03 respectively and the average results have been given in Appendix V(D).

The regression equation estimated is as follows:

$$SP = \alpha+\beta_1 RONW+\beta_2 EPS+\beta_3 ROCE+\beta_4 EVA+\varepsilon_t$$

TABLE 5.5

Correlation Results between EVA and Selected Variables

Years	Between					
	EVA and RONW		*EVA and ROCE*		*EVA and EPS*	
	r	R^2	*r*	R^2	*r*	R^2
(1)	*(2)*	*(3)*	*(4)*	*(5)*	*(6)*	*(7)*
1998-99	0.404**	0.163	0.464**	0.215	0.063 (.438)	0.004
1999-2000	-0.155 (.055)	0.024	0.719**	0.517	0.174* (.031)	0.030
2000-01	0.267** (.001)	0.071	0.530**	0.281	0.160* (.048)	0.026
2001-02	0.617**	0.381	0.586**	0.343	0.087 (.284)	0.008
2002-03	0.245** (.002)	0.060	0.725**	0.526	0.226** (.005)	0.051
Average	0.656**	0.430	0.654**	0.428	0.158 (.050)	0.025

* Correlation is significant at 0.05 level (2-tailed).

** Correlation is significant at 0.01 level (2-tailed).

When the above equation was estimated, following results are obtained:

For the Year 1998-99:

$$SP = -46.787 - 1.661\ EVA - 0.207\ RONW$$
$$\quad (-0.982) \quad (-0.733) \qquad (-0.349)$$
$$-0.448\ ROCE + 11.902\ EPS + \varepsilon_t$$
$$(-0.275) \qquad (15.303)$$
$$R^2 = 0.630;\ Adjusted\ R^2 = 0.620;\ F = 63.328$$

Results indicate that all the independent variables explain 63% variation in dependent variable i.e., share price but when adjusted for number of degree of freedom variation explained reduces to 62%. EPS is found to be the most significant variable at 0% level of significance in explaining the variation in share price of a company. However, share price is found to be negatively related to EVA, RONW and ROCE whereas it is positively related to EPS. This indicates that increase in EPS will have a positive impact on share price while decline in EVA, RONW and ROCE will increase the share price of a company.

For the Year 1999-2000:

$$SP = -32.575 + 0.131\ EVA - 0.037\ RONW$$
$$\quad (-0.654) \quad (-0.058) \qquad (-0.133)$$
$$-0.413\ ROCE + 11.864\ EPS + \varepsilon_t$$
$$(-0.240) \qquad (15.294)$$
$$R^2 = 0.623;\ Adjusted\ R^2 = 0.613;\ F = 61.657$$

Results indicate that all the independent variables explain 62.3% variation in dependent variable i.e., share price but when adjusted for number of degrees of freedom variation explained reduces to 61.3%. Again, EPS is found to be the most significant variable at 0% level of significance in explaining the variation in share price of a company. However, share price is found to be negatively related to RONW and ROCE whereas it is positively related to EVA and EPS. This indicates that increase in EPS and in EVA will have a positive impact on share price while decline in RONW and ROCE will increase the share price of a company.

For the Year 2000-2001:

$$SP = -289.886 - 2.914\ EVA - 4.500\ RONW + 7.662\ ROCE$$
$$(-2.238)\quad (-1.366)\qquad (-1.752)\qquad (1.530)$$
$$+39.348\ EPS + \varepsilon_t$$
$$(15.857)$$
$$R^2 = 0.641;\ \text{Adjusted } R^2 = 0.631;\ F = 66.536$$

Results indicate that all the independent variables explain 64.1% variation in dependent variable i.e., share price but when adjusted for number of degrees of freedom variation explained reduces to 63.1%. EPS is found to be the most significant variable at 0% level of significance in explaining the variation in share price of a company. However, share price is found to be negatively related to EVA and RONW whereas it is positively related to ROCE and EPS. This indicates that increase in ROCE and EPS will have a positive impact on share price while decline in EVA and RONW will increase the share price of a company.

For the Year 2001-02:

$$SP = -82.200 - 0.089\ EVA - 0.518\ RONW + 1.993\ ROCE$$
$$(-2.357)\quad (-0.443)\qquad (-1.100)\qquad (1.518)$$
$$+11.883\ EPS + \varepsilon_t$$
$$(15.287)$$
$$R^2 = 0.633;\ \text{Adjusted } R^2 = 0.623;\ F = 64.332$$

Results indicate that all the independent variables explain 63.3% variation in dependent variable, i.e., share price but when adjusted for number of degrees of freedom variation explained reduces to 62.3%. Again EPS is found to be the most significant variable at 0% level of significance in explaining the variation in share price of a company. However, share price is found to be negatively related to EVA and RONW whereas it is positively related to ROCE and EPS. This indicates that increase in EPS and ROCE will have a positive impact on share price while decline in EVA and RONW will increase the share price of a company.

For the Year 2002-03:

$$SP = -60.980 - 1.062\ EVA + 0.094\ RONW + 0.338\ ROCE$$
$$\quad (-1.654)\quad (-0.953)\qquad (-0.408)\qquad (0.302)$$
$$12.379\ EPS + e_t$$
$$(15.590)$$
$$R^2 = 0.630;\ Adjusted\ R^2 = 0.620;\ F = 63.398$$

Results indicate that all the independent variables explain 63% variation in dependent variable i.e., share price but when adjusted for number of degrees of freedom variation explained reduces to 62%. EPS is found to be the most significant variable at 0% level of significance in explaining the variation in share price of a company. However, share price is found to be negatively related to EVA whereas it is positively related to RONW, ROCE and EPS. This indicates that increase in RONW, ROCE and EPS will have a positive impact on share price while decline in EVA will increase the share price of a company.

Average Regression Results:

$$SP = -96.352 - 0.851\ EVA - 0.340\ RONW + 1.438\ ROCE$$
$$\quad (-1.433)\quad (-0.666)\qquad (-0.241)\qquad (0.549)$$
$$17.281\ EPS + e_t$$
$$(15.119)$$
$$R^2 = 0.630;\ Adjusted\ R^2 = 0.620;\ F = 63.487$$

Results indicate that all the independent variables explain 63% variation in dependent variable i.e., share price but when adjusted for number of degrees of freedom variation explained reduces to 62%. EPS is found to be the most significant variable at 0% level of significance in explaining the variation in share price of a company. However, share price is found to be negatively related to EVA and RONW whereas it is positively related to ROCE and EPS. This indicates that increase in ROCE and EPS will have a positive impact on share price while decline in EVA and RONW will increase the share price of a company.

5.3 CONCLUSIONS

The present chapter has made an in-depth analysis of the

financial performance of one hundred and fifty four companies based on both traditional performance metrics – RONW, ROCE, EPS and the new and hottest value-based performance metric-EVA. The relationship of share price with these performance measures is also analysed for the requisite period covered in the study. Following conclusions are drawn based on empirical results and their analysis:

(a) From the analysis of companies for five financial years, it was found that only 31% of companies resulted in value addition in terms of EVA with increasing trend. The remaining 69% of sample companies failed to deliver value to shareholders in five years.

(b) The traditional measure of estimation of value for shareholders, namely RONW and ROCE revealed different results with EVA. In case of RONW, only 6% of companies showed increasing trend of value and the remaining 94% of companies failed to deliver value to shareholders. With respect to ROCE, only 13% of companies revealed value addition over the study period and the remaining 87% of companies failed to add value to shareholders' wealth.

(c) Inter-firm analysis carried on with average yearly computed values of EVA revealed value erosion in case of 71% of companies. Only 29% of companies gained values for their shareholders, the important ones being Hero Honda Motors Ltd., Aurobindo Pharma Ltd., Visualsoft-Technologies Ltd., etc.

(d) The results of inter-firm analysis with RONW and ROCE exhibited almost opposite findings. As per RONW, 87% of companies added value for their shareholders indicating that these are profitable ones over the study period. Only 13% of companies resulted in value erosion. With respect to ROCE, 95% of companies added value over the study period and just 5% of sample companies resulted in value erosion.

(e) The correlation results of association between the new value added metric EVA with traditional performance metrics RONW, ROCE and EPS for the entire sample of one hundred and fifty-four companies revealed low but positive correlation of 0.15 with EPS; highly positive and significant correlation of 0.656 and 0.654 with RONW and ROCE respectively at 1% significant level.

(f) The coefficients of determination (R^2) computed for EPS, RONW and ROCE revealing the extent of variation in shareholder wealth explained by these performance measures is 5%, 43% and 53% respectively. Thus, these measures do not reflect the real value of shareholders. EVA is thereby proved to be most efficient to reflect the shareholder value as compared to these traditional performance measures.

(g) The correlation results* of association between share price and other variables—EVA, ROCE, RONW and EPS for the entire sample of one hundred and fifty-four companies revealed low but positive correlation of 0.091 with EVA, of 0.233 with ROCE and of 0.144 with RONW whereas the correlation between share price and EPS is found to be highly positive and significant at 1% level of significance of 0.793.

(h) The correlation results over the study period thus revealed EPS as the most significantly correlated variable with share price followed by ROCE, RONW and EVA.

(i) With regard to the relationship between share prices of the sample companies and the financial as well as economic variables of RONW, ROCE, EPS and EVA the regression results revealed EPS as the most significant variable in explaining the variation in share prices followed by EVA, ROCE and RONW.

(j) Regression results with average values of variables over the 5-year period is positively related to EPS and ROCE whereas it is negatively related to RONW and EVA, i.e. an increase in ROCE and EPS will have a positive impact on share price while decline in EVA and RONW will increase the share price of a company.

* For detailed correlation results between share price and other variables see Appendix-VD.

Hence, based on the above mentioned conclusions drawn from the empirical findings of the study Ho 1 i.e., EVA is superior in terms of examining shareholders' value addition/ destruction to RONW, ROCE and EPS holds good. However, Ho 2 i.e., no correlation exists between share prices and other variables is rejected.

CHAPTER

6

Disclosure Practices of EVA

The concept of EVA has gained importance over a period of time as a modified approach to corporate performance measurement. Number of companies that have turned to Economic Value Added (EVA) over the past few years as a new way to gauge financial performance is going up. Highly regarded corporations like Coca Cola, AT&T, Quaker Oats and Briggs and Stratton have set-up separate EVA measurement systems throughout their organisations. So far as Indian corporate world is concerned, it is also recognising the importance of EVA, though at a slow pace as compared to corporates in other countries. Many Indian companies have made EVA a part of their Annual Reports. Besides this some have started calculating EVA as an internal report. But, unlike in other countries, EVA has less significance in the Indian context due to accounting distortions and poor disclosure practices.

6.1 TREND OF REPORTING EVA

The concept of EVA has found a number of supporters in India. It has also earned favour with journalists and leaders in corporate reporting. What approach is being taken by India's most popular business houses to report EVA externally is taken a ground for depicting the trend of reporting EVA in the Indian corporate sector. For this purpose five case studies have been drawn from the Indian corporate sector. The companies, chosen randomly, are : (a) Infosys Technologies Limited; (b) Hindustan Lever Limited; (c) Global Telesystems; (d) Godrej Consumer Products Ltd; and (e) Moser Baer India.

CASE STUDY I

Infosys Technologies Limited

Infosys Technologies Limited, known for its transparency in financial statements, may be considered a pioneer in reporting EVA in annual report.

EVA TRENDS OF INFOSYS TECHNOLOGIES LIMITED (ITL)
EVA Statement of ITL as Published in the Annual Report 1999-2000 for the Year Ended March 31...

Particulars	*1997*	*1998*	*1999*	*2000*
Average Capital Employed (Rs. in lakhs)	9846.75	14289.67	24541.6	70386.70
Average Debt %/Total Capital (%)	2.16	NA	NA	NA
Beta variant	1.48	1.48	1.48	1.48
Risk-free debt cost (%)	13.60	12.15	12.00	10.45
Market Premium	10.00	10.00	9.00	8.00
Cost of equity (%)	28.40	26.95	25.32	22.29
Cost of debt (post-tax) (%)	7.70	NA	NA	NA
Weighted Average Cost of Capital (WACC) (%)	27.97	26.95	25.32	22.29
PAT as a percentage of average capital employed (%)	33.91	42.24	54.16	40.63
Economic Value Added:				
Operating Profit (PBT excluding extra-ordinary income)	3893.03	6586.33	15585.54	32564.86
Less: Tax	554.00	550.00	2294.00	3970.00
Less: Cost of Capital	2754.34	3851.07	6213.94	15689.19
Economic Value Added (EVA)	584.69	2186.26	7707.60	12905.67
EVA as a percentage of average capital employed (%)	5.94	15.29	28.84	18.34

Notes: (a) The cost of equity is calculated by using the following formula: Return on risk-free investment + Expected risk premium on equity investment adjusted for average beta variant for software stocks in US.

(b) Figures above are based on Indian GAAP financial statements.

A perusal of the EVA statement published by Infosys in its annual report for the year 1999-2000 reveals the following points:

(i) EVA computation is highly subjective i.e., the disclosure of assumptions based on which EVA is computed is not made that reduces the informative value of EVA very significantly, e.g., the cost of equity is estimated by using CAPM, but it is not very clear why a uniform beta variant of 1.48 is being used for all the years. Also the assumption based on which risk premium has been estimated as 8%, 9%, 10% and 10% for the years 2000, 1999, 1998 and 1997 respectively are not mentioned anywhere.

(ii) Further, the EVA statement also shows a reduction in the cost of equity from 27.97% in 1997 to 22.29% in 2000. This reduction is explained by the reduction in risk-free debt cost from 13.6% in 1997 to 10.45% in 2000 and the reduction in risk premium from 10% in 1997 to 8% in 2000. But, in fact, that reduction do not reflect the reality.

CASE STUDY 2

Hindustan Lever Ltd.

HLL is at present India's fast moving consumer goods (FMCG) company with leadership in Home and Personal Care, Food and Beverages and speciality chemicals. So far as the accounting disclosure is concerned, it has touched new heights i.e., has started disclosing in its Annual Report how much value it has added to shareholders' wealth. The reported EVA figures of HLL published in its Annual Report for the year ended Dec. 31, 2003 are exhibited on the next page.

The observations w.r.t. HLL reporting of EVA can be enlisted as under:

(i) No adjustments have been made for converting book capital into economic capital and the accounting profit into economic profit.

EVA Trends: 1994-2003 (Unaudited)

(*Rs. Crores*)

	1994	*1995*	*1996*	*1997*	*1998*	*1999*	*2000*	*2001*	*2002*	*2003*
(1)	*(2)*	*(3)*	*(4)*	*(5)*	*(6)*	*(7)*	*(8)*	*(9)*	*(10)*	*(11)*
Cost of Capital Employed (COCE):										
1. Average Debt	97	110	156	160	165	162	93	50	45	881
2. Average Equity	462	588	815	1127	1487	1908	2296	2766	3351	2899
3. Average Capital Employed (1) + (2)	559	698	971	1287	1652	2070	2389	2816	3396	3780
4. Cost of debt, post-tax (%)	7.36	7.56	7.88	8.82	9.10	0.61	8.16	7.72	6.45	4.88
5. Cost of Equity (%)	19.70	19.70	19.70	19.70	19.70	19.70	19.70	16.70	14.40	12.95
6. WACC (%)	17.57	17.79	17.80	18.34	18.64	18.83	19.27	16.54	14.30	11.07
7. COCE : (3) × (6)	98	124	173	236	308	390	460	466	486	418
8. Profit after tax, before exceptional items	190	239	413	580	837	1070	1310	1541	1716	1804
9. Add: Interest, after taxes	15	11	32	21	19	14	8	5	6	43
10. NOPAT	205	250	445	601	856	1084	1318	1546	1722	1847
11. COCE, as per (7) above	(98)	(124)	(173)	(236)	(308)	(390)	(460)	(466)	(486)	(418)
12. EVA: (10) – (11)	107	126	272	365	548	694	858	1080	1236	1429

(ii) Calculation of cost of equity is again questionable on account of using a uniform beta variant of 0.81 for all the ten years 1994-2003. The assumptions on which the estimation of market risk premium is based are not explained clearly.

CASE STUDY 3

Global Telesystems

Economic Value Added (EVA) Statement

	Year Ended March 31, 1999		*Rs. (in million)*
1.	Average Capital Employed		5421.31
2.	Average Debt/Average Capital Employed (%)		60.73
3.	Beta variant		1.06
4.	Risk-free debt cost (%)		12.05
5.	Market Premium (%)		10.00
6.	Cost of equity (%)		22.65
7.	Cost of debt (post-tax) (%)		11.42
8.	WACC (%)		15.83
9.	Economic Value Added (EVA)		43.50
	Profit before tax		708.19
	Add: Finance Costs (Gross)		421.17
	PBIT		1129.36
	Less: Non-recurring items:		
	(a) Other income	44.88	
	(b) Interest received	106 77	151.65
	PBT excluding non-recurring income		977.71
	Less: Tax		76.00
	NOPAT		901.69
	Less: Cost of Capital		858.19
	EVA		43.50

Source : Global Telesystems Annual Report, 1998-99.

CASE STUDY 4

Godrej

Godrej Consumer Products Ltd. (GCPL) was formed as a result of the de-merger of Godrej Soaps Limited—a major player in the FMCG market with leadership in the personal, hair-care, fabric and household segments. A system of internal corporate governance was needed which guides all managers and employees and motivates them to work for the best interests of the company. Meanwhile, the concept of EVA was catching on. After much debate and contemplation, the management decided to go ahead with EVA in the financial year 2001-02. And now GCPL is an Economic Value Added (EVA) company.

EVA Statement of GCPL

(*Rs. crore*)

Part 1 : Calculation of NOPAT	*2002-03*	*2001-02*
Profit before tax (PBT)	70.1	63.2
Interest	0.9	2.5
Net operating profit before tax	71.0	65.7
Cash operating tax on PBT	14.4	15.4
Cash operating tax on interest	0.4	0.9
Net operating Profit After Tax (NOPAT)	56.2	49.4
Part II: Calculation of WACC	*2002-03*	*2001-02*
Leverage Beta (β)	0.63	0.63
Market risk premium (P)	10%	10%
Equity risk premium (P X β)	6.3%	6.3%
Risk-free return (r)	9.3%	11.5%
Cost of equity [r + (P x β)]	15.6%	17.8 %
Equity/market value (e)	0.96	0.96
Weighted cost of equity [{r + (pβ)} e]	15.0%	17.1 %
Pre-tax cost of borrowing	10%	14%
Retention rate (1 – tax rate)	64.3%	65%
Debt/market value (d)	0.04	0.04
Weighted cost of debt {1 – (1–f)d}	0.3%	0.4%
WACC	15.3% (16%)	17.5% (18%)

GCPL's average capital employed for 2002-03 is Rs. 90.4 crore (Rs. 107.1 crore for 2001-02). Given a WACC of 16% (18% for 2001-02) this translates into Rs. 14.5 crore (Rs. 19.3 crore for 2001-02) cost of capital employed.

EVA = NOPAT – [{1 (1–tax rate) d} + { (r + pβ) e } × capital employed.

(Rs. Crores)

	2002-03	*2001-02*
NOPAT	56.2	49.4
Capital Charge	14.5	19.3
EVA	41.7	30.1

CASE STUDY 5

Moser Baer India (MBI)

Moser Baer presented EVA statement as one of the various sub-heads under Additional Information for Shareholders. EVA analysis starts with the premise that investors are primarily concerned with the cash return on their cash investment and the risk associated with that investment. This return can be directly compared with the return expected by them, the company's WACC. Value is created/destroyed if the business generates a return above/below its cost of capital. For Risk-free return (R_f), the yield on the 10-year government bond is being used. Equity Beta based on an analysis of comparable optical storage media companies in Asia as well as MBI's beta estimate from Bloomberg.

The above description shows that although the popularity of EVA has tempted the companies to report EVA as a public relations measure, its reporting is not yet upto the mark. A trend has set in to use EVA casually for external reporting. The requirement is to stall this trend and to bring more transparency in providing EVA information and its reporting. Otherwise such a reporting of EVA might mislead the users of these reports.

EVA Statement of MBI for the year ended March 31...

Sl. No.	*Particulars*	*2002*	*2001*	*2000*	*1999*	*1998*
	(1)	*(2)*	*(3)*	*(4)*	*(5)*	*(6)*
1.	Average capital employed (Rs. in million)	12018.9	6727.7	2714.9	1289.0	934.0
2.	Average debt (Rs. in million)	5927.8	3092.9	1709.4	813.4	601.7
3.	Beta variant	1.34	1.33	1.14	1.21	1.1
4.	Risk-free debt cost (%)	7.5	10.1	10.0	12.0	12.0
5.	Market risk premium	7.0	8.0	8.5	8.5	8.5
6.	Cost of equity (%)	16.9	20.7	19.6	22.2	21.3
7.	Post-tax cost of debt (%)	9.3	6.9	6.8	7.2	8.5
8.	Weighted average cost of capital (WACC) (%)	13.9	18.3	10.0	13.8	11.9
9.	PAT as a percentage of average capital employed (%)	18.0	20.6	16.3	15.9	14.1
10.	Economic Value Added (EVA) (Rs. in million):					
	Operating Profit (PBT excluding extra-ordinaries)	2575.8	1647.4	521.0	290.0	183.1
	Less: Tax	42.4	0.3	0.3	0.2	0.1
	Less: Cost of capital	1009	1201	457	178	111
	EVA	864	414	64	112	72
11.	Enterprise value : (Rs. in million)					
	Market value of equity	13119.1	14758.7	6113.2	642.6	223.1
	Add: Net debt	7137.5	2283.6	1499.0	513.5	602.4
	Enterprise Value	20256.6	17042.4	7612.1	1156.1	825.5
12.	Ratio:					
	EVA as a percentage of capital employed (%)	7.2	6.1	2.4	8.7	7.7
	Enterprise value/Average capital employed	1.7	2.5	2.8	0.9	0.9

6.2 HOW SOME COMPANIES HAVE USED EVA?

We will be missing one of the strategic issue related to EVA if we don't discuss the usage of EVA i.e., whether EVA has been adopted a measure of financial performance or it has been used as a base for determining incentives to managers or it has been used as a measure of internal corporate governance, both in case of Indian as well as non-Indian/foreign companies. To be more specific a few examples out of Indian and foreign corporate sector have been taken up to explain it and are arranged in the form of following Table:

TABLE 6.1
The Usage of EVA

S. No.	Company	The Usage of EVA
1.	The Coca Cola Co.	Focussed business managers on increasing shareholder value.
2.	AT & T Corp.	Used EVA as the lead indicator of a performance measurement system that included "people value added" and "customer value added".
3.	IBM	Conducted a study with Stern Stewart that indicated that outsourcing IT often led to short-term increases in EVA.
4.	Horman Miller Inc.	Tied EVA measure to senior manager's bonus and compensation system.
5.	Infosys	Here EVA is used as a tool to tell its clients that the value derived by Infosys is greater than what the clients pays for.
6.	Marico	As a signalling device to tell its employees that capital is important.
7.	TCS	Here EVA is linked to compensation and has been implemented in great detail.
8.	Godrej	EVA is used not only as a financial tool but also as a way of structuring performance-linked variable remuneration.
9.	Dr. Reddy's Laboratories	As a qualifying criterion to grant rewards such as variable pay, stock options and performance bonuses.
10.	HLL	Used EVA as a basis to measure the performance of each of its divisions.

6.2.1 EVA at Godrej

Continuous discussions among the management led to the conclusion that a system of internal corporate governance was needed which guides all managers and employees and motivates them to work for the best interest of the company. A leading consultant was called to make a presentation on the EVA option for Godrej. This is what the management learned :

- EVA implementation would improve overall capital efficiency and ensure that the company was moving forward in the right direction. It also integrated financial measurement with business imperatives in a comprehensible form.
- The key factor was that employees would begin to think like owners. They would also start worrying about where the capital is employed and what returns are being generated from it rather than sticking to just their own pay cheques and promotions. This mindset was crucial for the success of the company.
- EVA eliminated the problem of multi-step targets outlined earlier because it is a graph where incentives are plotted against the EVA earned and so every employee gets rewarded for the amount of work put in by him.
- EVA would make it possible to have bonus plans with no upside limits. Bonuses, whether meager or lavish, are earned by beating annually negotiated budgets. Under the old system, a manager's greatest incentive is to negotiate an easily achievable budget and because the bonus is capped, not to exceed it by too much for fear of raising expectations or damaging his or her credibility. EVA bonus targets, in contrast, would be automatically reset each year by formula. If EVA shot up, for example the following year's bonus would be based on improvement above the new, higher level of EVA.
- EVA is an excellent indicator of wealth creation. After much debate and contemplation, the management decided to go ahead with EVA. Godrej Consumer

Products Limited (GCPL) implemented EVA in the financial year 2001-02.

Six group companies of Godrej went in for EVA implementation. This was facilitated by Stern Stewart and company, a New York-based management consulting firm that pioneered the development of the EVA framework. GCPL has implemented the EVA programme at all non-unionised levels that involved various steps:

1. EVA of various businesses was measured and the implications of the numbers understood.
2. Targets on EVA improvement were then set over a three year time frame.
3. An exhaust manual was made about what each function could do to improve the EVA of the business. This was a detailed task involving the consultants, the functional heads and HR department. Details of what some of the functions did are provided below :

Human Resoures and Finance

- *Employee Benefits*: HR and Finance departments had plenty of reorganizing to do. One of the initiatives taken up by the HR department was outsourcing the housing loans to IDBI. Earlier, housing loans were given at a subsidised rate of 5% to the employees. IDBI was offering this facility at 11%. The remainder was passed on as a benefit to the employee. To the extent outsourced, the capital was freed up. The company may also outsource its vehicle loans and discontinue company owned cars.
- *Maintaining and developing talent*: During the year, the company implemented a system of performance linked variable remuneration (PLVE) of employees based on improvement in EVA of the company. This EVA-based PLVR accounts for about 35 percent of a senior managers total remuneration package, and 25 percent

of a junior manager. The PLVR scheme has been devised in such a manner that it provides an incentive for employees to create EVA on a long-term and sustained basis. The company also implemented another unique program by which employees participate in training programs through an online initiative, aptly called E-gyan. In collaboration with Satyam, this new knowledge initiative helps employees improve their skills and knowledge without having to remove themselves from their work environment.

Production

Lowering the cost of production by keeping working capital (WC) to the minimum and using better inventory management techniques. In fact, after EVA implementation, GCPL has been on a negative WC all along.

- EVA calculations supported the decision to put up a third manufacturing base in Guwahati.

Logistics and Distribution

- During the year, the company was able to increase the number of directly covered retail outlets and also increase its reach to smaller towns through the Super Sub-Stockist schemes. A complex Collaborative, Planning, Forecasting and Replenishment (CPFAR) web-based initiative was put into place to connect the entire GCPL sales and distribution network across India. The objective was to ensure that the supply chain runs smoothly and the right product is available at the right place in the right quantities, on a continuous replenishment basis. CPFAR involves reduction of inventories, improved efficiencies right through the extended supply chain, speeding up the investment turnover and educating CFAs on improved logistics methods.

Marketing and Sales

- The sales team was to be assessed not only on orders booked but also on optimal credit period as it is this that has a direct impact on the ROCE (Return On Capital Employed). EVA also eliminated the pitfalls of short-term targets as the three year implementation period allowed better investment decisions.

After laying out what each function could do, exhaustive training programmes were conducted on communicating what each department or individual could do to help improve the EVA of the company. The initial sessions were held by Stern Stewart with roll out programmes by the Senior Management and the training department.

The employees at GCPL were skeptical about EVA and this had to be overcome. The first response of every employee was typical: Is this a new management trick to deprive me of my money? These were met within the most friendly and approachable manner. The training workshops made it clear that EVA was not only a more equitable system but also would reward much more handsomely on achievement of targets. It has been a step-by-step implementation for GCPL, designed for better acceptance from employees. In the first year, emphasis was on business and team performance alone. In the second year, a multiplication factor ranging from 0 to 1.2 has been introduced in the compensation package to reflect individual performance. However, after a process of dissemination and management buy-in, EVA was accepted with great enthusiasm within the company.

GCPL was able to create a positive EVA of Rs. 30.1 crore during the year 2001-02. The EVA target set by the company for the financial year 2001-02 was not only met but exceeded. The company has achieved an EVA of Rs. 9.7 crore for the quarter ended 30th June 2002 as against Rs. 6.5 crore for the corresponding quarter last year, i.e., an increase of 49%. GCPL did a SWOT analysis of their experience with EVA which is summarised in the following table:

TABLE 6.2
SWOT Analysis of GCPL

Strengths	*Opportunities*
EVA serves as a one point indicator for business performance. It aligns employees', owners' and shareholders' interests.	It creates an opportunity for each individual and each function to analyse how each process can be made EVA friendly and hence more productive. It also gives top management the opportunity to eliminate non-value adding activities and business.
Weaknesses	*Threats*
The concept is time-consuming to understand. Communicating the concept requires that employees have tremendous faith in the management, otherwise the intentions may be misunderstood.	A typical criticism levelled against EVA was that it is anti-growth and anti-risk, e.g., taking up a new project could reduce the EVA for about 2-3 years. However, whether it remains on the downturn will depend on the nature of the risk in the project. A sound business plan should eventually result in better EVA.

For Godrej, the EVA implementation surely was a rewarding experience. Since the employees were clear about how they are contributing to increasing the EVA, it worked as a tremendous motivator for them. Moreover, the objective of continuously working towards increasing EVA ensured that capital efficiency improved and that shareholders were happy.

6.2.2 The EVA Story at Tata Consultancy Services (TCS)

Tata Consultancy Services (TCS) employs over 15,000 professionals, has offices in 23 countries and projects in 50 countries across the world, and revenues around $700 million. Among its clientele are number of Fortune 500 companies and it is in the league of 30 top IT consulting firms in the world.

TCS today is an Indian enterprise with a global reach. Its hiring and people care practices are in line with the industry practices and the compensation model has been traditional. The company has now sets its sights on becoming a truly global organisation. Its vision is to be among the top 10 IT consulting organisations in the world, a global employer of choice. It is looking towards institutionalising leading edge practices in hiring, training and people care, with and innovative EVA-based compensation model. This will make it the first organisation in India to implement this competitive salary structure, which determines compensation based on value delivered to the employer. TCS is playing a game where rules are stricter and opponents tougher. TCS hopes its adoption of EVA, in April 1999, will help it to survive in this intensely competitive business.

TCS faced many challenges while implementing EVA, but it successfully overcome them to complete the implementation ahead of schedule. The implementation coincided with corporate reorganisation. Also, given the nature of its projects, TCS had to design an incentive mechanism not only to retain talent but also to reward it accordingly.

TCS's EVA framework aligns corporate value with the performance of the constituent business units and the individuals who comprise those. It is a compensation model where the employees has a share in the profits of the organisation. At the individual level, an employee needs to know the drivers to enhance the EVA of the enterprise and the business unit, and his own contribution towards all these. There are three basic drivers: revenue, cost and capital charge. Revenue is driven by the rate or license price put into the product, sales, billable hours, response time and domain skills. Cost is managed through productivity, and is affected by sales and marketing costs, recruitment, etc. Receivables and training are the bulk of the capital charge.

The individual works towards the improvement of the benefit package, which essentially has three components: corporate EVA, business—unit EVA, and the individual performance factor. Out of the total EVA payment, a certain percentage goes to each employee on the basis of corporate EVA improvement. Besides, if one business unit does better than another business unit, one gets more than somebody in the other unit. It is a team reward concept. Further, TCS has also introduced the concept of 'bonus bank'. Whenever a stipulated corporate target is exceeded, the company declares a potential bonus for the individual. It is cumulated over years and the pay-out is a function of the cumulative balance. This approach ensures performance improvements and maintains a cumulative relationship between pay and performance. It enhances the sense of participation through the realisation of the share in the larger pie, and provides the motivation to contribute to enlarge the pie.

6.2.3 Tata Tea: EVA in a Tea Cup

Dissatisfied with traditional accounting measures, Mr. Homi Khusrokhan, managing director, Tata tea, had asked Stern Stewart to do a diagnostic study on value in Tata Tea. The aim of the study was to see whether information systems focussed on value and enabled good decision-making, and which areas had to be addressed in order to create positive value. Also, the value chain was not sufficiently de-aggregated to show where value was being created and where it was being destroyed. Later, Tata Tea started the measurement phase. This involved training its finance personnel in the adjustments to be made in the accounting figures. The 'company steering group' decided on how many and which EVA centres should be created within the company.

The EVA process was made possible through a workshop on plantation economics. The workshop was designed to provide a method for treating each plantation as an asset, with the value of the discounted value of future earnings from the teas produced at that plantation evaluated at auction—equivalent prices. The method looked at plantations as units of production that are capable of generating alternative streams of revenue, depending on inputs, agronomic practices and prices. This outlook allowed people to make choices on the basis of financial outcomes rather than gut feel.

Tata Tea has started building EVA as a 'key performance indicator' in the balanced scorecards, so that the performance—management system centres around EVA. The minimum number of such balanced scorecards will be nine, one for each of the EVA centres. Since EVA is influenced by decisions made within the centre, the impact of these decisions will be tracked on the balanced scorecards for the EVA centre. The idea is to identify where the value for the shareholder is being created. The company will test its first cut medium-term three-year business plan on this metric, and determine whether the plan delivers the required future growth value. If not, it will have to re-examine some of the strategies.

Implementing EVA was not easy for Mr. Khusrokhan and his team. They needed to change the mind sets and beliefs that were once held dear. For instance, brands became "captive to plantations" and the choices open to the company were narrowed down. Dependencies were created between plantations and brands, and these become difficult to severe. All own-plantation teas are sustainable and have a value that can be easily ascertainable. No unit of production can be rewarded a realisation that is higher than its true 'economic rent'.

To make the right choices, one needs to de-aggregate the value-chain and determine where value is being created and where it is being destroyed. The EVA-based way of looking at plantation values—at the auction equivalent price of the teas produced, rather than the aggregated realisation that can be got out of a brand—is a better and more correct way of looking at the true economics of plantations.

By creating EVA centres in the organisation, Tata Tea's top echelon is moving away from a top-down decision structure. The nine EVA centres are supported by EVA-measurement points, which will aid the spread of the methodology. The North India plantation operations are collectively an EVA centre; individual plantations like Powai or Chubwa are EVA-measurement points.

Mr. Khusrokhan, managing director, Tata Tea, expects a momentous change from EVA implementation. The most significant benefit that the group can derive out of the EVA methodology is an improvement in the quality of strategic decision-making within individual group companies.

6.2.4 Tata Steel: Rolling Out EVA

Tata steel is not content with being India's only world-class steel-maker. The urge to improve and to emerge as the most cost-efficient steel producer induced it to consider quality and performance—improvement initiatives. It adopted the value-engineering technique, ISO 9000, ISO 14000, QS 9000, Six Sigma, the JRD Quality value and EVA among other things. Tata Steel adopted a five-stage process for implementing EVA:

- *Sharing the vision*: creation of awareness among employees.
- *Value diagnostic*: identification of gaps and opportunities.
- Value audit and goal setting.
- Measurement and management.
- Training and knowledge transfer from working groups to employees.

So far the implementation has progressed along expected lines Tata Steel's experience with 'total operating performance' and the performance ethic programme (PEP) have helped. Tata steel did not have to spend time on identifying EVA centres and drivers as the PEP was already structured on those lines. The company was able to integrate all initiatives and make speedy progress on multiple initiatives. Targets have been set of turning EVA positive by 2007 to meet the expectations of investors.

6.3 CONCLUSION

Undoubtedly, a keen interest is taken in the Indian corporate world to opt EVA as a new performance measurement tool as well as to design the compensation on the basis of EVA. Certain companies like HLL, Infosys, etc. have started even disclosing EVA in their annual reports. Others like Godrej, Tata Consultancy Services, etc. have developed the EVA model. All this indicates that the trap of traditional performance measures like ROI, ROCE, EPS, etc. is breaking down but still people are skeptical about the success of EVA companies. One reason is the unsatisfactory disclosure of EVA. To be more specific the level of transparency is low regarding its measurement aspect. Secondly, difficulties have been experienced in breaking the resistance of middle and low level employees to adopt this new culture. Hence, by developing understanding of the concept first by arranging workshops and training sessions and then by improving communication levels ensuring them that EVA is not a new mean to take away their share in the corporate pie rather by adopting it something can be added to their big share if they are contributing to add value to the shareholders' wealth, problem can be solved to a large extent. So the need of the hour is to stall this trend of disclosing EVA casually for external reporting purposes.

CHAPTER

7

Policy Implications for Investors and Managers

7.1 OVERVIEW

Developing new management accounting and decision tools is a very current subject both in business and consultation practice, as well as in academic research as the success of the firm depends on its management having theoretically sound and in practice on operational tools for planning, decision-making and monitoring. During the last few years this development has become even more prominent thanks to several new techniques and concepts, both financial and non-financial. These include Activity Based Management, Balanced Scorecard, Benchmarking, Total Quality Management and the Economic Value Added (EVA), Market Value Added (MVA) and the Shareholder Value Added (SVA) variants.

The firm has a number of stakeholders with differing, sometimes conflicting goals. The stakeholders include the owners, lenders, management, personnel, customers, suppliers, creditors, government and regulatory agencies. In corporate governance agency theory the managers are regarded as agents of the owners in stockholders' wealth-maximisation. Among the management tools EVA, in particular, emphasizes the interests of the owners.

The concept of economic value added is a derivative of the traditional accounting concept of Residual Income (RI). The concept emerges in several variations and incarnations including the trade-marked Stern Stewart & Co's EVA with its copious accounting adjustments. In line with the theory of finance the RI derivative EVA is commonly advocated as a management tool because the goal of the firm is to add value to the owners' wealth. In other words, just as debt holders of a firm expect a specific rate of return, the other stakeholders of the firm i.e., the shareholders also expect a certain rate of return for taking the risk of investing in the firm; a maximum compensation over the cost of capital invested in the firm.

There are many traditional ways by which one can analyze the companies' performance like EPS, ROCE, P/E Ratio, RONW, etc. but these can be manipulated by accounting practice and doesn't provide clear understanding of the variables that drive value, such as, operating margins, cost of capital and the competitive advantage period. So we can use a new technique called EVA to address business and financial risk and allows the investor to gauge the magnitude and sustainability of returns. This methodology also allows investors to easily identify companies that pursue business strategies with the goal of shareholders' value creation.

The origin of the value added concepts date all the way back to the early 1900's. The concept resurfaced in 1990's much thanks to the consulting firm Stern Stewart and Co. successful launching of the economic value added as the trademark EVA and the subsequent adoption by several major corporations. In the academic world, a number of studies have been carried out on this burning topic abroad especially in the developed capital markets of U.S.A. and U.K. These studies have covered various aspects, viz., (a) presenting, promoting or discussing the EVA concept, (b) measuring the strength of the relation between market return (or market value added) and EVA compared to the relation between market return and the traditional income measures, (c) looking at EVA as a management tool from the point of view of the accounting measurement. Being relatively less popular phenomenon in India the concept of EVA has not received much attention of researchers. In fact, no comprehensive study has been undertaken to examine various aspects of EVA, especially empirical investigation of its' relationship with share prices of companies. The present study is aimed at examining this in India during the period covered in the study (i.e., 1998-99 to 2002-03) in terms of financial performance of the sample companies. An attempt has also been made to evaluate the superiority of EVA compared to the traditional performance measures like RONW, ROCE, EPS, etc.

The study focussed on four main aspects, viz., (a) examination of relationship between EVA and other financial variables—ROCE, RONW and EPS, (b) evaluation of performance in terms of value addition to shareholders, (c) studying the relationship of share price with EVA, RONW, ROCE and EPS, and (d) evaluating the disclosure of EVA information. Methodology followed for each of these four aspects is different. It is therefore useful to briefly recapitulate the methodology followed in the study.

In the first aspect the performance of all the 154 sample companies was analyzed in terms of value addition to shareholders. For this purpose, the metrics namely EVA, RONW and ROCE were computed for five financial years from 1998-99 to 2002-03. Further, intra-firm analysis and inter-firm analysis were conducted using the technique of clusture analysis.

The second aspect dealt with the analysis of sample companies to study the relationship between EVA and other financial variables RONW, ROCE and EPS using the correlation analysis. Further, the superiority of EVA over other performance measures is tested in terms of the extent of explanation of variation in total shareholders' wealth using coefficient of determination.

The third aspect was related to an in-depth analysis of the relationship between share price and the set of economic and financial variables—EVA, RONW, ROCE and EPS. For this part of analysis, statistical tool of Karl Person's Coefficient of Correlation and Multiple Regression are used.

The fourth aspect covered the evaluation of reporting practices w.r.t. EVA information. For this purpose, the case study method is used. Five companies have been taken up and discussed in detail w.r.t. disclosure of EVA information.

The following null hypotheses were tested in the study:

1. There is no significant difference between the financial performance results exhibited by the value-based measure—EVA and the profit-based measures EPS, RONW and ROCE.
2. There is no significant correlation between share prices and financial variables—EVA, EPS, RONW and ROCE.
3. EVA disclosures in the published annual report of Indian companies are not satisfactory.

7.2 MAIN EMPIRICAL FINDINGS

Shareholders' value addition and survival of the fittest are the buzzwords. The corporate sector has increasingly resorted to certain new value-based performance measures to gauge the financial soundness of a concern like Economic Value Added (EVA), Shareholder Value Added (SVA), Cash Value Added (CVA), Cash Flow Return on Investment (CFROI) in addition to the traditional performance measures—Return on Net Worth (RONW), Return on Capital Employed (ROCE), Earnings Per Share (EPS), Price Earning Ratio (P/E Ratio), etc. Even the investors can get a better picture of what the company is doing with the funds invested by them by looking at the annual EVA figures. Besides, EVA mechanism also proves to be an important incentive tool for the group of managers. The study has also focussed on this hottest financial idea—Economic Value Added (EVA).

The findings of the study are discussed under four major heads, viz., (a) performance evaluation of sample companies in terms of value addition to shareholders, (b) relationship between EVA and the financial variables—RONW, ROCE and EPS, (c) relationship between share price and economic as well as accounting variables—EVA, RONW, ROCE and EPS, (d) disclosures of EVA information in published annual reports.

7.2.1 Value-Added Performance Evaluation

As stated earlier, the performance of one hundred and fifty-four sample companies were examined with the help of value-added metrics, namely, EVA, RONW and ROCE. Statistical technique of clusture analysis, was employed to analyse and interpret the results. The findings of the analysis are summarized in two categories as follows:

1. Intra-firm Analysis

(1) The analysis of sample companies in terms of EVA revealed that 69% of the companies resulted in value erosion for its shareholders with decreasing or no visible trend in five financial years. Only 31% of companies exhibited positive value of shareholders which increased in these years. Hero Honda Motors Ltd., CMC Ltd. and Tata Elxsi Ltd. were few firms that gained heavily in these years.

(2) Similar analysis carried on with the traditional tool of measuring corporate's performance namely, RONW and ROCE revealed altogether different results. In case of RONW, only 6% of companies showed increasing trend of value and the remaining 94% of companies failed to deliver value to shareholders. With respect to ROCE only 13% of companies revealed value addition over the whole study period and the remaining 87% of companies failed to add value to shareholders' wealth.

2. Inter-Firm Analysis

(1) Result of inter-firm analysis based on comparison of average values of EVA in the study period revealed value erosion to the shareholders in case of 71% of sample companies. Only 29% of the companies gained shareholder value, the important achievers were Aurobindo Pharma Ltd., Hero Honda Motors Ltd., Visual Soft Technologies Ltd., etc.

(2) The result of inter-firm analysis with the measures of RONW and ROCE revealed almost different findings.

As per RONW, 87% of the companies gained value for their shareholders. Only 13% of companies were found to be non-profitable. The major gainers with the measure were Aarti Drugs Ltd., Dr. Reddy's Laboratories Ltd., Hero Honda Motors Ltd. and Infosys Technologies Ltd., etc. With regard to ROCE 95% of companies added value over the study period and just 5% of sample companies resulted in value erosion. Few companies like Hero Honda Motors Ltd., Apollo Tyres Ltd., ITC Ltd., Novartis India Ltd., Wipro Ltd., etc. were among the big gainers.

7.2.2 EVA *vs.* Traditional Performance Measures

The association between EVA and the traditional profit-based measures like RONW, ROCE, EPS is examined using Karl Pearson's correlation coefficient. The findings that emerge in terms of correlation between EVA and these financial variables—RONW, ROCE and EPS suggests that EVA is associated with these measures. Further it has been found that there exists significant correlation between these set of measures. Also the superiority of EVA over these measures was established using coefficient of determination. The summarized findings are as follows:

1. An in-depth analysis of sample companies revealed that there exists low but positive correlation between EVA and EPS and highly positive and significant correlation with RONW and ROCE.
2. It is further found that EPS explained just 5% of the total variation in shareholder wealth, RONW to the extent of 43% and ROCE to 53% of the total variation. Hence, EVA proved to be most efficient to reflect the shareholder value as compared to these performance measures.

7.2.3 Share Prices and Performance Metrics

After evaluating the performance of sample companies and establishing the superiority of EVA over the traditional measures, correlation and regression analysis were conducted to set the relationship between share prices and these value-based and profit-based performance measures—EVA, RONW, ROCE and EPS. The results revealed that the null hypothesis, namely, there exists on significant correlation between share prices and the variables—EVA, RONW, ROCE and EPS has been rejected and alternate hypothesis is accepted. The summarized results of this test are as follows:

1. The correlation results of association between share price and other variables—EVA, ROCE, RONW, EPS revealed low but positive correlation of share price with EVA, RONW and ROCE. Only between EPS and the share price, correlation is found to be highly positive and significant. Hence, EPS is a better measure for examining the relationship with share price than EVA.
2. Further, the regression results also revealed EPS as the most significant variable in explaining the variation in share prices followed by EVA, ROCE and RONW.

7.2.4 Disclosure of EVA Information

Disclosure of EVA information has been analysed on the basis of published annual reports of some companies. Based on the detailed analysis of EVA statements of five selected cases composed of Infosys Technologies Ltd., Hindustan Lever Ltd., Global Telesystems Ltd., Godrej Ltd. and Moser Baer India Ltd., following results have emerged:

1. There exists large inconsistency in reporting EVA by the companies in terms of its computation methodology and various assumptions being made therein.
2. A trend has set in to use EVA casually for external reporting purposes.
3. Not even in a single company's annual report EVA statement forms part of the audited financial results rather it is reported in the form of unaudited additional information given to shareholders.

7.3 MAIN CONCLUSIONS OF THE STUDY

The following conclusions have been drawn from the study:

1. To gauge the financial performance of a company it is not advisable to place the sole reliance on the traditional profit-based measures of performance. By using value-based metrics, like Economic Value Added (EVA), Market Value Added (MVA), etc. along with these traditional measures a better picture can be attained of the financial performance of companies.
2. While simply measuring EVA can give companies a better focus on how they are performing, its true value comes in using it as the foundation for a comprehensive financial management system that encompasses all the policies, procedures, methods and measures that guide operations and strategy. The EVA system covers the full range of managerial decisions including strategic planning, allocating capital, pricing acquisitions and setting annual goals even in day-to-day operating decisions. The uniform focus on continuously improving EVA provides the best insurance that all managers are making the right decisions for shareholders.
3. Most of the companies in India relied heavily on Return on Capital Employed (ROCE), Earning per Share (EPS) to measure the profitability of their concern. The results exhibited by these measures seem to be distorted when compared with the value-added results for the same companies using the value-based metric—EVA. The results of companies in India corroborate the conclusions of research work in this field with most of even high EPS companies turned out to be non-profitable or value destroyer to shareholders' wealth.
4. With regard to the relationship between share prices and the performance measures, highly value-added or high EVA companies should lead to an upward movement in its share prices or *vice-versa*. However,

broadly, the results of various research studies in this context falls into two broad categories; one strongly correlating share prices with EVA and the other totally disregarding the bondage between EVA and the share prices. The results of various analysis conducted in the present study conclude that there is no significant correlation between EVA and the share prices.

5. There still exists strong human resistance in India to shift to these new value-added measures of performance from the traditional ROCE, RONW, EPS, etc. Wherever efforts have been made to remove this resistance and develop an EVA-friendly environment again preciseness is low with respect to various assumptions made for its computation. Hence, more transparency is suggested both in its computation as well as in its reporting.

7.4 IMPLICATIONS OF THE STUDY

The present study and its empirical findings would be useful to investors as it provides evidence of value addition capability of investment outlets in India. Investors aim at adding more value to their investible wealth and therefore, they need to study and analyse the value addition character of companies before putting their money therein.

It is found that EVA has varied across companies as well as across periods for a single company. And, contrary to the popular belief—more profits more value, even the higher profit-making companies would tend to have negative EVA and *vice-versa*. An investor thus must choose to invest in a particular concern having value creating capability year after year. The focus of any new investment certainly should be on earning positive EVA over the life of the investment.

The findings of the study are of help to senior managers on two major aspects—one for making strategic decisions that impact the intrinsic value of the business and the other for managing performance by putting in place value-based performance management systems. In the first, focus is on the types of strategic decisions while making a major investment or divestment. What are the goals they have to set for creating wealth for shareholders? How much improvement in EVA is good enough? On performance management systems, it helps companies to recognize and understand that managing for improving the value is not simply a measurement. Disclosure of one's economic performance may be an important feature but it is not the starting and the ending point. It further help managers understand how to measure and hold accountability for economic performance and cascade accountability. The findings of the study also provide help to managers linking executive performance compensation to value enhancement. Various EVA-linked incentive schemes have been designed in the study that shares a portion of excess return which managers are creating for shareholders. These schemes are shareholder-friendly because by definition shareholders' expectations of return are built-in and have to be delivered. Performance in this aspect is fundamentally measured and not prone to capital market vagaries.

7.5 SUGGESTIONS FOR FURTHER WORK

The area of value-added metrics, especially, EVA, MVA, etc. has been extensively researched in many developed nations especially in USA and UK. However, not much work has been done in this area in India. The present study is a comprehensive attempt to empirically analyze the financial performance of companies through EVA during the period 1998-2003. But still there are some areas of research which require investigation. It would be worthwhile for the future researchers to enquire into these areas. These areas are listed below:

1. The present study has made an in-depth analysis of value-added performance of companies in India by using a single value-based metric EVA. However, there are other value-based metrics, like Market Value Added (MVA), Cash Value Added (CVA) and Shareholder Value Added (SVA). Hence, research in these other metrics need to be taken up.
2. The study has assessed superiority of EVA over the traditional measures of performance based on an in-depth analysis of one hundred and fifty-four

manufacturing companies only. This can also be assessed on a larger sample comprising of service concerns also.

3. Further, the long-run financial performance of companies can be gauged by taking a longer time period, say ten to fifteen years. For this, however, one would have to wait for few years to get the relevant data as most of the companies in India have been started using value-added metrices only in past few years.
4. The impact of performance measures such as EPS, ROCE, RONW and EVA on share price variation has been measured while there are other variables like dividend per share, price-earnings ratio, etc. which could be taken up by future researchers. Moreover, the association of MVA as a performance measure may be researched.

CHAPTER

8

EVA and Share Price Behavior : The Recent Analysis

8.1 OVERVIEW

In business schools, we get to learn the various measures adopted by analysts to gauge the performance of companies and are able to fathom abbreviations like EPS, ROCE and RONW but many of us are not comfortable with these matrices rather a set of new value-based measures like CVA, SVA, CFROI, EVA and WA have emerged on the screen. Out of these EVA has emerged as a clear cut winner to these traditional accounting measures. EPS, ROCE, RONW, etc. do not correlate well with the shareholder value creation . On the contrary, EVA offers a consistent approach to setting goals and measuring performance, communicating with investors, evaluating strategies and allocating capital. EVA as a value-based performance metric seeks to measure the periodic performance in terms of change in value. Maximising EVA means the same as maximizing long-term yield on shareholders' investment. It is the measure that captures the true economic profit of the organization.

Here an attempt has been made to examine the relationship between share price and Economic Value Added (EVA), considered to be the best indicator of shareholder value creator in relation to other performance measures like Return on net worth (RONW), Return on Capital Employed (ROCE), and Earning per Share (EPS).

8.2 METHOD OF INVESTIGATION AND ANALYSIS

The study takes the universe of all 500 Indian companies—the top Indian companies termed as India's biggest wealth creators as per the Stern-Stewart listing, the most accurate report card of India Inc's ability to create (or destroy) wealth. After the first phase of securitization we eliminate the companies for which the requisite financial data is not available for at least 3 out of 5 financial years covered in the study. Further, we eliminate the companies whose financial year is ending either in the month of December or June but not in the month of March. Additionally, we also eliminate the companies falling in the category of non-manufacturing industry. Thus, we take up a fairly representative sample group of Indian corporate sector having uniform accounting year with an assurance of the availability of data for at least 3 out of 5 financial years covered in the study. Finally, the sample comprises of top 135 companies. The company data has been collected for the period of the study. The required financial data is collected from the electronic database PROWESS, provided by Centre for Monitoring Indian Economy (CMIE), Mumbai. Apart from this, we have used the published annual reports of companies wherever required.

We take values of EPS, ROCE and RONW have been taken as given in the database while EVA is computed using Stern-Stewart formula, where EVA is the difference between NOPAT and the capital charge (i.e., WACC CE).

The share price of the 135 sample companies are taken as the average of the high, low, opening and closing values of that financial year. Since no huge transitions have occurred in the trends of stock prices over the period considered, the fluctuations are not far-off from the obtained average value.

The relationship between EVA and other traditional measures is examined using Pearson's Coefficient of correlation. Regression analysis has been used to examine the relationship of EVA, EPS, RONW and ROCE with share price.

8.3 RESULTS AND DISCUSSION

8.3.1 EVA and Traditional Measures of Performance

Table 8.1 shows the average financial measures over the entire period of study spanning from 1998-99 to 2002-03. The first column of the table represents the name of the companies and the rest of the columns show different financial measures. Column 2 of the aforesaid table consists of EVA values in Rupee terms followed by Column 3 containing EVACE in relative terms, Columns 4, 5, and 6 consisting the values of RONW, ROCE and EPS in relative terms. Finally, column 7 contains the share prices of the sample companies in absolute rupee terms.

As one can observe, there are wide variations in the financial measures across the companies, the largest being in the case of Economic Value Added. Economic Value Added (EVA) varies from –386.37% in the case of Timex Watches Ltd. to 20.43% in the case of Hero Honda Motors. Similarly one can observe variations in other financial factors across the companies from Table 8.1.

Correlating the traditional measures with EVA shows that the relationship is positive but very low and moderate with EPS (0.06), RONW (0.22) and ROCE (0.28). This is probably due to the fact that the definition of EVA itself separates it from the other three measures and also the traditional measures do not reflect the real value of shareholders. Hence, there is a need to measure EVA to understand increase/decrease in shareholder value.

In order to have a better inference, the EVACE a relative measure, is calculated and we ascertain the relationship of EVACE to EPS, RONW and ROCE through correlation analysis.

Table 8.1
Average Financial Variables: 1998-99 to 2002-03

Company Name	*EVA*	*EVACE*	*RONW*	*ROCE*	*EPS*	*SP*
(1)	*(2)*	*(3)*	*(4)*	*(5)*	*(6)*	*(7)*
ACC Ltd.	-231.42	-11.64	1.63	9.08	11.02	198.99
Aarti Drugs Ltd.	-29.73	-34.89	17.50	26.51	5.57	39.32
Aban Offshore Ltd.	-6.40	-2.93	-5.55	26.82	17.56	214.25
Ador Welding Ltd.	-2.08	-2.72	10.75	20.54	4.80	47.28
Ambalal Sarabhai Enterprises Ltd.	-31.04	-24.16	-40.76	-18.42	-4.13	5.03
Amtek Auto Ltd.	-1.20	-1.10	16.59	18.27	20.89	279.18
Apollo Tyres Ltd.	-22.09	-4.25	12.65	22.47	12.63	177.29
Asian Paints (India) Ltd.	5.33	0.82	26.74	33.74	19.10	474.27
Asian Star Co. Ltd.	-14.20	-10.57	20.85	45.86	21.85	1033.24
Aurobindo Pharma Ltd.	19.77	8.40	36.40	41.26	42.29	326.56
Avaya Globalconnect Ltd.	-22.56	-24.87	-5.51	16.38	12.77	142.77
B A S F India Ltd.	-20.19	-7.99	10.98	17.27	9.35	136.52
BPB India Gypsum Ltd.	-1.12	-1.60	11.87	17.41	0.79	25.59
B S L Ltd.	-3.60	-5.30	6.36	17.52	4.95	32.27
Bajaj Auto Ltd.	-252.86	-8.64	16.04	20.62	43.80	718.92
Balkrishna Industries Ltd.	-4.60	-3.66	9.72	13.97	11.73	69.05

Balmer Lawrie & Co. Ltd.	-16.00	-4.62	5.36	11.22	8.92	117.30
Berger Paints India Ltd.	-1.82	-1.56	22.30	29.92	11.40	101.37
Bharat Electronics Ltd.	15.79	1.97	21.02	34.41	12.44	322.78
Bharat Forge Ltd.	-64.68	-9.32	11.26	14.05	10.12	373.16
Bharat Heavy Electricals Ltd.	-492.39	-13.53	4.68	13.66	23.62	333.69
Bharat Petroleum Corpn. Ltd.	-32.08	-0.70	22.66	27.48	35.65	334.14
Birla Corporation Ltd.	-88.71	-20.79	-20.71	2.36	-8.41	19.50
Birla Ericsson Optical Ltd.	-9.18	-8.08	11.52	15.24	2.96	14.28
Blue Star Ltd.	-1.57	2.87	18.43	22.66	0.42	120.09
Bongaigaon Refinery & Petrochemicals Ltd.	-116.26	-28.76	-12.08	-9.01	-1.11	26.50
Bosch Chassis Systems India Ltd.	-5.14	-5.99	13.56	12.01	6.65	311.86
Britannia Industries Ltd.	7.26	0.46	22.88	33.98	20.17	748.53
Carrier Aircon Ltd.	-10.28	-10.02	15.34	22.93	5.25	125.60
Ciba Specialty Chemicals (India) Ltd.	-6.64	-6.99	10.62	21.84	9.19	151.57
Cipla Ltd.	24.48	2.94	28.81	37.96	38.65	1052.67
Clariant (India) Ltd.	3.90	5.56	26.80	42.21	15.34	186.12
Clariant Chemicals (India) Ltd.	-12.24	-7.74	9.77	15.91	109.17	325.89
Colgate-Palmolive (India) Ltd.	-7.28	-2.28	22.15	36.87	4.41	181.23
Cosmo Films Ltd.	-2.20	-2.53	5.76	13.04	5.85	95.70
Crompton Greaves Ltd.	-159.54	-22.37	-20.13	4.13	-8.97	86.45
Cummins India Ltd.	-10.93	-2.33	19.48	27.09	14.61	78.77

(Contd.)

TABLE 8.1 (Contd.)

(1)	(2)	(3)	(4)	(5)	(6)	(7)
DIL Ltd.	-2.98	-4.98	10.64	16.45	34.28	164.50
Dabur India Ltd.	-11.78	-2.98	19.87	20.79	13.16	56.59
Dr. Reddy's Laboratories Ltd.	56.38	0.29	29.08	33.67	30.90	1307.69
Eicher Motors Ltd.	-2.06	-3.94	20.73	23.26	7.78	115.48
Eimco Elecon (India) Ltd.	-1.25	-2.10	14.56	24.95	13.68	61.95
Electrosteel Castings Ltd.	12.68	3.82	32.17	33.00	63.45	331.84
Elgi Equipments Ltd.	-10.83	-10.82	8.55	15.58	15.05	27.42
Essel Propack Ltd.	-15.00	-2.35	12.84	17.92	17.29	194.505
F D C Ltd.	3.98	2.41	24.57	30.35	22.26	40.15
Floatglass India Ltd.	-45.55	-36.07	-109.65	0.69	-3.65	28.81
Force Motors Ltd.	-32.68	-19.83	-8.33	4.03	-8.88	143.13
Gabriel India Ltd.	-17.21	-7.96	3.91	11.68	4.39	107.44
Godavari Fertilisers & Chemicals Ltd.	-9.96	-7.04	10.60	22.61	2.18	47.93
Godfrey Phillips India Ltd.	6.46	3.06	27.88	42.60	46.41	431.13
Gujarat Sidhee Cement Ltd.	-38.35	-56.52	4.84	-26.87	-3.42	4.71
Hero Honda Motors Ltd.	122.07	20.43	52.11	70.98	29.70	286.66
Hi-Tech Gears Ltd.	0.30	0.45	24.33	32.47	12.55	115.58
Hikal Ltd.	1.00	0.62	28.64	11.00	13.36	146.39

Hindustan Motors Ltd.	-124.92	-22.16	-25.14	6.16	-1.33	11.54
Hindustan Petroleum Corpn. Ltd.	-157.90	-2.51	16.67	21.72	30.78	432.88
Hindustan Powerplus Ltd.	-10.74	-11.02	9.06	19.49	2.30	41.89
Honeywell Automation India Ltd.	-2.65	-4.34	33.21	38.50	16.17	356.25
I C I India Ltd.	-12.99	-3.66	10.32	17.52	10.90	172.13
I P Rings Ltd.	-1.40	-3.60	8.49	10.30	4.10	49.90
I T C Ltd.	225.15	5.40	31.94	42.67	32.93	983.58
Ind-Swift Ltd.	-0.07	-1.13	26.60	32.85	12.94	68.70
India Glycols Ltd.	-10.76	-4.97	10.43	13.45	6.82	56.15
Indo Rama Synthetics (India) Ltd.	-135.71	-8.81	-9.10	8.42	-2.38	40.96
Infomedia India Ltd.	-1.87	-0.24	35.80	32.76	14.91	142.02
Ingersoll-Rand (India) Ltd.	4.66	2.49	20.96	32.31	14.53	292.35
Ipca Laboratories Ltd.	-10.94	-5.56	16.81	21.74	18.76	261.66
J B Chemicals & Pharmaceuticals Ltd.	-0.34	-1.44	21.12	23.88	20.51	223.94
Jayant Agro Organics Ltd.	3.20	9.96	26.54	29.42	15.35	69.49
Jubilant Organosys Ltd.	-15.00	-4.12	15.29	19.92	31.08	221.85
Jupiter Bioscience Ltd.	0.60	0.69	21.57	21.03	7.63	54.54
Kansai Nerolac Paints Ltd.	-12.20	-5.40	16.37	22.56	18.44	236.46
Krebs Biochemicals Ltd.	1.76	3.06	32.96	29.06	25.50	138.42
Lakhani India Ltd.	-10.63	-16.09	3.47	11.09	2.12	135.54
Lakshmi Auto Components Ltd.	1.44	1.69	27.73	30.63	8.60	95.11

(Contd.)

TABLE 8.1 (Contd.)

(1)	(2)	(3)	(4)	(5)	(6)	(7)
Lumax Industries Ltd.	-7.40	-6.97	3.81	11.01	3.56	40.93
Madras Cements Ltd.	-58.39	-6.42	10.77	13.85	307.02	4919.29
Mangalore Refinery & Petrochemicals Ltd.	-952.73	-18.38	-44.55	4.02	-2.67	13.38
Medicorp Technologies India Ltd.	-6.40	-9.54	-8.62	5.53	-0.43	54.91
Micro Inks Ltd.	-4.84	3.16	25.89	31.82	33.67	387.40
Mirc Electronics Ltd.	-13.70	-5.78	25.06	24.13	45.71	533.89
Mirza Tanners Ltd.	0.50	1.65	23.50	35.46	12.37	46.91
Monsanto India Ltd.	-0.77	2.96	26.76	35.40	46.19	704.84
Moser Baer India Ltd.	-36.79	-6.20	30.36	21.89	19.88	368.39
Motherson Sumi Systems Ltd.	0.06	-0.97	25.47	34.38	10.91	106.11
Munjal Showa Ltd.	1.35	1.12	25.58	34.60	20.37	184.78
N R B Bearings Ltd.	-6.41	-6.25	12.65	20.07	9.76	94.69
Narmada Cement Co. Ltd.	-24.02	-24.02	63.04	-3.96	-3.69	38.66
Narmada Chematur Petrochemicals Ltd.	-26.46	-8.74	2.12	10.00	0.41	18.70
Nava Bharat Ventures Ltd.	-2.80	-1.15	2.42	15.88	7.46	57.23
Nicholas Piramal India Ltd.	-3.53	0.03	18.95	23.35	18.77	315.90
Nippo Baterries Co. Ltd.	0.89	1.23	21.71	31.09	43.98	489.21
Nirma Ltd.	-30.58	-2.16	27.33	22.46	42.05	360.33
Novartis India Ltd.	20.53	7.69	22.56	37.59	20.73	331.04

Orient Paper & Inds. Ltd.	-86.09	-19.91	-74.22	5.10	-22.92	21.62
PCS Technology Ltd.	-9.30	-16.77	-0.30	14.42	1.02	23.69
Panacea Biotec Ltd.	1.87	0.82	31.54	38.12	37.52	37.73
Parke-Davis (India) Ltd. [Merged]	6.14	6.20	24.53	33.25	13.15	220.19
Pidilite Industries Ltd.	11.20	5.69	26.91	39.10	25.92	329.86
Pricol Ltd.	-9.58	-7.35	14.17	20.46	18.35	227.36
Punjab Tractors Ltd.	45.07	13.75	37.62	51.86	42.51	181.88
Rain Commodities Ltd.	-16.69	-13.15	-2.92	23.35	0.19	11.98
Rallis India Ltd.	-31.52	-9.19	-5.93	20.11	9.10	82.64
Reliance Energy Ltd.	-185.08	-6.00	13.55	14.76	21.39	321.86
Reliance Industries Ltd.	-842.16	-4.14	19.08	15.87	21.40	408.23
Rico Auto Inds. Ltd.	-0.31	-0.80	30.31	26.74	18.22	151.69
Salora International Ltd.	-6.37	-8.00	9.56	16.48	7.03	56.23
Shasun Chemicals & Drugs Ltd.	1.60	1.79	21.33	26.87	13.71	137.37
Sona Koyo Steering Systems Ltd.	-8.08	-8.63	9.49	15.19	7.57	105.68
Sri Vishnu Cement Ltd.	-8.03	-12.97	5.73	14.64	0.67	208.63
Swaraj Engines Ltd.	7.56	16.53	45.59	55.29	37.74	260.912
Swaraj Mazda Ltd.	-2.13	-5.62	34.14	25.70	3.99	118.83
Tamilnadu Telecommunications Ltd.	-7.29	-16.40	8.35	15.40	0.97	12.76
Tata Metaliks Ltd.	2.00	4.55	20.56	25.39	2.06	42.20
Tata Motors Ltd.	-792.52	-16.82	-5.36	6.79	-2.82	228.54

(Contd.)

TABLE 8.1 (Contd.)

(1)	(2)	(3)	(4)	(5)	(6)	(7)
Tata Sponge Iron Ltd.	-1.00	-1.08	15.80	15.12	5.06	48.42
Thirumalai Chemicals Ltd.	-20.93	-10.79	5.53	11.52	6.01	59.32
Timex Watches Ltd.	-31.65	-386.37	-176.90	-63.41	-4.00	12.99
Timken India Ltd.	-6.97	-6.21	12.77	19.65	2.04	39.07
Titan Industries Ltd.	-49.54	-10.51	6.85	16.18	3.62	79.37
Torrent Gujarat Biotech Ltd.	-17.25	-18.30	152.61	-4.37	-5.15	8.53
Torrent Pharmaceuticals Ltd.	-14.84	-3.19	21.96	25.80	20.24	244.59
Ucal Fuel Systems Ltd.	-1.75	-2.65	24.09	22.20	16.53	227.85
Unichem Laboratories Ltd.	0.99	0.10	27.88	26.62	25.98	220.76
V I P Industries Ltd.	-15.40	-9.82	8.22	14.26	6.19	25.21
V S T Industries Ltd.	0.13	1.80	34.48	32.36	-0.56	144.56
Vikrant Tyres Ltd.	-17.79	-7.42	5.87	14.63	2.20	14.39
Voltas Ltd.	-40.30	-18.91	-7.87	7.61	1.90	74.76
West Coast Paper Mills Ltd.	-1.00	-0.96	20.23	30.02	20.98	142.82
Williamson Tea Assam Ltd.	-11.13	-8.68	24.51	31.41	11.89	92.62
Wimco Ltd.	-21.78	-37.90	-36.20	20.36	-3.86	37.56
Wyeth Ltd.	2.55	1.32	24.72	37.95	19.23	286.01
Yokogawa Blue Star Ltd.	-6.54	-9.85	9.44	15.07	5.98	95.06
Zandu Pharmaceutical Works Ltd.	-1.90	-3.98	16.69	24.88	118.06	1948.21

The results (Correlation results are given in Appendix VIII(A) show that:

EVACE and EPS r = 0.13
EVACE and ROCE r = 0.66
EVACE and RONW r = 0.67

There is low and moderate association between EVACE and EPS but there is high association between EVACE and ROCE and EVACE and RONW.

8.3.2 EVA and Share Price Behavior

The study examines the relationship between EVA, EVACE, EPS, RONW, ROCE and share price. After using Karl Pearson's Coefficient of Correlation we find that share price is highly correlated to EPS (r=0.90) and is significant at the 0.01 level (two-tailed), moderate and low with other financial measures (i.e., r=0.11) between RONW and share price; r=0.16 between ROCE and share price. The correlation between EVACE and share price is very low (r=0.08).

Further in order to find out which of the performance measures influence share prices, we conduct a linear regression analysis. All the four variables EVACE, EPS, RONW and ROCE collectively explained a variance of 80.5% of the share price. EPS turns out to be the most influencing variable in explaining the variations in the share price (b=0.91) followed by EVACE (b=0.01). EVA is the second most influencing variable in explaining variations in share price. Both EVACE and EPS are poorly correlated with a coefficient of 0.134, thus revealing that they are independent variables and add credibility to the regression results (Refer Appendix VIII(B)).

8.3.3 Disclosure Practices of EVA

Further, the implementation and application of EVA is discussed with special reference to the detailed case studies of Hindustan Lever Ltd. and Infosys.

The concept of EVA has gained importance over a period of time as a modified approach to corporate financial performance measurement. Number of companies that have turned to Economic value Added (EVA) over the past few years as a new way to gauge financial performance is going up. Highly regarded corporations like Coca Cola, AT&T, Quaker Oats and Briggs and Stratton have set-up separate EVA measurement systems throughout their organisations. So far as Indian corporate world is concerned, it is also recognising the importance of EVA, though at a slow pace as compared to corporates in other countries. Many Indian companies e.g., Hindustan Unilever Ltd. (formerly known as Hindustan Lever Ltd.), NIIT, Infosys Technologies, Hyderabad based Dr. Reddy Laboratories, Godrej Consumer Products Ltd. etc. have made EVA a part of their Annual Reports. Besides this others like Ranbaxy Laboratories, Samtel India Ltd., etc. have started calculating EVA as an internal report. ITC began consciously examining its shareholder value creating capabilities in 1996. According to the CEO of ITC, the concept of EVA has been followed as it enables the company to clearly identify value drivers from the perspective of the capital market, and once they are identified, it becomes possible for the company to focus their internal processes on them and take every strategic decision in a manner that contributes to the enhancement of shareholder value.

An attempt has been made here to analyse the EVA as applied by Hindustan Unilever Ltd. In HUL, the Fast Moving Consumer Goods (FMCG) giant, the goal of sustainable long-term value creation for shareholders is well understood by all the business groups. EVA trends of HUL for a period of 1998-2007 are exhibited in Exhibit 8.1.

Considering the change in EVA as measure of corporate performance, it can be well deduced that:

there has been continuous improvement in its value addition to shareholders, though the rate of growth in its EVA slowed down in 2004. Further, during the period 1998-2000 annual value addition by the firm was considerably low as compared to the average value addition of Rs. 1021.1 crores over this 10 year period (1998-2007). Since 2001-03 the tables have turned the other way round and the gap between average EVA and annual EVA figures

Exhibit 8.1
EVA TRENDS : 1998-2007

(Rs crores)

	1998	1999	2000	2001	2002	2003	2004	2005	2006	2007
(1)	(2)	(3)	(4)	(5)	(6)	(7)	(8)	(9)	(10)	(11)
Cost of Capital Employed (COCE)										
1. Average Debt	165	162	93	50	45	881	1588	360	163	382
2. Average Equity	1487	1008	2296	2700	3351	2899	2116	2200	2515	2402
3. Average Capital Employed (1)+(2)	1652	2070	2389	816	3396	3780	3704	2560	2677	2785
4. Cost of Debt, post-tax %	9.1	8.61	8.46	7.72	6.45	4.88	5.19	3.38	5.9	6.24
5. Cost of Equity %	19.7	19.7	19.7	16.7	14.4	12.95	14.77	15.5	16.38	17.59
6. Weighted Average Cost of Capital % (WACC)	18.64	18.83	19.27	16.54	14.3	11.07	10.66	13.8	15.74	16.03
7. COCE: (3)*(6)	308	390	460	466	486	418	395	353	421	446
Economic Value Added (EVA)										
8. Profitafter tax, before exceptional items	837	1070	1310	1541	1716	1804	1199	1355	1540	1769
9. Add: Interest, after taxes	19	14	8	5	6	43	82	12	7	17

(Contd.)

EXHIBIT 8.1 (Contd.)

(1)	(2)	(3)	(4)	(5)	(6)	(7)	(8)	(9)	(10)	(11)
10. Net Operating Profit After Taxes (NOPAT)	856	1084	1318	1546	1722	1847	1282	1367	1547	1786
11. COCE, as per (7) above	308	390	460	466	486	418	395	353	421	446
12. EVA (10)–(11)	548	694	858	1080	1236	1429	887	1014	1125	1340

Notes : (1) Methodology adopted for calculating EVA:

EVA = Net Operating Profit after Taxes (NOPAT) – Cost of Capital Employed (COCE).,

NOPAT = Profits after depreciation and taxes but before interest costs. NOPAT thus represents the total pool of profits available on an ungeared basis to provide a return to lenders and shareholders, and

COCE = Weighted Average Cost of Capital (WACC) * Average Capital Employed.

(2) Cost of debt is taken at the effective rate of interest applicable to an 'AAA' rated company like HUL, with an approximate mix of short, medium and long-term debt, net of taxes. We have considered a pre-tax rate of 9.45 % for 2007 (8.90% for 2006) after taking into account the trends over the years and market situtations.

(3) Cost of Equity is the return expected by the investors to compensate them for the variability in returns caused by fluctuating earnings and share prices.

Cost of Equity = Risk-free return equivalent to yield on long-term Government Bonds (taken at 7.95% for 2007)

+

Market risk premium (taken at 11%)* Beta variant for the Company (taken at 0.876) where Beta is a relative measure of risk associated with the Company's shares as against the market as a whole.

Thus HUL's cost of equity = 7.95% + 11% * 0.876 = 17.59%.

becomes positive i.e., the company has added value even higher than the average one. Again in the year 2004 and 2005 a U-turn in the value addition trends i.e., the gap between average EVA and annual EVA figures becomes negative. Further from the year 2006 the same value addition trend revives that has been observed in the period 2001-03.

Continuous value addition by HUL over the years can be well exhibited with the help of graphical presentation drawn in Exhibit 8.2.

EXHIBIT 8.2

EVA in Practice at HUL (1998-2007)

(*Rs. Crores*)

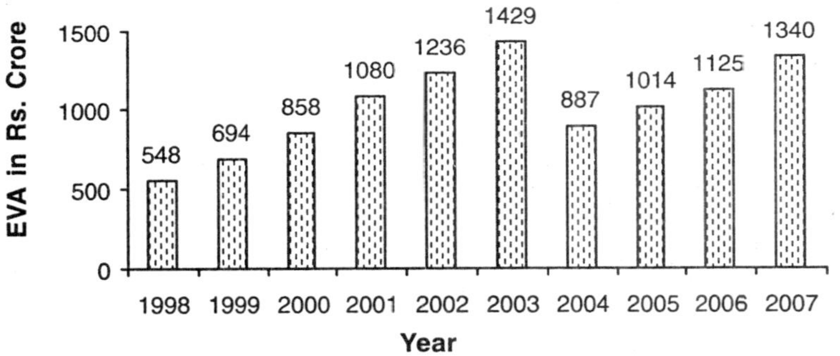

Analysing corporate performance of HUL based on Return on Net Worth (RONW), Return on Capital employed (ROCE)—the conventional benchmarks and on the new "trendier" one i.e., EVA the results can be well exhibited as shown in Exhibit 8.3.

Comparing EVA with other traditional performance measures, indicates that HUL depicts a rosy picture in terms of EPS, RONW and ROCE for almost all the ten years but not so with EVA. For the year 1998, ROCE is 58.65%—Rs. 58.65 return per 100 rupees of capital employed, RONW is 48.89%—Rs. 48.89 return per 100 rupees of Net Worth but the actual value addition to shareholder's value is just Rs. 27.71 per 100 rupees of capital employed. Same difference in the performance results as per traditional measures—RONW, ROCE and EPS and by using EVA as a new measure to performance is observed

EXHIBIT 8.3

Performance Measurement of HUL : 1998-2007

Year	*R.O.C.E. (%)*	*R.O.N.W. (%)*	*EVA (Rs. in Crores)*	*CE* (Rs. in Crores)*	*EVA as % of CE**	*EPS*
1998	58.65	48.89	548	1977.34	27.71	36.70
1999	61.84	50.87	694	2280.53	30.43	48.62
2000	64.55	52.65	858	2599.83	33.00	59.50
2001	62.38	50.63	1080	3127.43	34.53	74.60
2002	59.35	47.32	1236	3717.17	33.25	80.40
2003	60.15	84.37	1429	3843.03	37.18	80.50
2004	45.89	57.31	887	3563.82	24.89	54.40
2005	68.72	58.75	1014	2362.56	42.92	64.00
2006	66.97	56.53	1125	2796.09	40.23	84.10
2007	144.63	122.92	1340	1527.76	87.71	87.30

Note : ROCE is profit before interest and taxation divided by debt pius equity as at the end of the year.

RONW is profit tax divided by net worth as at the end of the year.

CE Capital Employed = Share Capital + Reserve and Surplus + Loan Funds

* As the net worth and capital employed figures during the year 2007 have decreased from 2723.49 crores in 2006 to 1439.23 crores in 2007 and from 2796.09 crore in 2006 to 1527.76 crores in 2007, ROCE and RONW have shown higher percentaage.

over other accounting periods. Thus, the comparison shows the divergence exists between the perormance results given by traditional measures and EVA. The traditional measures do not reflect the real value addition to shareholder's wealth. Hence, EVA has to be measured to have an idea about the real value addition or subtraction to shareholder's wealth.

More profits is not equal to more value add. For instance, the EVA of Infosys Technologies Ltd. for the year ending 31st March 2003 to 2007 is given in Table 8.2.

From the Table 8.2 we find that absolute profits have increased tremendously except in the year 2006 and PAT/ Average capital employed ratio reflects this. But EVA is depicting another story, a declining trend in the EVA/Average capital employed Ratio after the year 2005. Also the absolute

TABLE 8.2
EVA Generated by Infosys

(Rs. in crores)

Particulars	*2003*	*2004*	*2005*	*2006*	*2007*
Operating profit (excluding extraordinary income)	1079	1357	2048	2654	3877
Less: Tax	201	228	326	313	386
Cost of Capital	424	440	590	801	1369
Economic Value Added (EVA)	454	689	1132	1540	2122
Average Capital Employed	2493	3125	4331	6177	9147
PAT/Average Capital Employed	38.3	39.8	42.6	40.1	42.2
EVA/Average Capital Employed	18.2	22.1	24.9	24.9	23.2

EVA figure does not depicted as much increase over the period as shown by the operating Profit figure.

8.4 CONCLUSION

The analysis shows that Economic Value Added as a percentage of Capital Employed (EVACE) is a better performance measure influencing the share price behavior than the traditional measures like RONW, ROCE, etc. in the Indian corporate sector. However, neither EVACE nor any single measure alone can explain share price variance more significantly. A combination of traditional measures with the new value-based measures may impact share price behavior. Despite its computational difficulties, the concept of EVA contributes to the strategic financial planning process of an organization. Further, it emphasizes the intrinsic truth for all the financial managers that the equity capital of an organization is very expensive and risky and an organization, which is capable of monitoring the net profit position along with the cost of capital, will be capable of generating values for its owners in the long-run.

The day is not very far when everybody even in the Indian corporate sector will follow the maxim—"*Forget EPS, ROI and ROE, remember EVA* as this value-based management tool tells the real story of corporate financial performance. Though the premise behind EVA that business must cover its capital costs is neither new nor peculiar except the companies where equity is viewed as a free source of funds and prformance is measured by some earnings figure, yet it helps in creating a mind-set throughout the organisation that encourages managers and employees to behave like owners. Organisations should change their mind-set and focus on EVA for adding more wealth to the shareholders as EVA as a concept is very valuable and is the first real attempt to try and align goals of all the major stakeholders e.g., managers, shareholders and employees.

APPENDIX V(A)
List of Sample Companies

Sl. No.	Company Name	Industry Type
(1)	(2)	(3)
1.	Aarti Drugs Ltd.	Manufacturing
2.	Aban Loyd Chiles Offshore Ltd.	Manufacturing
3.	Advani-Oerlikon Ltd.	Manufacturing
4.	Ambalal Sarabhai Enterprises Ltd.	Manufacturing
5.	Amtek Auto Ltd.	Manufacturing
6.	Apollo Tyres Ltd.	Manufacturing
7.	Asian Paints (India) Ltd.	Manufacturing
8.	Asian Star Co. Ltd.	Manufacturing
9.	Associated Cement Cos. Ltd.	Manufacturing
10.	Aurobindo Pharma Ltd.	Manufacturing
11.	B A S F India Ltd.	Manufacturing
12.	B S E L Information Systems Ltd.	Manufacturing
13.	B S E S Ltd.	Manufacturing
14.	B S L Ltd.	Manufacturing
15.	Bajaj Auto Ltd.	Manufacturing
16.	Bajaj Tempo Ltd.	Manufacturing
17.	Balkrishna Industries Ltd.	Manufacturing
18.	Balmer Lawrie & Co. Ltd.	Manufacturing
19.	Berger Paints India Ltd.	Manufacturing
20.	Bharat Electronics Ltd.	Manufacturing
21.	Bharat Forge Ltd.	Manufacturing
22.	Bharat Heavy Electricals Ltd.	Manufacturing
23.	Bharat Petroleum Corpn. Ltd.	Manufacturing
24.	Birla Corporation Ltd.	Manufacturing
25.	Birla Ericsson Optical Ltd.	Manufacturing
26.	Blue Star Ltd.	Manufacturing
27.	Bongaigaon Refinery & Petrochemicals Ltd.	Manufacturing
28.	Britannia Industries Ltd.	Manufacturing
29.	C M C Ltd.	Manufacturing
30.	Cadila Healthcare Ltd.	Manufacturing

(*Contd.*)

APPENDIX V(A) (*Contd.*)

(1)	(2)	(3)
31.	Carrier Aircon Ltd.	Manufacturing
32.	Ciba Specialty Chemicals (India) Ltd.	Manufacturing
33.	Cipla Ltd.	Manufacturing
34.	Clariant (India) Ltd.	Manufacturing
35.	Colgate-Palmolive (India) Ltd.	Manufacturing
36.	Colour-Chem Ltd.	Manufacturing
37.	Cosmo Films Ltd.	Manufacturing
38.	Crompton Greaves Ltd.	Manufacturing
39.	Cummins India Ltd.	Manufacturing
40.	Dabur India Ltd.	Manufacturing
41.	Dr. Reddy's Laboratories Ltd.	Manufacturing
42.	Duphar-Interfran Ltd.	Manufacturing
43.	Eicher Motors Ltd.	Manufacturing
44.	Eimco Elecon (India) Ltd.	Manufacturing
45.	Electrosteel Castings Ltd.	Manufacturing
46.	Elgi Equipments Ltd.	Manufacturing
47.	Essel Propack Ltd.	Manufacturing
48.	F D C Ltd.	Manufacturing
49.	Floatglass India Ltd.	Manufacturing
50.	Gabriel India Ltd.	Manufacturing
51.	George Williamson (Assam) Ltd.	Manufacturing
52.	German Remedies Ltd.	Manufacturing
53.	Godavari Fertilisers & Chemicals Ltd.	Manufacturing
54.	Godfrey Phillips India Ltd.	Manufacturing
55.	Goodlass Nerolac Paints Ltd.	Manufacturing
56.	Gujarat Sidhee Cement Ltd.	Manufacturing
57.	Hero Honda Motors Ltd.	Manufacturing
58.	Hi-Tech Gears Ltd.	Manufacturing
59.	Hikal Ltd.	Manufacturing
60.	Hindustan Inks & Resins Ltd.	Manufacturing
61.	Hindustan Motors Ltd.	Manufacturing
62.	Hindustan Petroleum Corpn. Ltd.	Manufacturing

(*Contd.*)

APPENDIX V(A) (Contd.)

(1)	(2)	(3)
63.	Hindustan Powerplus Ltd.	Manufacturing
64.	I C I India Ltd.	Manufacturing
65.	I P Rings Ltd.	Manufacturing
66.	I T C Ltd.	Manufacturing
67.	I T W Signode India Ltd.	Manufacturing
68.	Ind-Swift Ltd.	Manufacturing
69.	India Glycols Ltd.	Manufacturing
70.	India Gypsum Ltd.	Manufacturing
71.	Indo National Ltd.	Manufacturing
72.	Indo Rama Synthetics (India) Ltd.	Manufacturing
73.	Infosys Technologies Ltd.	Manufacturing
74.	Infotech Enterprises Ltd.	Manufacturing
75.	Ingersoll-Rand (India) Ltd.	Manufacturing
76.	Ipca Laboratories Ltd.	Manufacturing
77.	J B Chemicals & Pharmaceuticals Ltd.	Manufacturing
78.	J K Synthetics Ltd.	Manufacturing
79.	Jayant Agro Organics Ltd.	Manufacturing
80.	Jubilant Organosys Ltd.	Manufacturing
81.	Jupiter Bioscience Ltd.	Manufacturing
82.	Kalyani Brakes Ltd.	Manufacturing
83.	Krebs Biochemicals Ltd.	Manufacturing
84.	Lakhani India Ltd.	Manufacturing
85.	Lakshmi Auto Components Ltd.	Manufacturing
86.	Larsen & Toubro Ltd.	Manufacturing
87.	Lumax Industries Ltd.	Manufacturing
88.	Madras Cements Ltd.	Manufacturing
89.	Mangalore Refinery & Petrochemicals Ltd.	Manufacturing
90.	Medicorp Technologies India Ltd.	Manufacturing
91.	Mirc Electronics Ltd.	Manufacturing
92.	Mirza Tanners Ltd.	Manufacturing
93.	Monsanto India Ltd.	Manufacturing
94.	Moser Baer India Ltd.	Manufacturing

(*Contd.*)

APPENDIX V(A) (*Contd.*)

(1)	(2)	(3)
95.	Motherson Sumi Systems Ltd.	Manufacturing
96.	Munjal Showa Ltd.	Manufacturing
97.	N R B Bearings Ltd.	Manufacturing
98.	Narmada Cement Co. Ltd.	Manufacturing
99.	Narmada Chematur Petrochemicals Ltd.	Manufacturing
100.	Nava Bharat Ferro Alloys Ltd.	Manufacturing
101.	Nicholas Piramal India Ltd.	Manufacturing
102.	Nirma Ltd.	Manufacturing
103.	Novartis India Ltd.	Manufacturing
104.	Orient Information Technology Ltd.	Manufacturing
105.	Orient Paper & Inds. Ltd.	Manufacturing
106.	P C S Industries Ltd.	Manufacturing
107.	Panacea Biotec Ltd.	Manufacturing
108.	Parke-Davis (India) Ltd. [Merged]	Manufacturing
109.	Pidilite Industries Ltd.	Manufacturing
110.	Polaris Software Lab Ltd.	Manufacturing
111.	Premier Instruments & Controls Ltd.	Manufacturing
112.	Priyadarshini Cement Ltd.	Manufacturing
113.	Punjab Tractors Ltd.	Manufacturing
114.	Rallis India Ltd.	Manufacturing
115.	Ramco Industries Ltd.	Manufacturing
116.	Reliance Industries Ltd.	Manufacturing
117.	Rico Auto Inds. Ltd.	Manufacturing
118.	Salora International Ltd.	Manufacturing
119.	Satyam Computer Services Ltd.	Manufacturing
120.	Shasun Chemicals & Drugs Ltd.	Manufacturing
121.	Sona Koyo Steering Systems Ltd.	Manufacturing
122.	Sonata Software Ltd.	Manufacturing
123.	Sri Vishnu Cement Ltd.	Manufacturing
124.	Sundaram Fasteners Ltd.	Manufacturing
125.	Swaraj Engines Ltd.	Manufacturing

(*Contd.*)

APPENDIX V(A) (Contd.)

(1)	(2)	(3)
126.	Swaraj Mazda Ltd.	Manufacturing
127.	Tamilnadu Telecommunications Ltd.	Manufacturing
128.	Tata Elxsi Ltd.	Manufacturing
129.	Tata Engineering & Locomotive Co. Ltd.	Manufacturing
130.	Tata Honeywell Ltd.	Manufacturing
131.	Tata Infomedia Ltd.	Manufacturing
132.	Tata Infotech Ltd.	Manufacturing
133.	Tata Metaliks Ltd.	Manufacturing
134.	Tata Sponge Iron Ltd.	Manufacturing
135.	Tata Telecom Ltd.	Manufacturing
136.	Thirumalai Chemicals Ltd.	Manufacturing
137.	Timex Watches Ltd.	Manufacturing
138.	Timken India Ltd.	Manufacturing
139.	Titan Industries Ltd.	Manufacturing
140.	Torrent Gujarat Biotech Ltd.	Manufacturing
141.	Torrent Pharmaceuticals Ltd.	Manufacturing
142.	Ucal Fuel Systems Ltd.	Manufacturing
143.	Unichem Laboratories Ltd.	Manufacturing
144.	V I P Industries Ltd.	Manufacturing
145.	V S T Industries Ltd.	Manufacturing
146.	Vikrant Tyres Ltd.	Manufacturing
147.	Visualsoft Technologies Ltd.	Manufacturing
148.	Voltas Ltd.	Manufacturing
149.	West Coast Paper Mills Ltd.	Manufacturing
150.	Wimco Ltd.	Manufacturing
151.	Wipro Ltd.	Manufacturing
152.	Wyeth Ltd.	Manufacturing
153.	Yokogawa Blue Star Ltd.	Manufacturing
154.	Zandu Pharmaceutical Works Ltd.	Manufacturing

APPENDIX V(B)
Financial and Non-financial Data Collected for each Sample Company (1998-99)

Sl. No.	Year	CE	EVA	EVACE	RONW	ROCE	EPS	OP	HP	LP	CP	AOHLCP
(1)	(2)	(3)	(4)	(5)	(6)	(7)	(8)	(9)	(10)	(11)	(12)	(13)
1.	1998-2003	56.93	0	0	14.25	26.91	8.79	26.3	27	26.3	27	26.65
2.	1998-2003	170.71	0	0	-20.56	16.93	11.37	145	145	137	143.8	142.7375
3.	1998-2003	97.08	-3.4	-3.50	16.45	24.54	6.87	33	33.5	33	33	33.125
4.	1998-2003	101.13	-39.18	-38.74	-41.14	-13.04	-2.25	3.65	3.65	3.4	3.55	3.5625
5.	1998-2003	68.05	0	0.00	19.38	19.31	20.72	192.7	194	191	191	192.0875
6.	1998-2003	438	-36.7	-8.38	21.54	32.43	25.59	114	121	114	122.1	118.625
7.	1998-2003	373.44	-16.9	-4.53	24.5	33.29	22.49	337	337	321	322.2	329.1375
8.	1998-2003	77.73	0	0.00	16.32	40.29	21.41	702	714	702	710	706.9375
9.	1998-2003	1904.92	0	0.00	-1.67	5.84	6.08	140.5	142	138	141.3	140.4625
10.	1998-2003	109.55	15.98	14.59	40.9	45.08	34.21	222.1	225	219	218.6	221.0375
11.	1998-2003	248.8	-36.87	-14.82	10.04	13.9	11.34	94.5	94.5	92.5	92.95	93.6125
12.	1998-2003	5.32	0	0.00	0.19	0.19	0.39	11.6	11.6	11.6	11.55	11.575
13.	1998-2003	3028.53	-302.2	-9.98	14.9	14.68	11.79	223.5	225	218	222.8	222.3
14.	1998-2003	96.18	0	0.00	1.92	16.89	1.2	22.25	22.3	22.3	22.25	22.25
15.	1998-2003	2362.63	-384.7	-16.28	20.57	29.21	52.57	509.1	511	500	503.8	505.9625
16.	1998-2003	185.65	-40.41	-21.77	1.46	12.28	19.17	97.85	98	96.5	97	97.3375

17.	1998-2003	93.36	0	0.00	16.29	20.07	17.69	46.05	46.1	46	46	46.025
18.	1998-2003	327.76	0	0.00	10.83	15.59	11.36	82.5	83	80.6	81.25	81.8375
19.	1998-2003	89.02	-1.79	-2.01	25.28	39.61	11.95	69.05	69.1	69.1	69.05	69.05
20.	1998-2003	483.7	0	0.00	15.7	33.31	34.36	211	215	205	208.9	210.0125
21.	1998-2003	755.6	-82.83	-10.96	11.68	13.16	21.51	245.1	259	245	256	251.25
22.	1998-2003	2982.24	0	0.00	17.5	30.22	21.13	227	232	222	229.2	227.4
23.	1998-2003	3545.42	0	0.00	23.44	26.06	39.19	232.5	239	229	234.7	233.8125
24.	1998-2003	481.13	-123.1	-25.58	-24.77	-1.32	0.54	13.05	13.9	13.1	13.85	13.4625
25.	1998-2003	108.32	-4.78	-4.41	1.63	10.03	-1.1	9.8	10	9.8	9.95	9.8875
26.	1998-2003	128	-10.64	-8.31	14.7	19.39	16.99	86	88	85.7	87.4	86.7625
27.	1998-2003	634.43	0	0.00	12.67	14.61	2.39	17.5	17.6	16.8	16.9	17.1875
28.	1998-2003	139.9	-11.47	-8.20	25.08	33.25	80.7	512.1	525	512	522.3	517.85
29.	1998-2003	62.71	0	0.00	13.21	26.81	23.17	455	485	445	477.1	465.525
30.	1998-2003	106.42	0	0.00	29.77	33.73	12.95	123.3	125	122	122.3	123.1375
31.	1998-2003	79.51	3.32	4.18	38.87	50.53	0.57	84.25	86.5	84	86	85.175
32.	1998-2003	87.87	-14.88	-16.93	10.32	21.05	14.38	105.9	106	106	105.9	105.9
33.	1998-2003	365.11	-11.2	-3.07	34.16	43.29	41.27	740	750	732	733.5	738.85
34.	1998-2003	47.18	0.34	0.72	27.51	41.54	16.76	128.8	129	129	128.5	128.625
35.	1998-2003	288.71	-26.62	-9.22	30.23	47.6	5.92	124	125	122	123.8	123.5
36.	1998-2003	189.72	-13.59	-7.16	-4.48	10.32	12.17	221	223	220	221.4	221.35
37.	1998-2003	110.54	0	0.00	-9.21	3.19	23.55	61.25	63	61.3	61.85	61.8375

(Contd.)

Appendix V(B) (Contd.)

(1)	(2)	(3)	(4)	(5)	(6)	(7)	(8)	(9)	(10)	(11)	(12)	(13)
38.	1998-2003	747.3	-123.5	-16.52	3.49	14.89	5.24	57	60.7	55.5	58.6	57.95
39.	1998-2003	379.97	-8.85	-2.33	24.75	34.89	4.31	51	55	51	53.75	52.6875
40.	1998-2003	368.22	-27.49	-7.47	22.27	21.06	2.71	37.2	40	36.5	39.7	38.35
41.	1998-2003	314.17	-36.23	-11.53	20.51	24.53	48.78	934	934	845	854.8	891.9375
42.	1998-2003	55.28	-2.85	-5.16	6.19	10.33	9.43	116	116	112	112	114
43.	1998-2003	74.75	-24.12	-32.27	6.36	14.51	18.73	78.05	80	78.1	80	79.025
44.	1998-2003	54.29	-4.26	-7.85	13.75	26.14	8.01	41.5	43.5	41.5	42.05	42.1375
45.	1998-2003	[illegible]	0	0.00	35.07	32.48	46.97	228.5	230	227	229.5	228.6875
46.	1998-2003	104.51	-11.34	-10.85	8.47	18.62	2.36	19	19	18.4	18.7	18.775
47.	1998-2003	262.06	0	0.00	12.82	16.95	13.78	133.5	138	133	133.3	134.3125
48.	1998-2003	76.92	-5.09	-6.62	17.75	20.84	4.57	26.8	28.5	26.5	27.5	27.3125
49.	1998-2003	317.03	-87.75	-27.68	-215.5	-2.07	2.21	19	19.5	18.9	19.25	19.1625
50.	1998-2003	234.49	-33.04	-14.09	7.86	13.5	15.99	75	75	72	72	73.5
51.	1998-2003	126.84	0	0.00	35.88	40.75	7.95	65	65.1	63.9	63.85	64.4375
52.	1998-2003	81.18	0.59	0.73	33.76	39.96	22.76	215	215	215	215	215
53.	1998-2003	155.04	-7.8	-5.03	37.28	28.82	-1.85	33.25	33.3	33.3	33.3	33.275
54.	1998-2003	131.03	2.06	1.57	34.07	54.4	49.22	305	305	287	290.1	296.6875
55.	1998-2003	196.29	-12.56	-6.40	22.99	30.6	26.03	160	160	157	159.1	159.0375

56.	1998-2003	122.98	-33.55	-27.28	-289	3.14	10.88	3.25	3.25	3.1	3.1	3.175
57.	1998-2003	281.11	33.26	11.83	45.61	53.99	29.08	195	208	195	205.9	200.875
58.	1998-2003	22.24	0	0.00	12.46	20.23	14.66	80.8	80.8	80.8	80.8	80.8
59.	1998-2003	123.27	0	0.00	4.67	2.75	21.8	100.6	101	101	100.6	100.55
60.	1998-2003	49.01	7.88	16.08	23.48	35.46	26.65	270	275	260	267	268
61.	1998-2003	613.55	-131.1	-21.37	13.39	18.24	-0.48	7.95	8	7.75	7.9	7.9
62.	1998-2003	5046.72	0	0.00	16.21	20.87	39.14	305.7	310	300	304.3	304.875
63.	1998-2003	109.07	-15.2	-13.94	15.66	22.57	1.71	29	29	29	29	29
64.	1998-2003	324.54	-23.02	-7.09	18.51	28.46	41.58	115.5	116	114	115.5	115.0375
65.	1998-2003	38.02	0	0.00	11.85	13.02	4.1	37	37	37	37	37
66.	1998-2003	2915.45	-90.25	-3.10	38.16	42.54	54.31	660	690	660	674.9	671.25
67.	1998-2003	134.97	-30.8	-22.82	8.54	20.15	9.31	76.55	76.6	76.6	76.55	76.55
68.	1998-2003	16.82	0	0.00	21.24	26.91	23.87	46.1	47.5	45.5	46.3	46.35
69.	1998-2003	151.71	-8.82	-5.81	14.09	18.54	8.2	37.25	39.2	37.3	38.7	38.1
70.	1998-2003	21.25	0.61	2.87	25.97	27.65	0.12	14.4	14.6	14.4	14.55	14.475
71.	1998-2003	61.77	1.65	2.67	29.24	38.1	59.63	326	326	315	315.1	320.525
72.	1998-2003	1600.75	-325.6	-20.34	-17.05	4.41	8	29.5	29.5	28	28.1	28.775
73.	1998-2003	172.96	-19.53	-11.29	43.29	46.29	144.61	3131	3131	2420	2618	2824.925
74.	1998-2003	13.07	0	0.00	32.49	32.18	10.9	92	97.3	86.3	94.1	92.4
75.	1998-2003	173.85	6.28	3.61	32.11	48.36	12.73	195.3	200	195	199	197.3125
76.	1998-2003	163.07	-11.78	-7.22	15.51	21.45	45.61	179	181	173	174.9	176.75

(Contd.)

APPENDIX V(B) (Contd.)

(1)	(2)	(3)	(4)	(5)	(6)	(7)	(8)	(9)	(10)	(11)	(12)	(13)
77.	1998-2003	115.51	-12.99	-11.25	29.23	30.71	31.86	152.5	153	150	151.8	151.7375
78.	1998-2003	158.36	0	0.00	119.05	-34.67	-6.02	2.9	3.35	2.9	3.35	3.125
79.	1998-2003	21.18	0	0.00	15.1	16.53	7.33	48	48	47.2	47.2	47.5875
80.	1998-2003	268.36	0	0.00	29.2	27.74	30.35	145	148	145	148.4	146.7
81.	1998-2003	17.15	0	0.00	19.84	14.52	17.01	36.05	37.5	36	36.85	36.6
82.	1998-2003	81.31	-12.71	-15.63	13.49	12.65	15.03	211	211	211	211	211
83.	1998-2003	46.26	5.09	11.00	60.92	43.97	29.65	91.35	92.8	89	91.45	91.15
84.	1998-2003	59.18	-8.76	-14.80	10.03	19.05	1.65	94.75	95	94.8	95	94.875
85.	1998-2003	31.77	0.2	0.63	34.46	44.01	14.76	65.5	65.5	65.5	65.5	65.5
86.	1998-2003	5609.89	-684.5	-12.20	13.17	13.16	14.25	189.8	190	185	186.4	187.75
87.	1998-2003	86.17	0	0.00	13.35	18.05	2.14	26.9	26.9	25.5	25.5	26.2
88.	1998-2003	761.43	-61.93	-8.13	10.78	15.86	142.4	3402	3402	3400	3400	3401.025
89.	1998-2003	4062.51	-984	-24.22	5.52	14.8	-3.62	8.6	8.75	8.4	8.7	8.6125
90.	1998-2003	36.12	0	0.00	-17.36	-2.43	-1.01	39.05	39.1	39.1	39.05	39.05
91.	1998-2003	187.72	-20.66	-11.01	23.62	26.78	82.04	350	364	350	364	357
92.	1998-2003	51.49	3.18	6.18	29.06	43.39	11.04	31.1	32.6	31.1	32.5	31.825
93.	1998-2003	24.8	0	0.00	40.81	59.83	65.52	476	489	475	485.7	481.4125
94.	1998-2003	103.52	-7.5	-7.24	31.34	20.56	50.68	243	251	236	247.8	244.45

95.	1998-2003	65.8	-2.92	-4.44	22.58	31.8	7.13	67.95	68	68	67.95	67.95
96.	1998-2003	50.07	-1.71	-3.42	34.94	45.14	33.81	118.5	123	118	121	120.25
97.	1998-2003	97.21	-7.62	-7.84	17.7	27.67	13.31	59	65.5	59	65.5	62.25
98.	1998-2003	115.89	-24.93	-21.51	-8.92	-0.44	-8.08	26	27	26	26	26.25
99.	1998-2003	334.9	0	0.00	2.65	2.6	2.75	12	13.2	12	13.2	12.6
100.	1998-2003	233.78	0	0.00	3.83	17.82	23.74	40	40.2	40	40.2	40.1
101.	1998-2003	541.21	-29.46	-5.44	19.6	17.73	31.08	212	212	209	211.1	211.025
102.	1998-2003	731.84	-34.77	-4.75	36.99	29.28	23.89	222.5	236	221	236	228.875
103.	1998-2003	238.61	18.55	7.77	18.21	33.31	24.00	225.0	227	225	220.2	225.9025
104.	1998-2003	8.02	0.09	1.12	42.24	39.39	-1.76	31.25	32.7	30.4	31.9	31.5375
105.	1990-2003	442.76	-134	-30.27	-11.22	5.02	-9.5	14.5	16.7	14.5	16.7	15.6
106.	1998-2003	46.97	0	0.00	1.71	13.64	0.91	16.3	16.3	15.7	15.65	15.975
107.	1998-2003	45.17	0	0.00	26.96	31.64	3.29	26.75	26.8	26.6	26.75	26.7
108.	1998-2003	41.38	-6.32	-15.27	28.86	29.01	13.27	153.3	157	153	156.4	154.95
109.	1998-2003	141.43	5.25	3.71	28.4	34.15	23.8	225.4	230	225	230	227.6875
110.	1998-2003	21.32	0	0.00	34.58	35.87	8.43	122.3	129	114	127.2	123.075
111.	1998-2003	103.56	-13.35	-12.89	18.24	25.86	26.92	151.5	154	152	154	152.75
112.	1998-2003	70.51	-7.55	-10.71	26.99	42.49	-20.55	8.35	8.9	8.3	8.9	8.6125
113.	1998-2003	236.84	53.19	22.46	49.66	66.58	6.96	122.6	125	122	122.2	122.8125
114.	1998-2003	292.55	-21.84	-7.47	15.5	33.95	17.86	56	58.1	55	56.5	56.4
115.	1998-2003	192.33	0	0.00	14.31	15.22	37.71	134	134	123	122.5	128.25

(Contd.)

APPENDIX V(B) (Contd.)

(1)	(2)	(3)	(4)	(5)	(6)	(7)	(8)	(9)	(10)	(11)	(12)	(13)
116.	1998-2003	18485.8	-2200	-11.90	17.81	13.39	29.39	284	294	284	293.1	288.7625
117.	1998-2003	66.74	-3.29	-4.93	18.9	22.95	19.22	98.2	98.2	98.2	98.2	98.2
118.	1998-2003	57.78	0	0.00	9.6	15.93	9.97	37.55	38.9	37	37.35	37.6875
119.	1998-2003	215.6	-10.31	-4.78	26.65	25.1	9.77	151	154	127	144.8	144.3625
120.	1998-2003	84.72	0	0.00	7.95	21.32	17.23	88	90.1	87	88.55	88.4
121.	1998-2003	94.42	-12.89	-13.65	20.49	23.78	6.89	67.95	74.4	68	74.35	71.15
122.	1998-2003	21.79	-0.84	-3.85	41.82	45.29	1.48	12.15	13.1	12	12.95	12.55
123.	1998-2003	65.12	-6.02	-10.58	17.03	21.31	-2.23	141	141	141	141	141
124.	1998-2003	188.35	-9.43	-5.01	21.86	24.57	34.44	332.5	340	333	340	336.25
125.	1998-2003	44.43	6.54	14.72	48.36	42.74	21.26	180.3	182	180	182	181.125
126.	1998-2003	34.79	-3.61	-10.38	78.94	29.93	13.71	74.1	78.1	74.1	78	76.0625
127.	1998-2003	28.87	0	0.00	-0.54	8.7	-7.85	9.4	9.4	9.35	9.35	9.375
128.	1998-2003	37.13	-4.97	-13.39	7.32	18.48	3.75	68	69.7	65.4	68.7	67.9375
129.	1998-2003	5200.43	-1084	-20.84	9.12	15.1	10.14	168	168	159	160.6	163.775
130.	1998-2003	55.02	-7.52	-13.67	18.46	27.85	19.04	244	244	232	238.7	239.675
131.	1998-2003	85.7	0	0.00	11.96	17.11	8.38	69.55	69.6	68.3	68.25	68.9
132.	1998-2003	118.9	-0.08	-0.07	28.41	47.69	8.04	146	161	142	150.5	149.8625
133.	1998-2003	48.46	0	0.00	10.87	18.87	4.49	29.25	29.5	29	29	29.1875

134.	1998-2003	91.55	0	0.00	16.04	12.71	7.14	33.3	33.7	33.1	33.15	33.3125
135.	1998-2003	85.28	-36.9	-43.27	2.97	21.39	12.77	90.25	95.7	90.1	94.75	92.6875
136.	1998-2003	180.13	-24.93	-13.84	11.33	12.55	7.2	42	43	41.6	41.7	42.075
137.	1998-2003	96.16	-18.59	-19.33	-3.57	7.37	-2	9.1	9.25	9.1	9.1	9.1375
138.	1998-2003	109.69	0	0.00	19.45	26.91	2.6	25.05	26.5	25.1	26.2	25.7
139.	1998-2003	494.96	-60.28	-12.18	7.55	15.85	2.12	55.35	55.4	52	53.15	53.9625
140.	1998-2003	184.21	0	0.00	-126.8	-11.59	1.98	6.05	6.2	6	6	6.0625
141.	1998-2003	369.95	-40.38	-10.91	24.82	25.55	46.17	170	170	169	169	169.5
142.	1998-2003	64.45	-4.65	-7.21	35.48	28.68	42.31	150	152	149	150.9	150.3375
143.	1998-2003	81.58	-6.26	-7.67	31.66	28.43	36.51	151	153	150	152	151.475
144.	1998-2003	165.33	-23.03	-13.93	9.47	15.81	2.44	17.9	17.9	16.9	17	17.4125
145.	1998-2003	172.68	-27.37	-15.85	6.75	17.68	24.76	99.9	99.9	99.9	99.9	99.9
146.	1998-2003	164.27	-8.87	-5.40	28.39	32.3	-0.19	10.75	10.8	9.7	9.9	10.275
147.	1998-2003	9.74	0.59	6.06	38.22	37.2	16.28	130	139	120	136.9	131.375
148.	1998-2003	310.55	-43.49	-14.00	-7.93	12.42	7.43	52	52.5	50	50	51.125
149.	1998-2003	109.33	0	0.00	10.07	23.62	39.29	94.8	94.8	94	94.8	94.6
150.	1998-2003	66.24	-19.9	-30.04	-19.41	8.81	1.56	25.9	26.2	25.5	25.9	25.8625
151.	1998-2003	441.2	-4.91	-1.11	38.75	36.93	34.97	1040	1100	900	929.1	992.25
152.	1998-2003	97.15	0	0.00	28.88	42.48	19.58	195	198	195	195.5	195.7375
153.	1998-2003	71.74	0	0.00	25.71	32.86	2.86	65.4	65.5	65.4	65.45	65.425
154.	1998-2003	44.19	-5.66	-12.81	20.5	25.97	182.54	1352	1360	1350	1352	1353.513

(Contd.)

APPENDIX V(B) (Contd.)

Financial and Non-financial Data Collected for each Sample Company (1999-2000)

Sl. No.	Year	CE	EVA	EVACE	RONW	ROCE	EPS	OP	HP	LP	CP	AOHLCP
(1)	(2)	(3)	(4)	(5)	(6)	(7)	(8)	(9)	(10)	(11)	(12)	(13)
1.	1999-2003	56.49	-1.65	-2.92	12.74	26.96	8.79	26.25	27	26.25	27	26.625
2.	1999-2003	167.94	0	0.00	6.12	30.44	11.37	143	147.85	143	145.3	144.7875
3.	1999-2003	83.1	0	0.00	14.34	22.71	6.87	32.5	32.65	32.35	32.35	32.4625
4.	1999-2003	69.96	0	0.00	-45.05	-23.84	-2.25	3.35	3.45	3.25	3.35	3.35
5.	1999-2003	98.75	0	0.00	15.84	16.08	20.72	191.9	193.9	190.7	193	192.3625
6.	1999-2003	507.04	32.21	6.00	15.22	25.14	25.59	123	123	120.35	122.4	122.1875
7.	1999-2003	453.14	-5.47	-1.21	24.12	27.69	22.49	328	328	320	323	324.75
8.	1999-2003	88.81	0	0.00	17.98	38.93	21.41	696	710	696	710	703
9.	1999-2003	1861.69	-298.1	-16.01	-1.23	8.43	6.08	140	141	134.65	135.1	137.6875
10.	1999-2003	197.3	16.88	8.56	51.74	51.42	34.21	222	222	218	218.6	220.1375
11.	1999-2003	247.34	-20.08	-8.12	10.28	15.5	11.34	93.1	94.45	93.1	94.25	93.725
12.	1999-2003	13.89	3.3	23.76	58.2	60.91	0.39	10.05	10.25	10.05	10.25	10.15
13.	1999-2003	3058.88	-201.2	-6.58	13.1	15.39	11.79	224.5	225	220.6	221.9	222.975
14.	1999-2003	89.8	0	0.00	7.8	17.17	1.2	21.2	21.2	21.2	21.2	21.2
15.	1999-2003	3010.35	-154.6	-5.14	19.98	26.21	52.57	493	505	493	498	497.25
16.	1999-2003	161.49	-60.99	-37.77	-17.89	-6.18	19.17	98.5	100	98	100	99.125

17.	1999-2003	93.5	0	0.00	10.08	14.79	17.69	38.2	48.95	38.2	47.8	43.2875
18.	1999-2003	362.21	0	0.00	-4.44	7.06	11.36	80	82	80	82	81
19.	1999-2003	137.04	-5.3	-3.87	22.01	30.3	11.95	70	70	69.55	69.55	69.775
20.	1999-2003	545.87	-5.06	-0.93	14.15	28.42	34.36	209.9	223.5	206.75	220	215.025
21.	1999-2003	737.01	-133.6	-18.12	8.73	10.93	21.51	257.1	257.05	253.25	255	255.575
22.	1999-2003	3250.24	-456.9	-14.06	8.87	21.76	21.13	231.5	231.5	225.75	228.9	229.4
23.	1999-2003	4000.7	-54.4	-1.36	24.62	30.1	39.19	225	229.85	222	228.5	226.3375
24.	1999-2003	420.82	-126.5	-30.07	-35.25	-0.63	0.54	13.85	13.85	13.85	13.85	13.85
25.	1999-2003	115.32	-5.14	-4.46	16.53	18.28	-1.1	10.35	10.35	9.8	9.8	10.075
26.	1999-2003	158.03	-11.19	-7.08	15.59	19.81	16.99	88	89.6	88	89.45	88.7625
27.	1999-2003	658.45	-81.29	-12.35	5.47	6.5	2.39	17.2	17.45	16.6	17.2	17.1125
28.	1999-2003	199.36	-4.25	-2.13	24.29	33.89	80.7	521.1	524	521.1	521.2	521.8375
29.	1999-2003	64.42	-7.57	-11.75	10.75	24.4	23.17	492.4	500.9	470.5	485.7	487.3625
30.	1999-2003	183.51	3.82	2.08	42.51	31.24	12.95	123	123.95	121.6	123	122.8875
31.	1999-2003	101.9	8.28	8.13	30.66	39.92	0.57	87.95	87.95	86.1	87.05	87.2625
32.	1999-2003	99.31	-6.33	-6.37	6.33	18.85	14.38	102	104	102	104	103
33.	1999-2003	460.31	7.58	1.65	28.41	38.34	41.27	740	745.85	735	738.8	739.9125
34.	1999-2003	57.28	4.17	7.28	31.54	47.58	16.76	127	127	127	127	127
35.	1999-2003	295.71	1.24	0.42	14.7	24.68	5.92	124	125	122.55	124.8	124.075
36.	1999-2003	180.74	-11.63	-6.43	23.25	20.84	12.17	225	225	223.2	223.7	224.2
37.	1999-2003	106.22	0	0.00	-3.84	6.69	23.55	65	65.5	61.5	64.55	64.1375

(Contd.)

APPENDIX V(B) (Contd.)

(1)	(2)	(3)	(4)	(5)	(6)	(7)	(8)	(9)	(10)	(11)	(12)	(13)
38.	1999-2003	879.36	-108.2	-12.30	3.94	14.55	5.24	60.8	60.9	58.35	59.35	59.85
39.	1999-2003	434.74	-29.8	-6.85	18.97	27.41	4.31	53.75	54	53.05	53.1	53.475
40.	1999-2003	431.11	-18.39	-4.27	17.63	18.74	2.71	39.5	40	39.35	39.85	39.675
41.	1999-2003	388.57	-29.89	-7.69	16.19	20.74	48.78	871	933	870	912.1	896.525
42.	1999-2003	59.85	-0.06	-0.10	12.59	20.62	9.43	112	115.05	112	112.1	112.7875
43.	1999-2003	83.89	-0.16	-0.19	14.11	17.64	18.73	80	80	77.3	79.95	79.3125
44.	1999-2003	59.44	0	0.00	15.6	28.31	8.01	40.05	44	40.05	43.85	41.9875
45.	1999-2003	266.35	19.41	7.29	40.77	40.91	46.97	226	231.5	224	231.5	228.25
46.	1999-2003	102.17	-9.82	-9.61	10.54	16.61	2.36	18.9	19	18.65	18.95	18.875
47.	1999-2003	248.39	0	0.00	17.16	23.61	13.78	134.6	136	133	135.3	134.725
48.	1999-2003	85.36	0	0.00	26.84	34.89	4.57	28	28	27.5	27.55	27.7625
49.	1999-2003	269.45	0	0.00	-109.4	-1.35	2.21	19.25	20	19.1	19.95	19.575
50.	1999-2003	226.78	0	0.00	-2.39	8.84	15.99	71.35	72.05	71.35	72	71.6875
51.	1999-2003	142.35	-16.63	-11.68	36.08	40.66	7.95	62.6	64.25	62.6	63.95	63.35
52.	1999-2003	99.55	7.44	7.47	33.67	42.86	22.76	210.1	213.9	209	213.9	211.725
53.	1999-2003	153.55	0	0.00	22.62	34.35	-1.85	32.75	32.75	32.1	32.1	32.425
54.	1999-2003	176.13	1.22	0.69	29.39	44.6	49.22	292	295	290	292.8	292.45
55.	1999-2003	210.56	-13.44	-6.38	17.9	23.46	26.03	160.5	160.5	157.5	157.5	159

56.	1999-2003	98.98	-68.19	-68.89	196.45	-31.64	10.88	3.1	3.25	3.1	3.15	3.15
57.	1999-2003	360.49	47.08	13.06	48.49	61.7	29.08	204.9	207.5	194.4	195.5	200.575
58.	1999-2003	24.22	-1.52	-6.28	18.51	24.8	14.66	80.8	80.8	78.05	78.05	79.425
59.	1999-2003	138.77	0	0.00	-11.49	4.02	21.8	100	100	98.5	100	99.625
60.	1999-2003	75.76	8.93	11.79	43.44	48.87	26.65	276	285	263	268	273
61.	1999-2003	639.81	-131.5	-20.55	-14.05	7.75	-0.48	8	8	7.85	7.95	7.95
62.	1999-2003	5773.78	-451.5	-7.82	17.84	24.58	39.14	291	301.9	285	300.5	294.5875
63.	1999-2003	84.81	-7.48	-8.82	7.55	18.97	1.71	28.5	28.5	28.5	28.5	28.5
64.	1999-2003	380.47	-29.94	-7.87	9.35	19.21	41.58	114.1	118	114.05	118	116.0375
65.	1999-2003	38.61	0	0.00	7.82	9.06	4.1	34.55	35	34.55	35	34.775
66.	1999-2003	3249.11	-100	-3.08	31.63	36.81	54.31	679	683.9	669	671.9	675.9375
67.	1999-2003	106.17	-39.1	-36.83	-26.27	-17.46	9.31	77.05	77.05	77.05	77.05	77.05
68.	1999-2003	20.26	-1.36	-6.71	23.08	29.77	23.87	48.75	48.75	45.4	45.95	47.2125
69.	1999-2003	174.4	0	0.00	7.29	11.09	8.2	38.5	39	38.15	38.35	38.5
70.	1999-2003	24.09	0.77	3.20	23.98	26.91	0.12	17.2	17.2	17	17	17.1
71.	1999-2003	71.28	1.8	2.53	26.66	36.65	59.63	324.1	324.5	324	324	324.1375
72.	1999-2003	1512.41	0	0.00	-40.26	1.55	8	30.45	30.5	26.55	27.8	28.825
73.	1999-2003	574.43	18.75	3.26	38.58	43.66	144.6	2725	2913.8	2725	2863	2806.563
74.	1999-2003	21.22	3.63	17.11	44.44	42.52	10.9	97	100.9	96.5	97.75	98.0375
75.	1999-2003	204	19.02	9.32	28.81	42.07	12.73	201	201.9	201	201	201.225
76.	1999-2003	193.38	-13.9	-7.19	18.72	24.04	45.61	179.8	179.8	174	176.2	177.45

(Contd.)

Appendix V(B) (Contd.)

(1)	(2)	(3)	(4)	(5)	(6)	(7)	(8)	(9)	(10)	(11)	(12)	(13)
77.	1999-2003	133.98	-5.71	-4.26	13.04	15.13	31.86	154.7	154.7	153	153.9	154.075
78.	1999-2003	73.3	0	0.00	37.12	-30.39	-6.02	2.9	2.9	2.75	2.9	2.8625
79.	1999-2003	20.17	0	0.00	10.41	12.72	7.33	47	47.5	47	47.5	47.25
80.	1999-2003	312.92	0	0.00	19.7	20.2	30.35	145	145	145	145	145
81.	1999-2003	22.8	0	0.00	19.32	15.92	17.01	36.1	37.25	36	36.95	36.575
82.	1999-2003	78.31	0	0.00	3.38	4.8	15.03	210	210	210	210	210
83.	1999-2003	59.24	0.71	1.20	37.79	27.32	29.65	95	99.8	93	94.4	95.55
84.	1999-2003	72.81	-11.39	-15.64	1.2	9.68	1.65	95	95	88	95	93.25
85.	1999-2003	76.94	0	0.00	37.71	31.66	14.76	63.3	63.3	63.3	63.3	63.3
86.	1999-2003	6272.79	-598.6	-9.54	11.04	12.67	14.25	187.6	188.5	185.55	187.3	187.225
87.	1999-2003	107.7	0	0.00	6.13	11.7	2.14	25.5	27.7	25.5	27.7	26.6
88.	1999-2003	724.26	0	0.00	11.95	15.37	142.4	3430	3440	3430	3440	3435
89.	1999-2003	5906.23	-789.7	-13.37	-1.12	8.51	-3.62	8.65	9.3	8.65	9.2	8.95
90.	1999-2003	37.6	0	0.00	6.53	9.52	-1.01	37.25	37.5	37.25	37.5	37.375
91.	1999-2003	229.78	-17.85	-7.77	25.77	26.36	82.04	361	368	360	366.8	363.9375
92.	1999-2003	67.48	5.33	7.90	30.95	46.4	11.04	34	34	32	32.35	33.0875
93.	1999-2003	33.68	2.17	6.44	35.19	47.74	65.52	492	495	482.3	482.3	487.9
94.	1999-2003	153.98	-3.43	-2.23	29.99	23.15	50.68	254.7	255.5	243.1	246	249.8125

95.	1999-2003	64.58	-2.79	-4.32	19.06	28.07	7.13	68.95	71.5	68.95	70.1	69.875
96.	1999-2003	63.3	0.48	0.76	23.35	30.89	33.81	130	130	130	130	130
97.	1999-2003	96.63	-7.41	-7.67	10.75	16.2	13.31	68	69	65.3	67.1	67.35
98.	1999-2003	127.79	-43.15	-33.77	-72.94	-15.81	-8.08	25	26	24.7	26	25.425
99.	1999-2003	330.3	-56.29	-17.04	-10.36	4.51	2.75	12.6	12.95	12.5	12.95	12.75
100.	1999-2003	243.91	0	0.00	-11.3	11.82	23.74	39.3	39.3	39.3	39.3	39.3
101.	1999-2003	417.12	5.82	1.40	14.4	17.65	31.08	210	213.9	210	213.3	211.8
102.	1999-2003	1062.04	-9.11	-0.86	30.62	24.65	23.89	230	253	229.95	250	240.7375
103.	1999-2003	281.59	19.09	6.78	27.45	44.99	24.99	227.1	233.95	227.1	233	230.2875
104.	1999-2003	18.31	1.25	6.83	41.61	40.64	-1.76	32.8	33.7	32.25	32.75	32.875
105.	1999-2003	417.32	-117.4	-28.14	-61.29	-4.7	-9.5	15.15	15.15	15.1	15.1	15.125
106.	1999-2003	44.67	-6.51	-14.57	2.45	15.43	0.91	16	16.45	15.7	15.9	16.0125
107.	1999-2003	66.45	-3.67	-5.52	26.69	28.72	3.29	26.05	26.25	25.4	25.6	25.825
108.	1999-2003	55.44	0	0.00	46.07	33.34	13.27	151.5	153.9	150.6	150.8	151.6875
109.	1999-2003	138.43	9.77	7.06	30.61	44.09	23.8	225	228	224.25	228	226.3125
110.	1999-2003	38.6	8.45	21.89	50.84	50.47	8.43	127	131.7	122.35	124.5	126.3875
111.	1999-2003	122.69	-12.56	-10.24	8.91	15.55	26.92	155	158	153	158	156
112.	1999-2003	68.3	-12.9	-18.89	10.78	25.55	-20.6	8.05	8.1	8.05	8.1	8.075
113.	1999-2003	306.29	59.15	19.31	47.71	66.28	6.96	125	126	122.5	123.4	124.2
114.	1999-2003	343.02	-27.76	8.08	20.6	30.5	17.86	57.5	57.5	56.85	57.45	57.325
115.	1999-2003	226.29	-27.44	-12.13	12.58	14.38	37.71	130	137	130	137	133.5

(*Contd.*)

APPENDIX V(B) (Contd.)

(1)	(2)	(3)	(4)	(5)	(6)	(7)	(8)	(9)	(10)	(11)	(12)	(13)
116.	1999-2003	20921.6	-1521	-7.27	17.31	12.88	29.39	291.5	294.9	274.25	283.5	286.0375
117.	1999-2003	80.16	-10.27	-12.81	22.23	21.62	19.22	98	101.1	98	100.4	99.375
118.	1999-2003	69.07	-8.85	-12.81	12.87	18.7	9.97	38	38.55	37.8	37.9	38.0625
119.	1999-2003	394.25	0.74	0.19	54.08	34.06	9.77	147	155	147	152.3	150.3125
120.	1999-2003	84.07	0	0.00	19.1	26.49	17.23	90	90.9	90	90	90.225
121.	1999-2003	110.63	-8.51	-7.69	8.93	13.57	6.89	75.5	76	72	72	73.875
122.	1999-2003	55.74	-1.11	-1.99	31.9	35.29	1.48	13.5	13.55	13	13.45	13.375
123.	1999-2003	56.16	-5.24	-9.33	2.87	14.79	-2.23	143.7	143.65	143.65	143.7	143.65
124.	1999-2003	206.92	-4.52	-2.18	21.29	23.94	34.44	395	395	350	350	372.5
125.	1999-2003	41.88	7.27	17.36	54.62	54.87	21.26	181	181	178	178	179.5
126.	1999-2003	41.33	-3.04	-7.36	16.95	19.34	13.71	78.5	80	78.5	80	79.25
127.	1999-2003	48.77	-14.47	-29.67	10.16	11.28	-7.85	8.2	8.2	8.2	8.2	8.2
128.	1999-2003	32.77	-6.91	-21.09	8.94	22.12	3.75	69.95	70.8	68.65	69.3	69.675
129.	1999-2003	5292.37	-1223	-23.11	-2.58	6.88	10.14	161.1	161.05	154.5	156	158.1375
130.	1999-2003	63.36	-3.73	-5.89	42.86	45.68	19.04	241	254.95	240	243.9	244.9625
131.	1999-2003	90.25	-8.55	-9.47	12.02	17.98	8.38	70	70	68.5	69	69.375
132.	1999-2003	156.58	-7.44	-4.75	32.17	47.64	8.04	155	157.45	149.1	150.7	153.0625
133.	1999-2003	49.72	0	0.00	0.6	12.96	4.49	28.9	29	28.8	28.9	28.9

134.	1999-2003	102.26	0	0.00	12.19	11.78	7.14	33	33	32.55	32.95	32.875
135.	1999-2003	94.1	-40.91	-43.48	-43.75	-2.41	12.77	96.8	98.9	95.55	96.25	96.875
136.	1999-2003	204.02	-23.72	-11.63	5.55	11.54	7.2	39.05	40.95	39	40.95	39.9875
137.	1999-2003	83.1	-28.66	-34.49	-50.11	-5.56	-2	9.2	9.2	8.8	8.85	9.0125
138.	1999-2003	117.51	-11.84	-10.08	8.8	15.35	2.6	26.55	27	26	26.25	26.45
139.	1999-2003	486.38	-44.4	-9.13	8.66	17.01	2.12	54.1	55.5	53.5	54.35	54.3625
140.	1999-2003	112.3	-55.24	-49.19	846.1	-7.24	1.98	6	6.4	6	6	6.1
141.	1999-2003	445.92	-47.83	-10.73	18.83	21.71	46.17	165	169	165	167	166.5
142.	1999-2003	72.57	-4.09	-5.64	20.27	19.5	42.31	153	153	150.2	151.3	151.875
143.	1999-2003	91.54	-0.77	-0.84	24.57	25.5	36.51	148.1	151	148.1	150.9	149.5125
144.	1999-2003	172.97	-18.97	-10.97	9.51	14.89	2.44	17.25	17.25	17	17	17.125
145.	1999-2003	132.42	0	0.00	5.88	17.77	24.76	95.05	95.05	95.05	95.05	95.05
146.	1999-2003	190.06	-10.1	-5.31	17.62	20.78	-0.19	10.6	10.65	9.1	9.25	9.9
147.	1999-2003	19.74	8.62	43.67	83.14	82.7	16.28	139.5	141.95	132.1	135	137.125
148.	1999-2003	266.32	-46.03	-17.28	-9.66	10.17	7.43	51	51.85	50	51.55	51.1
149.	1999-2003	112.71	0	0.00	15	26.84	39.29	94.1	95.5	94	95.5	94.775
150.	1999-2003	73.21	0	0.00	-42.67	7.97	1.56	25.5	25.8	25.35	25.8	25.6125
151.	1999-2003	559.72	48.44	8.65	42.97	41.66	34.97	950	1028	941.35	981.5	975.2125
152.	1999-2003	110.28	-3.23	-2.93	26.58	37.95	19.58	192	209	190	191	195.5
153.	1999-2003	71.21	-3.71	-5.21	7.35	14.05	2.86	65.45	65.5	65.45	65.45	65.4625
154.	1999-2003	48.45	-1.82	-3.76	20.9	25.97	182.5	1325	1325	1300	1300	1312.5

(Contd.)

APPENDIX V(B) (*Contd.*)

Financial and Non-financial Data Collected for each Sample Company (2000-01)

Sl. No.	*Year*	*CE*	*EVA*	*EVACE*	*RONW*	*ROCE*	*EPS*	*OP*	*HP*	*LP*	*CP*	*AOHLCP*
(1)	*(2)*	*(3)*	*(4)*	*(5)*	*(6)*	*(7)*	*(8)*	*(9)*	*(10)*	*(11)*	*(12)*	*(13)*
1.	2000-03	70.53	-5	-7.09	21.48	30.58	8.79	26.55	27	26.25	26.75	86.49
2.	2000-03	166.15	-11	-6.62	-29.5	20.86	11.37	155	155	144.8	147.5	491.61
3.	2000-03	83.52	0	0.00	7.62	16.65	6.87	33.05	33.05	31.6	32.3	105.78
4.	2000-03	163.23	-48	-29.41	-47.18	-22.36	-2.25	3.4	3.6	3.4	3.4	11.25
5.	2000-03	132.8	-8	-6.02	16.22	15.95	20.72	192.45	193.9	191.1	193	625.70
6.	2000-03	609.14	-21	-3.45	19.17	23.51	25.59	122.5	124.7	121.9	122.2	399.65
7.	2000-03	459.89	12	2.61	29.35	35.55	22.49	322.5	328.9	319	324	1051.35
8.	2000-03	110.58	-21	-18.99	30.84	55.78	21.41	710	713	710	713	2311.25
9.	2000-03	2001	-422	-21.09	-7.84	4.31	6.08	138.5	138.5	135.5	136.8	446.65
10.	2000-03	312.63	38	12.15	43.3	45.16	34.21	221	221	218.5	220	715.50
11.	2000-03	244.66	-20	-8.17	11.07	18.93	11.34	94.5	94.5	92.25	92.45	304.36
12.	2000-03	29.09	7	24.06	77.76	78.73	0.39	10.3	10.3	10.3	10.3	33.48
13.	2000-03	3066.2	-197	-6.42	13.07	16.11	11.79	221.55	223.5	221	221.9	721.51
14.	2000-03	81.16	-7	-8.62	9.84	18.72	1.2	22.25	22.25	22.25	22.25	72.31
15.	2000-03	3598.2	-253	-7.03	15.58	20.42	52.57	500	502.4	494	496.8	1620.59
16.	2000-03	176.79	0	0.00	-11.91	1.76	19.17	98	99.7	96.5	96.55	318.34

17.	2000-03	104.12	0	0.00	9.41	12.87	17.69	48.8	48.8	46.55	46.55	155.79
18.	2000-03	376.75	-36	-9.56	11.65	12.47	11.36	81	81	80.05	80.5	262.18
19.	2000-03	145.78	-6	-4.12	20.61	25.95	11.95	70.4	70.4	70.4	70.4	228.80
20.	2000-03	600.99	0	0.00	22.82	34.59	34.36	212.7	228	212.7	227.5	710.26
21.	2000-03	718.21	-66	-9.19	15.08	15.94	21.51	255.05	257	253.5	253.7	828.96
22.	2000-03	3361.3	-551	-16.39	7.91	17.83	21.13	229.5	230.5	225.5	228.5	742.63
23.	2000-03	4605.4	-105	-2.28	22	26.42.	39.19	230	230	223.3	227	740.04
24.	2000-03	388.65	-85	-21.87	-25.61	2.55	0.54	13.4	13.6	13	13	43.25
25.	2000-03	104.64	-13	-12.42	14.67	16.94	-1.1	9.8	9.85	9.8	9.8	31.90
26.	2000-03	148.42	-8	-5.39	20.64	22.35	16.99	87.05	89	87.05	88.05	285.11
27.	2000-03	617.53	-71	-11.50	5.14	6.47	2.39	17.5	18.55	17.25	18.25	57.86
28.	2000-03	224.28	4	1.78	26.78	36.22	81.94	511.65	512	511.6	511.7	1663.18
29.	2000-03	76.19	-7	-9.19	20.12	33.78	23.17	490	492	482	490.1	1586.51
30.	2000-03	680.62	0	0.00	13.47	15.08	12.95	123.15	123.2	122.3	122.6	399.20
31.	2000-03	105.05	-16	-15.23	9.64	15.4	0.57	87.5	87.5	86	86	282.50
32.	2000-03	108.24	-9	-8.31	17.23	27.82	14.38	104	104	103.5	103.5	337.38
33.	2000-03	569.81	12	2.11	25.89	33.74	41.27	748	748	732.1	734.2	2411.59
34.	2000-03	65.58	4	6.10	25.91	42.29	16.76	127.2	129.1	127.2	129	415.70
35.	2000-03	306.96	-27	-8.80	18.09	30.45	5.92	124.25	124.3	122.5	123	401.75
36.	2000-03	156.68	-6	-3.83	17.47	22.3	12.17	222.65	225.7	222.7	225.7	727.43
37.	2000-03	97.13	-12	-12.35	5.37	12.05	23.55	66.95	67	63.45	64.7	213.58

(*Contd.*)

APPENDIX V(B) (Contd.)

(1)	(2)	(3)	(4)	(5)	(6)	(7)	(8)	(9)	(10)	(11)	(12)	(13)
38.	2000-03	781.21	-289	-36.99	-34.33	-3.19	5.24	60.2	60.25	58.55	59.95	193.99
39.	2000-03	510.96	2	0.39	21.19	29.7	4.31	53.1	53.65	52	53.5	172.13
40.	2000-03	461.15	-29	-6.29	19.22	19.83	2.71	39.95	40	38.55	38.9	128.23
41.	2000-03	412.87	-38	-9.20	16.76	20.8	48.78	920.1	925	900	901.7	2970.51
42.	2000-03	68.36	0	0.00	19.39	28.5	9.43	113.2	113.2	113.2	113.2	367.90
43.	2000-03	97.72	0	0.00	27.08	24.82	18.73	78.75	79.4	77.5	77.9	255.13
44.	2000-03	71.82	0	0.00	15.68	26.02	8.01	41.35	41.35	41.35	41.35	134.39
45.	2000-03	350.13	36	10.28	41.97	43.49	46.97	220	232	220	231.8	729.94
46.	2000-03	107.67	-15	-13.93	7.89	13.72	2.36	18.3	18.3	17.9	18.15	59.04
47.	200103	377.19	-5	-1.33	18.61	23.14	13.78	136	136.9	135	135.7	441.76
48.	2000-03	101.61	5	4.92	25.99	35.5	4.57	28	28.7	27	27.15	90.49
49.	2000-03	78.7	-75	-95.30	-165.98	-22.67	2.21	19.5	19.8	19.5	19.8	63.75
50.	2000-03	213.99	-26	-12.15	3.25	11.14	15.99	70.2	72.6	70.2	72.6	231.15
51.	2000-03	129.66	-21	-16.20	27.65	36.23	7.95	62.1	64.4	62	63.65	204.41
52.	2000-03	120.14	11	9.16	32.08	38.46	22.76	203.2	208	203.2	207.9	666.36
53.	2000-03	142.11	-25	-17.59	8.98	21.52	-1.85	32.15	33.2	32.15	33	105.75
54.	2000-03	199.11	9	4.52	30.5	44.53	49.22	296	296	296	296	962.00
55.	2000-03	224.09	-9	-4.02	17.26	24.34	26.03	160.5	164	158	161	522.75

56.	2000-03	79.9	0	0.00	60.33	-48.97	10.88	3.25	3.25	3.2	3.25	10.51
57.	2000-03	494.66	103	20.82	50.09	71.98	29.08	195.65	197	192.5	194.4	633.69
58.	2000-03	30.15	0	0.00	34.8	40.39	14.66	78.05	78.05	78.05	78.05	253.66
59.	2000-03	167.77	7	4.17	61.59	17.77	21.8	100	100	98	98.8	322.70
60.	2000-03	162.93	-6	-3.68	27.57	30.74	26.65	273.75	274	268.8	271.5	884.38
61.	2000-03	640.33	-166	-25.92	-30.99	7.04	-0.48	8.05	8.05	7.8	7.8	25.85
62.	2000-03	6765	-195	-2.88	19.57	22.72	39.14	300	303.4	295.5	296.2	972.94
63.	2000-03	91.33	-10	-10.95	7.31	21.04	1.71	29.05	29.05	28.1	28.25	93.26
64.	2000-03	357.4	-12	-3.36	13.14	16.32	41.68	118	110.4	117.7	117.7	304.40
65.	2000-03	40.62	0	0.00	9.59	11.11	4.1	31.05	35.35	31.05	35.1	106.23
66.	2000-03	3177	305	9.60	29.77	43.39	54.31	675	680.7	674.3	686.4	2209.60
67.	2000-03	102.67	0	0.00	2.81	5.93	9.31	77	77	77	77	250.25
68.	2000-03	25.06	-1	-3.99	31.15	34.38	23.87	46.95	47	45	45.7	150.38
69.	2000-03	199.18	-12	-6.02	11.09	14.54	8.2	38.7	38.7	37.6	38.3	124.58
70.	2000-03	45.85	0	0.00	5.13	8.26	0.12	17	18.7	17	17.3	57.03
71.	2000-03	79.04	2	2.53	21.57	32.4	59.63	347	347.3	347	347	1127.94
72.	2000-03	1471.1	-222	-15.09	-4.11	10.9	8	28.7	28.7	27.65	27.75	91.99
73.	2000-03	833.3	22	2.64	40.66	46.33	144.6	2889.9	3045	2865	3025	9555.90
74.	2000-03	54.96	-6	-10.92	39.11	31.24	10.9	98	99.95	94.75	95.4	316.55
75.	2000-03	229.43	9	3.92	22.93	33.97	12.73	198.55	201.5	198.6	200	648.60
76.	2000-03	199.49	-15	-7.52	14.28	19.44	45.61	179.35	182	177.5	179.7	583.71

(*Contd.*)

APPENDIX V(B) (Contd.)

(1)	(2)	(3)	(4)	(5)	(6)	(7)	(8)	(9)	(10)	(11)	(12)	(13)
77.	2000-03	147.43	-3	-2.03	17.61	17.85	31.86	155	157.9	154.3	154.9	505.86
78.	2000-03	27.11	-108	-398.38	22.71	-47.34	-6.02	2.9	2.9	2.85	2.9	9.38
79.	2000-03	24.91	2	8.03	33.58	37.71	7.33	48.5	48.5	48.5	48.5	157.63
80.	2000-03	359.66	-45	-12.51	-0.17	13	30.35	148	148	148	148	481.00
81.	2000-03	44.88	-2	-4.46	14.46	18.68	17.01	37.5	37.5	36.25	36.5	120.38
82.	2000-03	80.55	-6	-7.45	16.22	13.27	15.03	212.1	212.1	212.1	212.1	689.33
83.	2000-03	92.38	-2	-2.16	26.6	28.04	29.65	96.95	97	92.1	93.65	309.46
84.	2000-03	70.80	-13	-18.31	2.17	0.62	1.65	95	95	90	90	302.50
85.	2000-03	82.11	1	1.22	27.49	25.44	14.76	64.6	65.5	62.5	62.5	208.23
86.	2000-03	6593.8	-683	-10.36	6.85	12.32	14.25	189.4	191.9	187.1	187.4	615.20
87.	2000-03	103.82	-12	-11.56	5.46	12.74	2.14	29.7	29.7	29.7	29.7	96.53
88.	2000-03	848.23	-83	-9.79	11.12	13.59	142.4	3200	3500	3200	3499	10774.69
89.	2000-03	5812.9	-1143	-19.66	-29	-0.02	-3.62	9.15	9.4	9.1	9.2	29.95
90.	2000-03	53.47	-5	-9.35	19.69	18.78	-1.01	35.6	35.6	35.55	35.55	115.64
91.	2000-03	318.28	-8	-2.51	34.68	27.23	82.04	367	374.9	362	371.9	1196.81
92.	2000-03	112.89	0	0.00	25.01	33.02	11.04	32.8	32.9	32.5	32.6	106.35
93.	2000-03	42.93	6	13.98	30.49	36.89	65.52	485	485	480	481	1570.25
94.	2000-03	397.27	-43	-10.82	31.71	18.97	50.68	246	255.6	246	253.6	810.99

95.	2000-03	76.34	0	0.00	30.5	34.06	7.13	70	70.1	70	70.1	227.63
96.	2000-03	74.65	-1	-1.34	19.58	25.47	33.81	129	129	129	129	419.25
97.	2000-03	104.95	-7	-6.67	14.91	21.19	13.31	61	70	61	70	209.50
98.	2000-03	79.46	0	0.00	-139.44	-3.38	-8.08	26	26.5	26	26.5	85.13
99.	2000-03	289.17	-49	-16.95	-9.3	7.86	2.75	12.55	12.8	12.5	12.6	41.00
100.	2000-03	259.53	0	0.00	-3.82	12.58	23.74	38.55	38.55	38.55	38.55	125.29
101.	2000-03	480.03	-26	-5.42	15.94	20.82	31.08	211.85	216.9	211	215.4	693.59
102.	2000-03	1990.7	-89	-4.47	31.47	21.08	23.89	252	252	244	250	810.49
103.	2000-03	330.00	38	10.91	29.39	48.9	24.99	233.5	234	228	228.5	752.61
104.	2000-03	67.96	-9	-13.24	23.85	24.97	-1.76	33.35	33.35	32	32.25	106.76
105.	2000 03	430.24	-108	-25.10	-115.25	-1.21	-9.5	14.65	15	14.6	14.6	47.90
106.	2000-03	58.34	-15	-25.71	1.61	16.74	0.91	16	16.5	15.85	15.85	52.31
107.	2000-03	131.71	8	6.07	44.99	44.35	3.29	26.25	26.25	25	25	83.75
108.	2000-03	79.35	5	6.30	23.22	44.25	13.27	152	155	150	152	494.99
109.	2000-03	184.57	10	5.42	29.91	47.16	23.8	225.1	230	225.1	229.9	737.61
110.	2000-03	137.81	-4	-2.90	42.62	47.93	8.43	124.3	127.5	121.7	123.1	404.21
111.	2000-03	146.91	-7	-4.76	17	21.69	26.92	156	156	153.5	153.5	503.88
112.	2000-03	176.21	-31	-17.59	-16.86	17.69	-20.55	8.25	8.25	8.25	8.25	26.81
113.	2000-03	384.66	66	17.16	39.56	56	6.96	124.5	126.5	122.6	125.3	404.88
114.	2000-03	424.76	-16	-3.77	19.4	26.27	17.86	58	58	56.5	56.5	186.63
115.	2000-03	172.73	-63	-36.47	15.46	13.99	37.71	137	140	137	140	449.00

(Contd.)

APPENDIX V(B) (Contd.)

(1)	(2)	(3)	(4)	(5)	(6)	(7)	(8)	(9)	(10)	(11)	(12)	(13)
116.	2000-03	22083	-499	-2.26	22.6	16.29	29.39	280	285.5	280	283.6	916.40
117.	2000-03	96.98	0	0.00	37.78	23.98	19.22	97.35	102.1	97.35	102.1	322.33
118.	2000-03	76.52	-4	-5.23	14.85	25	9.97	37.3	39	37.25	38.85	123.26
119.	2000-03	537.05	-29	-5.40	52.1	38.95	9.77	153	158.2	152.1	157.4	502.64
120.	2000-03	89.35	7	7.83	42.84	40.94	17.23	96.95	96.95	90.1	90.1	306.53
121.	2000-03	102.44	-5	-4.88	13.02	19.01	6.89	70	71	68.5	70.1	227.03
122.	2000-03	63.62	5	7.86	42.54	42.28	1.48	13.5	13.75	12.85	13.2	43.40
123.	2000-03	71.66	-17	-23.72	-63	2.21	-2.23	145	145	145	145	471.25
124.	2000-03	264.5	0	0.00	26.92	27.89	34.44	331.2	348	331.2	344.8	1096.60
125.	2000-03	50.21	8	15.93	52.52	64.46	21.26	180	180	177.5	179.9	582.46
126.	2000-03	41.67	-3	-7.20	17.65	17.76	13.71	82.75	85.95	82.75	85.1	272.73
127.	2000-03	41.71	-8	-19.18	10.26	12.53	-7.85	8.75	8.75	8.75	8.75	28.44
128.	2000-03	34.97	-5	-14.30	20.98	38.5	3.75	69.8	70	69.1	69.55	226.29
129.	2000-03	4823.9	0	0.00	-6.62	6.12	10.14	155.5	158.3	155.5	157	508.54
130.	2000-03	77.92	3	3.85	54.58	54.88	19.04	242.1	242.1	234.5	235.3	777.51
131.	2000-03	95.67	-6	-6.27	14.79	20.76	8.38	68	69.4	68	69.4	222.75
132.	2000-03	161.63	-45	-27.84	4.03	6.27	8.04	151.95	153.7	147	149	489.89
133.	2000-03	53	-3	-5.66	11.23	15.3	4.49	28.75	29	28.75	28.85	93.71

134.	2000-03	96.19	-2	-2.08	21	18.52	7.14	32.7	33.5	32.7	32.7	107.08
135.	2000-03	89.54	-23	-25.69	-14.17	10.68	12.77	97	100	96.2	99.3	318.03
136.	2000-03	203.24	-19	-9.35	10.2	13.99	7.2	40.5	41	40	41	131.75
137.	2000-03	69.33	-25	-36.06	-52.85	-1.64	-2	8.9	9.15	8.85	8.85	29.11
138.	2000-03	103.31	0	0.00	17.64	26.87	2.6	26.95	27	26.25	26.6	86.85
139.	2000-03	454.75	-59	-12.97	4.51	15.3	2.12	55	55	54	54.85	177.71
140.	2000-03	80.79	0	0.00	24.54	-0.73	1.98	5.75	6	5.55	5.85	18.76
141.	2000-03	304.1	-4	-1.32	28.4	29.64	46.17	169.4	169.4	167.7	167.9	548.48
142.	2000-03	98.87	-6	-6.07	18.65	17.73	13.31	151	153	151	152.0	400.00
143.	2000-03	104.77	-3	-2.86	24.93	22	36.51	150	152	149.4	151	489.15
144.	2000-03	172.68	0	0.00	13.42	15.53	2.44	17.5	17.6	17	17.15	56.39
145.	2000-03	106.39	1	0.94	56.25	32.11	24.76	96	103.5	96	103.5	321.31
146.	2000-03	273.35	0	0.00	11.54	11.83	-0.19	9.6	10.15	9.6	9.9	31.83
147.	2000-03	88.21	-1	-1.13	54.93	56.34	16.28	136.5	136.9	128.3	129.8	434.10
148.	2000-03	211.35	-30	-14.19	2.88	13.23	7.43	50	53.25	50	53	166.50
149.	2000-03	131.95	-9	-6.82	17.43	27.67	39.29	94.5	100	94.5	100	314.00
150.	2000-03	48.59	-34	-69.97	-83.08	-13.02	1.56	25.65	26.25	25.6	26.1	84.03
151.	2000-03	713.88	53	7.42	54.71	61.01	34.97	994.8	1005	900.5	964	3141.29
152.	2000-03	127.33	2	1.57	23.28	37.54	19.58	190.5	197	190	195.9	626.48
153.	2000-03	67.1	-7	-10.43	14.89	18.16	2.86	65.5	65.5	65.5	65.5	212.88
154.	2000-03	48.38	-3	-6.20	7.78	16.28	182.5	1350	1350	1345	1345	4381.25

Appendix V(B) (*Contd.*)

Financial and Non-financial Data Collected for each Sample Company (2001-02)

Sl. No.	*Year*	*CE*	*EVA*	*EVACE*	*RONW*	*ROCE*	*EPS*	*OP*	*HP*	*LP*	*CP*	*AOHLCP*
(1)	*(2)*	*(3)*	*(4)*	*(5)*	*(6)*	*(7)*	*(8)*	*(9)*	*(10)*	*(11)*	*(12)*	*(13)*
1.	2001-03	79.13	-3	-3.79	17.99	22.78	8.79	27	27.9	26.75	26.75	27.10
2.	2001-03	181.02	-7	-3.87	1.38	27.09	11.37	162	162	141	145	152.49
3.	2001-03	71.71	-4	-5.58	5.14	18.62	6.87	33.5	33.5	31.95	32.1	32.76
4.	2001-03	126.13	-40	-31.71	-44.01	-22.69	-2.25	3.4	3.5	3.3	3.35	3.39
5.	2001-03	178.16	-1	-0.56	19.32	20.74	20.72	193.4	194	191.1	191.2	192.43
6.	2001-03	616.76	-54	-8.76	5.83	14.95	25.59	121.9	122.95	121	121.5	121.84
7.	2001-03	544.84	5	0.92	27.77	35.23	22.49	322.5	330	322.3	322.5	324.33
8.	2001-03	138.06	-26	-18.83	23.67	52.82	21.41	700	720	680	720	705.00
9.	2001-03	2127.9	-285	-13.39	6.35	11.77	6.08	137	138.5	135.2	137.2	136.96
10.	2001-03	387.32	21	5.42	27.27	37.37	34.21	218	219.1	217.9	219.1	218.53
11.	2001-03	262.55	-15	-5.71	9.56	16.65	11.34	93.55	95.4	93.5	94.85	94.33
12.	2001-03	42.84	-1	-2.33	33.13	32.03	0.39	10.5	10.5	9.85	9.85	10.18
13.	2001-03	3210.6	-162	-5.05	13.13	13.35	11.79	224.2	224.7	217.5	219.3	221.43
14.	2001-03	78.58	-3	-3.82	10.39	19.63	1.2	21.75	23	21.5	23	22.31
15.	2001-03	3078.2	-310	-10.07	10.26	9.98	52.57	485	498	477	481.6	485.39

16.	2001-03	158.72	-49	-30.87	-14.64	2.55	19.17	99.35	99.4	95.15	95.15	97.26
17.	2001-03	125	-15	-12.00	3.04	7.48	17.69	47.85	48.4	47	47.55	47.70
18.	2001-03	358.22	-22	-6.14	6.11	11.58	11.36	80	81	79	81	80.25
19.	2001-03	160.08	-2	-1.25	21.4	27.4	11.95	69.1	69.1	69	69.05	69.06
20.	2001-03	709.14	40	5.64	26.52	36.94	34.36	221.4	227.4	219.6	226.6	223.74
21.	2001-03	492.28	-20	-4.06	8.83	14.16	21.51	252	253	250	253	251.99
22.	2001-03	3722.1	-1127	-30.28	-14.28	-12.79	21.13	226.1	230.55	225.5	229.1	227.81
23.	2001-03	5953.5	-140	-2.35	20.67	25.25	39.19	226.5	232.45	226	231.4	229.08
24.	2001-03	418.58	-65	-15.53	-12.07	4.7	0.54	12.75	12.75	12.75	12.75	12.76
25.	2001-03	117.07	-10	-8.54	16.76	20.58	-1.1	9.75	9.8	9.5	9.5	9.64
26.	2001-03	115.05	-1	-0.87	20.26	25.19	16.99	87.75	89.1	87.75	89.1	88.43
27.	2001-03	555.87	-147	-26.45	-11.25	-9.14	2.39	18.3	18.5	17.95	18.35	18.28
28.	2001-03	323.82	2	0.62	23.11	37.22	81.94	523	523	508.3	517.9	518.04
29.	2001-03	93.13	-25	-26.84	33.75	46.48	23.17	468	495	468	489.6	480.14
30.	2001-03	591.03	-19	-3.21	12.27	13.05	12.95	121.05	123	121.1	122.6	121.91
31.	2001-03	105.64	-20	-18.93	2.67	8.9	0.57	85.05	85.05	85.05	85.05	85.05
32.	2001-03	120.1	-6	-5.00	7.67	20.78	14.38	105.75	105.75	104	104	104.88
33.	2001-03	718.82	43	5.98	27.06	36.33	41.27	737	737.9	727	732.8	733.66
34.	2001-03	73.5	4	5.44	23.46	39.92	16.76	129	129	129	129	129.00
35.	2001-03	252.16	-4	-1.59	21.64	36.71	5.92	123	125.8	122	125	123.94
36.	2001-03	145.03	-17	-11.72	5.78	11.47	12.17	226	227.7	224.4	227	226.26

(Contd.)

Appendix V(B) (Contd.)

(1)	(2)	(3)	(4)	(5)	(6)	(7)	(8)	(9)	(10)	(11)	(12)	(13)
37.	2001-03	100.86	-3	-2.97	14.88	18.56	23.55	67	71.15	65.5	71.1	68.69
38.	2001-03	599.89	-222	-37.01	-65.11	-14.9	5.24	60	60	56.4	58.5	58.73
39.	2001-03	590.02	2	0.34	19.59	25.96	4.31	52.7	53.5	52.7	52.85	52.94
40.	2001-03	507.52	6	1.18	24.01	24.97	2.71	39	39.5	38.55	38.95	39.00
41.	2001-03	590.69	36	6.09	34.62	43.81	48.78	901.5	911	898.3	903.1	903.46
42.	2001-03	59.96	-9	-15.01	6.49	9.99	9.43	113.25	118	111	111	113.31
43.	2001-03	117.03	6	5.13	32.16	27.57	18.73	77.9	80.9	77.9	79	78.93
44.	2001-03	75.71	-2	-2.64	14.1	23.97	8.01	41.25	41.25	41.25	41.25	41.25
45.	2001-03	474.06	-2	-0.42	21.51	24.77	46.97	226	228.5	224.5	226.1	226.28
46.	2001-03	98.51	-13	-13.20	4.68	9.77	2.36	17.55	18.4	17.5	18	17.86
47.	2001-03	664.06	-17	-2.56	7.78	13.17	13.78	135.05	135.9	130	132.8	133.43
48.	2001-03	118.31	5	4.23	22.87	27.41	4.57	27.8	27.95	26.8	27	27.39
49.	2001-03	104.68	-40	-38.21	-69.72	-19.78	2.21	19.5	20	19.5	19.5	19.63
50.	2001-03	207.08	-16	-7.73	5.49	11.91	15.99	73	73	70.3	72.5	72.20
51.	2001-03	120.76	-9	-7.45	13.93	24.22	7.95	65.45	65.45	62.75	64	64.41
52.	2001-03	143.32	0	0.00	25.52	32.4	22.76	206	211	206	207.7	207.68
53.	2001-03	188.02	0	0.00	-14.85	8.95	-1.85	32.6	32.6	32.6	32.6	32.60
54.	2001-03	225.13	12	5.33	24.01	36.92	49.22	300	300	300	300	300.00

55.	2001-03	250.37	-15	-5.99	11.98	17.95	26.03	164	164	159	159	161.50
56.	2001-03	50.31	-60	-119.26	40.02	-48.58	10.88	3.1	3.3	3.1	3.15	3.16
57.	2001-03	675.47	116	17.17	47.52	70.98	29.08	195	195	185.5	186.2	190.43
58.	2001-03	33.4	0	0.00	25.6	35.34	14.66	80	80	80	80	80.00
59.	2001-03	187.63	-3	-1.60	48.12	15.54	21.8	100	100	100	100	100.00
60.	2001-03	340.86	-20	-5.87	19.01	20.9	26.65	273.95	273.95	267.2	270	271.26
61.	2001-03	486.8	-118	-24.24	-62.18	-3.12	-0.48	7.8	7.85	7.75	7.75	7.79
62.	2001-03	8701.2	-52	-0.60	16.89	21.4	39.14	296.5	297.5	293.5	294.9	295.60
63.	2001-03	97.45	-10	-10.26	8.14	19.98	1.71	28.2	28.25	28.05	28.25	28.19
64.	2001-03	394.35	0	0.00	5.2	11.38	41.58	117.05	117.9	117.1	117.4	117.35
05.	2001-03	41.81	-3	-7.21	8.28	10.8	4.1	31	34.95	31	34.05	32.75
66.	2001-03	3920.2	420	10.71	30.38	47.33	54.31	682	684.9	675.1	683.5	681.38
67.	2001-03	114.62	-4	-3.49	12.19	22.81	9.31	77.1	77.1	77.1	77.1	77.10
68.	2001-03	40.3	0	0.00	31.14	36.9	23.87	46	46	43.9	44.3	45.05
69.	2001-03	232.85	-10	-4.29	11.9	13.59	8.2	37.7	38.5	37.7	38.3	38.05
70.	2001-03	47.16	-4	-8.48	2.76	11.42	0.12	19.7	19.75	18.25	18.55	19.06
71.	2001-03	81.75	-5	-6.12	11.26	18.22	59.63	330	330	330	330	330.00
72.	2001-03	1536.2	-86	-5.60	6.08	13.05	8	27.9	28	27.5	27.7	27.78
73.	2001-03	1389.6	224	16.12	57.58	64.19	144.61	2921.4	2998	2811	2966	2924.03
74.	2001-03	79.23	-4	-5.05	35.01	26.86	10.9	94	94.7	90.7	92	92.85
75.	2001-03	251.62	-13	-5.17	5.67	14.66	12.73	204.9	204.9	200	201.5	202.81

(Contd.)

Appendix V(B) (Contd.)

(1)	(2)	(3)	(4)	(5)	(6)	(7)	(8)	(9)	(10)	(11)	(12)	(13)
76.	2001-03	237.92	-14	-5.88	12.76	17.69	45.61	177	179.9	175.6	176	177.11
77.	2001-03	170.83	4	2.34	21.81	26.24	31.86	153	154.5	152.1	152.4	152.99
78.	2001-03	-91.27	-96	105.18	18.73	73.21	-6.02	2.75	3	2.7	2.95	2.85
79.	2001-03	32.08	8	24.94	42.5	47.13	7.33	48	48	48	48	48.00
80.	2001-03	387.86	-16	-4.13	10.48	18.05	30.35	148.9	162.8	145	162.8	154.88
81.	2001-03	53.47	2	3.74	26.66	28	17.01	36.75	37	36.4	36.45	36.65
82.	2001-03	101.28	-6	-5.92	15.06	11.68	15.03	215	215	215	215	215.00
83.	2001-03	93.44	1	1.07	20	21.99	29.65	92.55	95.65	92.55	94.35	93.78
84.	2001-03	66.39	-11	-16.57	1.9	8.39	1.65	95	95	90	90.2	92.55
85.	2001-03	83.39	1	1.20	19.79	25.02	14.76	62.5	63	62.05	63	62.64
86.	2001-03	6809.5	-588	-8.63	5.5	11.74	14.25	186.5	189.4	185.9	188	187.45
87.	2001-03	105.84	-17	-16.06	-7.54	3.96	2.14	28.7	28.7	26.75	26.75	27.73
88.	2001-03	1117.3	-82	-7.34	12.3	12.86	142.4	3380	3489	3380	3489	3434.50
89.	2001-03	5325.6	-936	-17.58	-34.14	-0.65	-3.62	9.2	9.2	9.05	9.1	9.14
90.	2001-03	66.05	-11	-16.65	-13.23	1.88	-1.01	37.9	39	35.55	35.65	37.03
91.	2001-03	293.14	-18	-6.14	20.3	19.37	82.04	367	369	366	367	367.25
92.	2001-03	102.44	-5	-4.88	16.14	25.29	11.04	32	32.9	32	32.85	32.44
93.	2001-03	217.44	-14	-6.44	13.3	15.69	65.52	480	480	475	479	478.50

94.	2001-03	957.12	-49	-5.12	31.87	25.07	50.68	252.25	271	249	267	259.79
95.	2001-03	108.6	0	0.00	31.04	42.86	7.13	76.25	76.25	68	69.95	72.61
96.	2001-03	83.29	0	0.00	19.21	27.02	33.81	125	125	123.3	123.3	124.15
97.	2001-03	112.36	-8	-7.12	9.63	17.48	13.31	72.85	72.85	68	70.7	71.10
98.	2001-03	90.82	-32	-35.23	-491.4	-2.83	-8.08	21.7	26	21.7	25.95	23.84
99.	2001-03	288.42	-13	-4.51	17.84	18.37	2.75	12.25	12.7	12.2	12.65	12.45
100.	2001-03	244.09	-11	-4.51	6.07	16.96	23.74	39.95	39.95	39.2	39.25	39.59
101.	2001-03	517.06	-1	-0.19	17.69	20.97	31.08	218.9	218.9	215	216.9	217.41
102.	2001-03	2166.3	-55	-2.54	23.02	17.93	23.89	227.45	263	227.5	259.9	244.45
103.	2001-03	236.1	14	5.00	14.20	20.20	24.99	230	231	228.4	227.9	228.83
104.	2001-03	110.94	-10	-9.01	22.51	23.72	-1.76	31.95	31.95	31	31.2	31.53
105.	2001-03	435.78	-41	-9.41	-71.4	13.45	-9.5	15.05	15.05	14.6	14.6	14.83
106.	2001-03	58.66	-11	-18.75	2.16	17.13	0.91	16	16.6	15.35	16.2	16.04
107.	2001-03	107.81	0	0.00	30.15	42.39	3.29	26.25	26.25	26.25	26.25	26.25
108.	2001-03	79.35	25	31.51	13.33	37.25	13.27	151	151	148	149.1	149.76
109.	2001-03	221.48	9	4.06	23.41	36.01	23.8	228	231	227	231	229.25
110.	2001-03	192.44	7	3.64	36.37	36.77	8.43	121	121	107.8	110.4	115.05
111.	2001-03	180.18	-2	-1.11	17.52	22.68	26.92	160	160	147	147.4	153.59
112.	2001-03	175.19	-9	-5.14	5.61	22.82	-20.55	8.45	8.5	8.1	8.1	8.29
113.	2001-03	447.31	37	8.27	28.58	42.32	6.96	123.25	127.95	122.7	126.7	125.14
114.	2001-03	389.55	-55	-14.12	-21.18	11.08	17.86	56.5	56.5	55	55.1	55.78

(*Contd.*)

APPENDIX V(B) (Contd.)

(1)	(2)	(3)	(4)	(5)	(6)	(7)	(8)	(9)	(10)	(11)	(12)	(13)
115.	2001-03	182.09	-14	-7.69	14.61	16.35	37.71	130.7	139.85	130.7	139.9	135.28
116.	2001-03	21793	328	1.51	22.66	18.43	29.39	282	283	276	278.1	279.78
117.	2001-03	100.37	1	1.00	31.73	24.68	19.22	99	106	99	104	102.00
118.	2001-03	89.31	-10	-11.20	4.63	10.91	9.97	38.25	39.3	38.25	38.25	38.51
119.	2001-03	950.42	160	16.83	54.59	49.8	9.77	153	153.9	140	144.2	147.78
120.	2001-03	108.49	-1	-0.92	17.36	22.39	17.23	91.05	93.5	91	91.05	91.65
121.	2001-03	93.53	-10	-10.69	2.43	9	6.89	69.1	69.75	67	67.4	68.31
122.	2001-03	91.15	9	9.87	43.16	44.45	1.48	12.7	13.9	12.7	13.65	13.24
123.	2001-03	80.17	-6	-7.48	45.8	18.88	-3.29	141	141	141	141	141.00
124.	2001-03	242.87	-6	-2.47	18.22	23.25	34.44	344.8	345	341	341	342.95
125.	2001-03	45.98	7	15.22	37.22	54.77	21.26	178	178	178	178	178.00
126.	2001-03	40.87	-2	-4.89	22.02	28.86	13.71	82	82.25	82	82.25	82.13
127.	2001-03	44.34	-5	-11.28	20.41	30.61	-7.85	8.1	8.4	8.1	8.35	8.24
128.	2001-03	40.47	-2	-4.94	38.45	58.11	3.75	69.65	69.65	67.5	67.8	68.65
129.	2001-03	4173.8	-1149	-27.53	-19.01	-0.05	10.14	156	156.1	153.5	154.6	155.04
130.	2001-03	83.51	-5	-5.99	30.17	38.68	19.04	275	275	246	246	260.48
131.	2001-03	101.22	-7	-6.92	13.1	21.74	8.38	69.2	69.8	69	69	69.25
132.	2001-03	176.02	-34	-19.32	14.42	21.76	8.04	149	150	142	143.4	146.10
133.	2001-03	50.46	6	11.89	45.82	36.27	4.49	29	29.15	28.65	28.9	28.93

134.	2001-03	91.47	-2	-2.19	16.02	15.79	7.14	34	34	32.6	32.6	33.30
135.	2001-03	101.91	-9	-8.83	5.76	19.96	12.77	98	98.25	96.5	97.75	97.63
136.	2001-03	213.9	-27	-12.62	-3.92	7.15	7.2	41	41	40	41	40.75
137.	2001-03	3.34	-54	-1616.77	-402.7	-102.1	-2	9	9	8.75	9	8.94
138.	2001-03	123.2	-6	-4.87	18.91	26.38	2.6	26.05	26.5	25.75	26.25	26.14
139.	2001-03	475.99	-43	-9.03	6.9	15.95	2.12	55	55	54	54.05	54.51
140.	2001-03	73.78	-18	-24.40	10.68	-2.52	1.98	6	6	5.75	5.8	5.89
141.	2001-03	283.84	3	1.06	17.44	24.15	46.17	168	168	167.2	167.9	167.75
142.	2001-03	116.86	0	0.00	22.24	20.19	42.31	151	155	150	152	152.00
143.	2001-03	122.74	2	1.63	24.96	23.87	36.51	150.5	151.5	149.5	150	150.36
144.	2001-03	155.75	-16	-10.27	5.33	12.76	2.44	17.35	17.6	17.15	17.4	17.38
145.	2001-03	142.25	7	4.92	52.4	34.76	24.76	101	101	101	101	101.00
146.	2001-03	269.44	-42	-15.59	-9.88	2.35	-0.19	10	10.35	9.9	10.35	10.15
147.	2001-03	144.89	24	16.56	54.72	55.33	16.28	127.9	128	118.8	122.9	124.40
148.	2001-03	168.17	-42	-24.97	-10.69	3.24	7.43	50.6	52.2	50.5	51.9	51.30
149.	2001-03	173.94	2	1.15	30.82	41.41	39.29	101	104.5	100	103	102.13
150.	2001-03	63.65	-45	-70.70	-52.11	-22.99	1.56	27.5	29	23	23.7	25.80
151.	2001-03	1900.3	111	5.84	50.16	58.03	34.97	919	919	825	884.4	886.85
152.	2001-03	151.33	3	1.98	21.36	35.66	19.58	194.5	194.5	192.5	194	193.88
153.	2001-03	69.04	-12	-17.38	2.74	7.82	2.86	66	66	65.5	65.5	65.75
154.	2001-03	48.67	-1	-2.05	15.31	24.74	182.54	1326	1360	1326	1353	1341.30

(*Contd.*)

APPENDIX V(B) (Contd.)
Financial and Non-financial Data Collected for each Sample Company (2002-03)

Sl. No.	Year	CE	EVA	EVACE	RONW	ROCE	EPS	OP	HP	LP	CP	AOHLCP
(1)	(2)	(3)	(4)	(5)	(6)	(7)	(8)	(9)	(10)	(11)	(12)	(13)
1.	2002-03	86.53	-139	-160.64	21.03	25.33	8.79	29.5	30.5	29.5	29.5	29.75
2.	2002-03	335.77	-14	-4.17	14.81	38.76	11.37	142	142	137.2	137.35	139.64
3.	2002-03	66.4	-3	-4.52	10.21	20.16	6.87	32.25	32.5	32	32.25	32.25
4.	2002-03	133.7	-28	-20.94	-26.4	-10.16	-2.25	3.5	3.7	3.5	3.6	3.58
5.	2002-03	273.49	3	1.10	12.19	19.25	20.72	193.4	194.7	191.1	194	193.30
6.	2002-03	466.61	-31	-6.64	1.47	16.32	25.59	122.75	126.4	122.15	125.2	124.13
7.	2002-03	507.16	32	6.31	27.98	36.95	22.49	345	346	337.25	338.8	341.76
8.	2002-03	159.64	-24	-15.03	15.45	41.46	21.41	740	740	740	740	740.00
9.	2002-03	1975.88	-152	-7.69	12.52	15.03	6.08	132.5	134.3	132.2	133.8	133.19
10.	2002-03	538.79	7	1.30	18.8	27.26	34.21	258.9	261	254.3	256.1	257.58
11.	2002-03	287.99	-9	-3:13	13.97	21.36	11.34	96.9	98	95.5	95.9	96.58
12.	2002-03	38.85	-9	-23,17	-0.15	0.86	0.39	10.1	10.1	10	10	10.05
13.	2002-03	3215.89	-63	-1.96	13.54	14.25	11.79	223.95	224	218	218.3	221.06
14.	2002-03	56.93	-8	-14.05	1.85	15.2	1.2	22.4	24.15	22.4	24.15	23.28
15.	2002-03	3447.24	-162	-4.70	13.79	17.3	52.57	481	494	481	485.65	485.41
16.	2002-03	148.64	-13	-8.75	1.35	9.73	19.17	104.5	104.5	102	103.3	103.58

17.	2002-03	127.42	-8	-6.28	9.78	14.66	17.69	52.05	53.5	52	52.15	52.43
18.	2002-03	296.94	-22	-7.41	2.67	9.38	11.36	81.25	81.25	81.25	81.25	81.25
19.	2002-03	174.07	6	3.45	22.22	26.36	11.95	69.05	72.25	67	72.25	70.14
20.	2002-03	860.79	44	5.11	25.89	38.77	34.36	256.8	257.3	250.7	254.75	254.88
21.	2002-03	494.3	-21	-4.25	11.99	16.06	21.51	280.55	285.8	272	273.8	278.03
22.	2002-03	4735.94	-327	-6.90	3.42	11.27	21.13	240	244.6	238	242.3	241.23
23.	2002-03	5616.49	139	2.47	22.55	29.55	39.19	236	248.4	235.2	246.1	241.41
24.	2002-03	402.67	-44	-10.93	-5.85	6.48	0.54	13.65	14.8	13.65	14.65	14.19
25.	2002-03	122.79	-13	-10.59	8	10.35	-1.1	10.15	10.15	9.55	9.8	9.91
26.	2002-03	109.54	8	7.30	20.98	26.55	16.99	91	92	90.7	91.75	91.36
27.	2002-03	301.6	-282	03.50	72.44	-03.51	2.39	22	22.35	21.9	22	22.06
28.	2002-03	450.69	46	10.21	15.12	29.33	81.04	525	525	515.05	521.95	521.75
29.	2002-03	104.03	-15	-14.42	36.07	51.51	23.17	504.95	509	460	502.25	494:05
30.	2002-03	690.45	-29	-4.20	12.06	14.16	12.95	120.25	122.5	119.3	120.35	120.59
31.	2002-03	95.57	-27	-28.25	-5.14	-0.08	0.57	.88	88	88	88	88.00
32.	2002-03	179.76	3	1.67	11.54	20.69	14.38	106.1	107.9	106.1	106.8	106.71
33.	2002-03	884.64	71	8.03	28.51	38.08	41.27	636	647	630	644.3	639.31
34.	2002-03	84.6	7	8.27	25.6	39.71	16.76	129	131.5	129	131.5	130.25
35.	2002-03	256.89	20	7.79	26.08	44.89	5.92	133	134	132	132.5	132.88
36.	2002-03	135.88	-13	-9.57	6.81	14.6	12.17	229.5	232	229.05	230.3	230.21
37.	2002-03	148.2	4	2.70	21.62	24.72	23.55	71	71	69.3	69.65	70.24

(Contd.)

Appendix V(B) (*Contd.*)

(1)	(2)	(3)	(4)	(5)	(6)	(7)	(8)	(9)	(10)	(11)	(12)	(13)
38.	2002-03	609.23	-55	-9.03	-8.62	9.32	5.24	62.5	63.3	60.5	60.65	61.74
39.	2002-03	628.8	-20	-3.18	12.92	17.47	4.31	63.05	63.4	61	63.05	62.63
40.	2002-03	510.73	10	1.96	16.22	19.37	2.71	38.5	38.5	36.75	37.1	37.71
41.	2002-03	1471.25	350	23.79	57.3	58.48	48.78	879.95	880	868	876.05	875.99
42.	2002-03	65.06	-3	-4.61	8.55	12.8	9.43	115	115	114	114	114.50
43.	2002-03	104.74	8	7.64	23.96	31.74	18.73	84.05	86.5	84	85.5	85.01
44.	2002-03	76.32	0	0.00	13.65	20.29	8.01	50	50	50	50	50.00
45.	2002-03	516.12	10	1.94	21.54	23.37	46.97	248	248	244	244.1	246.03
46.	2002-03	76.65	-5	-6.52	11.15	19.16	2.36	21.95	23.75	21.4	23.15	22.56
47.	200212	675.19	-53	-7.85	7.82	12.72	13.78	127.5	129.8	127.5	128.2	128.25
48.	2002-03	157.82	15	9.50	29.38	33.11	4.57	27.75	27.95	27.7	27.7	27.78
49.	2002-03	130.33	-25	-19.18	12.39	49.3	2.21	22.05	22.4	21.6	21.7	21.94
50.	2002-03	188.39	-11	-5.84	5.33	13	15.99	90	90.25	86.95	87.5	88.68
51.	2002-03	111.53	-9	-8.07	9	15.19	7.95	66.5	66.5	66.5	66.5	66.50
52.	2002-03	149.95	2	1.33	16.82	23.77	22.76	207	207.5	206	206.45	206.74
53.	2002-03	135.08	-17	-12.59	-1.02	19.4	-1.85	35	36.3	35	36	35.58
54.	2002-03	249.83	8	3.20	21.42	32.55	49.22	305	305	304	304	304.50
55.	2002-03	259.84	-11	-4.23	11.74	16.46	26.03	177	184.5	177	181.6	180.03

56.	2002-03	44.68	-30	-67.14	16.42	-8.32	10.88	3.6	3.6	3.4	3.55	3.54
57.	2002-03	791.98	311	39.27	68.82	96.27	29.08	206	211	205	209	207.75
58.	2002-03	35.18	3	8.53	30.28	41.59	14.66	84	84	84	84	84.00
59.	2002-03	183.57	1	0.54	40.3	14.94	21.8	108	112.5	107.6	108.15	109.06
60.	2002-03	594.15	-15	-2.52	15.96	23.13	26.65	242.1	245	237	237.35	240.36
61.	2002-03	416.56	-78	-18.72	-31.86	0.91	-0.48	8.15	8.3	8.05	8.25	8.19
62.	2002-03	7339.34	-91	-1.24	12.84	19.01	39.14	294	300.5	292.1	298.9	296.38
63.	2002-03	98.85	-11	-11.13	6.65	14.88	1.71	29.75	31.5	29.75	30.9	30.48
64.	2002-03	419.08	0	0.00	5.39	13.21	41.58	126	131	125.5	128.5	127.75
65.	2002-03	37.08	-4	-10.79	4.92	7.7	4.1	37	41	36.95	40.05	38.75
66.	2002-03	4599.65	591	12.85	20.77	43.29	54.31	678	685	674.35	681.6	679.74
67.	2002-03	127.56	0	0.00	12.93	23.43	9.31	77.1	77.2	77.1	77.2	77.15
68.	2002-03	39.55	2	5.06	26.4	36.27	23.87	55.4	56.3	53	53.3	54.50
69.	2002-03	264.03	-23	-8.71	7.8	9.47	8.2	41.1	42.1	41	41.95	41.54
70.	2002-03	53.81	-3	-5.58	1.51	12.82	0.12	20.3	20.3	20.3	20.3	20.30
71.	2002-03	88.29	4	4.53	19.81	30.09	59.63	346.25	346.3	340	341.25	343.44
72.	2002-03	1480.32	-45	-3.04	9.83	12.21	8	27.8	27.95	26.95	27	27.43
73.	2002-03	2080.31	242	11.63	46.57	54.69	144.6	2960	3069	2894.9	2987.4	2977.83
74.	2002-03	126.99	-3	-2.36	27.97	31.02	10.9	109	114.5	108	109.55	110.26
75.	2002-03	272.44	2	0.73	15.26	22.49	12.73	205	222.5	205	214.7	211.80
76.	2002-03	227.91	0	0.00	22.8	26.06	45.61	193.4	195.9	191	192.7	193.25

(*Contd.*)

Appendix V(B) (Contd.)

(1)	(2)	(3)	(4)	(5)	(6)	(7)	(8)	(9)	(10)	(11)	(12)	(13)
77.	2002-03	199.98	16	8.00	23.92	29.48	31.86	155.75	157.2	153	154.2	155.04
78.	2002-03	-123.1	-58	47.12	8	-6.36	-6.02	3	3	2.75	2.8	2.89
79.	2002-03	35.61	6	16.85	31.11	33	7.33	47.9	47.9	46.1	46.1	47.00
80.	2002-03	352.43	-14	-3.97	17.26	20.59	30.35	182	183.8	180.4	180.5	181.68
81.	2002-03	71.76	3	4.18	27.58	28.03	17.01	43	43	42	42	42.50
82.	2002-03	106.08	-1	-0.94	19.67	17.67	15.03	233	235.8	232	235	233.95
83.	2002-03	95.58	4	4.18	19.47	23.99	29.65	102	104.3	101	101.45	102.18
84.	2002-03	59.56	-9	-15.11	2.04	8.8	1.65	94	95	94	95	94.50
85.	2002-03	92.13	5	5.43	19.21	27.04	14.76	75	76.75	75	76.75	75.88
86.	2002-03	5953.35	-412	-6.92	8.34	12.84	14.25	201	208	201	207.45	204.36
87.	2002-03	110.44	-8	-7.24	1.65	8.61	2.14	27.5	28.15	26.9	27.8	27.59
88.	2002-03	950.96	-65	-6.84	7.69	11.59	142.4	3507	3599	3500	3599	3551.25
89.	2002-03	5343.97	-911	-17.05	-164	-2.54	-3.62	10.2	10.45	10.15	10.15	10.24
90.	2002-03	73.83	-16	-21.67	-38.75	-0.11	-1.01	45.65	46	45.05	45.1	45.45
91.	2002-03	267.94	-4	-1.49	20.92	20.91	82.04	386	387.6	381.25	382.85	384.43
92.	2002-03	104.24	-1	-0.96	16.35	29.2	11.04	31.25	31.75	30.1	30.25	30.84
93.	2002-03	241.73	2	0.83	14.01	16.83	65.52	507.9	507.9	504	504.8	506.15
94.	2002-03	1444.47	-81	-5.61	26.91	21.68	50.68	274.85	281.5	271.6	279.65	276.90

95.	2002-03	154.12	6	3.89	24.16	35.13	7.13	91	95.9	91	92.05	92.49
96.	2002-03	93.7	9	9.61	30.81	44.49	33.81	130.95	133.1	125	131.95	130.25
97.	2002-03	103.09	-2	-1.94	10.27	17.81	13.31	60.5	66	60.5	66	63.25
98.	2002-03	67.56	-20	-29.60	1027.9	2.66	-8.08	30.2	37.9	30.2	32.25	32.64
99.	2002-03	268.59	-14	-5.21	9.79	16.68	2.75	16.15	16.15	13	13.5	14.70
100.	2002-03	244.91	-3	-1.22	17.32	20.24	23.74	42	42	41.5	42	41.88
101.	2002-03	335.68	33	9.83	27.14	39.57	31.08	244	248.5	244	246.3	245.69
102.	2002-03	1913.82	35	1.83	14.56	19.38	23.89	279	279	275	275.35	277.09
103.	2002-03	211.96	15	7.08	23.45	34.51	24.99	216.9	219	216.25	217.05	217.50
104.	2002-03	95.67	-27	-28.22	5.63	6.06	-1.76	33.1	33.6	32.35	32.75	32.95
105.	2002-03	452.35	-30	-6.63	-111.9	12.93	-9.5	14.65	14.65	14.6	14.6	14.63
106.	2002-03	56.41	-14	-24.82	-9.44	9.18	0.91	17.1	19.5	17.1	18.7	18.10
107.	2002-03	140.85	5	3.55	28.89	43.52	3.29	26.25	26.25	26	26	26.13
108.	2002-03	82.45	7	8.49	11.18	22.42	13.27	148.3	152	148.3	149.7	149.56
109.	2002-03	267.74	22	8.22	22.2	34.07	23.8	229.9	231	226.25	226.65	228.45
110.	2002-03	244.08	1	0.41	27.44	29.2	8.43	128.45	133.4	125.75	127.45	128.76
111.	2002-03	167.59	-13	-7.76	9.16	16.53	26.92	172	173.8	165	171.65	170.60
112.	2002-03	171.29	-23	-13.43	-41.12	8.21	-20.6	8.1	8.1	8.1	8.1	8.10
113.	2002-03	648.31	10	1.54	22.58	28.1	6.96	132.5	134.7	131	131.35	132.38
114.	2002-03	294.97	-37	-12.54	-63.96	-1.27	17.86	57.2	58.3	56.25	56.5	57.06
115.	2002-03	155.89	-13	-8.34	11.57	15.18	37.71	146.75	149.5	144.05	145.75	146.51

(Contd.)

Appendix V(B) (Contd.)

(1)	(2)	(3)	(4)	(5)	(6)	(7)	(8)	(9)	(10)	(11)	(12)	(13)
116.	2002-03	41854.1	-318	-0.76	15.02	18.38	29.39	270.45	272.6	268	269.65	270.16
117.	2002-03	86.34	11	12.74	40.92	40.45	19.22	137.05	137.1	135	137	136.53
118.	2002-03	83.68	-9	-10.76	5.85	11.85	9.97	42.5	45.5	42.5	44.05	43.64
119.	2002-03	1936.24	33	1.70	35.78	36.78	9.77	167.05	168.6	162.7	167.35	166.43
120.	2002-03	99.21	2	2.02	19.41	23.22	17.23	110.45	111.4	108.5	109.95	110.06
121.	2002-03	63.94	-4	-6.26	2.58	10.61	6.89	90.9	90.9	85	85.35	88.04
122.	2002-03	136.95	-11	-8.03	14.9	15.58	1.48	12.85	12.95	12.55	12.65	12.75
123.	2002-03	36.4	-5	-13.74	-4.03	13.01	-3.29	146.25	146.3	146.25	146.25	146.25
124.	2002-03	187.58	5	2.67	16.76	26.78	34.44	371	390	371	380.95	378.24
125.	2002-03	46.3	9	19.44	35.24	59.62	21.26	184	184	183	183	183.50
126.	2002-03	57.23	1	1.75	35.12	32.62	13.71	83	85	83	85	84.00
127.	2002-03	41.19	-9	-21.85	1.45	13.87	-7.85	9.5	9.75	9.2	9.75	9.55
128.	2002-03	43.91	3	6.83	41.86	58.5	3.75	66.5	68	66.4	66.9	66.95
129.	2002-03	4010.08	-507	-12.64	-7.72	5.89	10.14	154.8	160.2	154.1	159.85	157.23
130.	2002-03	90.45	0	0.00	19.97	25.43	19.04	265	265.3	250	254.2	258.61
131.	2002-03	98.87	-13	-13.15	9.62	15.02	8.38	73.8	75	73.55	74.75	74.28
132.	2002-03	191.14	-39	-20.40	3.85	5.92	8.04	141.5	145.3	141	142.9	142.66
133.	2002-03	42.41	7	16.51	34.26	43.54	4.49	30.2	30.6	30	30.35	30.29

134.	2002-03	87.96	-1	-1.14	13.75	16.8	7.14	34.2	37.1	34.2	36.6	35.53
135.	2002-03	97.68	-3	-3.07	21.63	32.27	12.77	108	111	107	108.45	108.61
136.	2002-03	153.11	-10	-6.53	4.51	12.39	7.2	42	42.1	42	42	42.03
137.	2002-03	14.21	-32	-225.19	-375.3	-215.2	-2	8.6	9	8.6	8.85	8.76
138.	2002-03	105.58	-17	-16.10	-0.95	2.74	2.6	32.5	32.5	27.5	28.4	30.23
139.	2002-03	443.85	-41	-9.24	6.63	16.77	2.12	57.75	57.75	54.5	55.25	56.31
140.	2002-03	72.56	-13	-17.92	8.56	0.23	1.98	5.85	5.9	5.7	5.8	5.81
141.	2002-03	251.72	15	5.96	20.29	27.94	46.17	172	174.9	168	168	170.71
142.	2002-03	105.98	6	5.66	23.81	24.91	42.31	186	202	186	193.85	191.96
143.	2002-03	126.82	13	10.25	33.28	33.31	36.51	161.9	165	161.9	164.3	163.28
144.	2002-03	136.17	-19	-13.95	3.38	12.31	2.44	17.25	18.4	17.25	18	17.73
145.	2002-03	105.21	20	19.01	51.12	59.47	24.76	107	107	104	104	105.50
146.	2002-03	258.88	-28	-10.82	-18.31	5.89	-0.19	9.6	10	9.6	10	9.80
147.	2002-03	166.35	-13	-7.81	16.33	17.19	16.28	140.9	148.3	139.6	143.5	143.08
148.	2002-03	166.15	-40	-24.07	-13.94	-1.01	7.43	53.95	54.1	53.1	53.9	53.76
149.	2002-03	226.52	2	0.88	27.83	30.56	39.29	107.95	110	107.95	108.5	108.60
150.	2002-03	53.18	-10	-18.80	16.27	121.03	1.56	26.65	26.95	26	26.35	26.49
151.	2002-03	2538.81	235	9.26	38.29	43.03	34.97	889	934	883	912.7	904.68
152.	2002-03	183.75	11	5.99	23.49	36.1	19.58	220.05	221	215	217.85	218.48
153.	2002-03	61.59	-10	-16.24	-3.5	2.48	2.86	65.75	65.85	65.75	65.75	65.78
154.	2002-03	40.68	2	4.92	18.94	31.46	182.5	1350	1355	1350	1355	1352.50

APPENDIX V(C)

A. Correlation Results between Share Price and Selected Variables

	Between			
Year	*Sp & EVA*	*SP & ROCE*	*SP & RONW*	*SP & EPS*
1998-1999	0.008	0.190*	0.117	0.792*
1999-2000	0.130	0.179*	0.012	0.789*
2000-2001	0.078	0.185*	0.138	0.794*
2001-2002	0.052	0.219**	0.125	0.791*
2002-2003	0.133	0.159*	0.036	0.792*
Average	0.091	0.233*	0.144	0.793**

*Correlation is significant at 0.05 level (2-tailed).

**Correlation is significant at 0.01 level (2-tailed).

B. Regression Results between Share Price and Selected Variables

For the Year 1998-1999

Variables Entered/Removed[b]

Model	Variables Entered	Variables Removed	Method
1	EPS, EVACE, RONW, ROCE[a]		Enter

a. All requested variables entered.

b. Dependent Variable: AOHLCP

Model Summary

Model	R	R-Square	Adjusted R-Square	Std. Error of the Estimate
1	.794[a]	.630	.620	238.93856

a. Predictors: (Constant), EPS, EVACE, RONW, ROCE

ANOVA[b]

Model		Sum of Squares	df	Mean Square	F	Sig.
1	Regression	14462108	4	3615527.017	63.328	.000[a]
	Residual	8506653	149	57091.633		
	Total	22968761	153			

a. Predictors: (Constant), EPS, EVACE, RONW, ROCE

b. Dependent Variable: AOHLCP

Coefficients[a]

Model		Unstandardized Coefficients		Standardized Coefficients	t	Sig.
		B	Std. Error	Beta		
1	(Constant)	-46.787	47.659	—	-.982	.328
	EVACE	-1.661	2.266	-.043	-.733	.465
	RONW	.207	.594	.020	.349	.728
	ROCE	-.448	1.629	-.017	-.275	.784
	EPS	11.902	.778	.796	15.303	.000

a. Dependent Variable: AOHLCP

For the Year 1999-2000

Variables Entered/Removed[b]

Model	Variables Entered	Variables Removed	Method
1	EPS, RONW, EVACE, ROCE[a]		Enter

a. All requested variables entered.

b. Dependent Variable: AOHLCP

Model Summary

Model	R	R-Square	Adjusted R-Square	Std. Error of the Estimate
1	.790[a]	.623	.613	241.110440

a. Predictors: (Constant), EPS, RONW, EVACE, ROCE

ANOVA[b]

Model		Sum of Squares	df	Mean Square	F	Sig.
1	Regression	14337533	4	3584383.294	61.657	.000[a]
	Residual	8662002	149	58134.244		
	Total	22999536	153			

a. Predictors: (Constant), EPS, RONW, EVACE, ROCE

b. Dependent Variable: AOHLCP

Coefficients[a]

Model		Unstandardized Coefficients		Standardized Coefficients	t	Sig.
		B	Std. Error	Beta		
1	(Constant)	-32.575	49.826	—	-.654	.514
	EVACE	.131	2.277	.004	.058	.954
	RONW	-.037	.282	-.007	-.133	.894
	ROCE	-.413	1.721	-.018	-.240	.811
	EPS	11.864	.776	.793	15.294	.000

a. Dependent Variable: AOHLCP

For the Year 2000-01

Variables Entered/Removed[b]

Model	Variables Entered	Variables Removed	Method
1	EPS, EVACE, RONW, ROCE[a]		Enter

a. All requested variables entered.

b. Dependent Variable: AOHLCP

Model Summary

Model	R	R-Square	Adjusted R-Square	Std. Error of the Estimate
1	.801[a]	.641	.631	765.7679004

a. Predictors: (Constant), EPS, EVACE, RONW, ROCE

ANOVA[b]

Model		Sum of Squares	df	Mean Square	F	Sig.
1	Regression	1.56E+08	4	39016551.42	66.536	.000[a]
	Residual	87373671	149	586400.477		
	Total	2.43E+08	153			

a. Predictors: (Constant), EPS, EVACE, RONW, ROCE

b. Dependent Variable: AOHLCP

Coefficients[a]

Model		Unstandardized Coefficients		Standardized Coefficients	t	Sig.
		B	Std. Error	Beta		
1	(Constant)	-289.886	129.509	—	-2.238	.027
	EVACE	-2.914	2.134	-.079	-1.366	.174
	RONW	-4.500	2.569	-.111	-1.752	.082
	ROCE	7.662	5.009	.109	1.530	.128
	EPS	39.348	2.481	.809	15.857	.000

a. Dependent Variable: AOHLCP

For the Year 2001-02

Variables Entered/Removed[b]

Model	Variables Entered	Variables Removed	Method
1	EPS, EVACE, ROCE, RONW[a]		Enter

a. All requested variables entered.

b. Dependent Variable: AOHLCP

Model Summary

Model	R	R-Square	Adjusted R-Square	Std. Error of the Estimate
1	.796[a]	.633	.623	240.7380

a. Predictors: (Constant), EPS, EVACE, ROCE, RONW

ANOVA[b]

Model		Sum of Squares	df	Mean Square	F	Sig.
1	Regression	14913432	4	3728357.967	64.332	.000[a]
	Residual	8635261	149	57954.774		
	Total	23548693	153			

a. Predictors: (Constant), EPS, EVACE, ROCE, RONW

b. Dependent Variable: AOHLCP

Coefficients[a]

Model		Unstandardized Coefficients		Standardized Coefficients	t	Sig.
		B	Std. Error	Beta		
1	(Constant)	-82.200	34.868	—	-2.357	.020
	EVACE	-.089	.202	-.030	-.443	.659
	RONW	-.518	.471	-.075	-1.100	.273
	ROCE	1.993	1.313	.101	1.518	.131
	EPS	11.883	.777	.786	15.287	.000

a. Dependent Variable: AOHLCP

For the Year 2002-03

Variables Entered/Removed[b]

Model	Variables Entered	Variables Removed	Method
1	EPS, RONW, EVACE, ROCE[a]		Enter

a. All requested variables entered.

b. Dependent Variable: AOHLCP

Model Summary

Model	R	R-Square	Adjusted R-Square	Std. Error of the Estimate
1	.794[a]	.630	.620	246.98817

a. Predictors: (Constant), EPS, RONW, EVACE, ROCE

ANOVA[b]

Model		Sum of Squares	df	Mean Square	F	Sig.
1	Regression	14913432	4	3728357.967	64.332	.000[a]
	Residual	8635261	149	57954.774		
	Total	23548693	153			

a. Predictors: (Constant), EPS, EVACE, ROCE, RONW

b. Dependent Variable: AOHLCP

Coefficients[a]

Model		Unstandardized Coefficients		Standardized Coefficients	t	Sig.
		B	Std. Error	Beta		
1	(Constant)	-82.200	34.868	—	-2.357	.020
	EVACE	-.089	.202	-.030	-.443	.659
	RONW	-.518	.471	-.075	-1.100	.273
	ROCE	1.993	1.313	.101	1.518	.131
	EPS	11.883	.777	.786	15.287	.000

a. Dependent Variable: AOHLCP

For the Year 2002-03

Variables Entered/Removed[b]

Model	Variables Entered	Variables Removed	Method
1	EPS, RONW, EVACE, ROCE[a]		Enter

a. All requested variables entered.

b. Dependent Variable AOHLCP

Model Summary

Model	R	R-Square	Adjusted R-Square	Std. Error of the Estimate
1	.794[a]	.630	.620	246.98817

a. Predictors: (Constant), EPS, RONW, EVACE, ROCE

ANOVA[b]

Model		Sum of Squares	df	Mean Square	F	Sig.
1	Regression	15470030	4	3867507.470	63.398	.000[a]
	Residual	9089470	149	61003.156		
	Total	24559500	153			

a. Predictors: (Constant), EPS, RONW, EVACE, ROCE

b. Dependent Variable: AOHLCP

Coefficients[a]

Model		Unstandardized Coefficients		Standardized Coefficients	t	Sig.
		B	Std. Error	Beta		
1	(Constant)	-60.980	36.869	—	-1.654	.100
	EVACE	-1.062	1.114	-.069	-.953	.342
	RONW	.094	.231	.021	.408	.684
	ROCE	.338	1.118	.022	.302	.763
	EPS	12.379	.794	.802	15.590	.000

a. Dependent Variable: AOHLCP

APPENDIX V(D)

Average Results (1998-99 to 2002-03)

Variables Entered/Removed[b]

Model	Variables Entered	Variables Removed	Method
1	Av. EPS, Av. EVACE, Av. RONW, Av. ROCE[a]		Enter

a. All requested variables entered.

b. Dependent Variable: Av. SP

Model Summary

Model	R	R-Square	Adjusted R-Square	Std. Error of the Estimate
1	.794[a]	.630	.620	348.6162098

a. Predictors: (Constant), Av. EPS, Av. EVACE, Av. RONW, Av. ROCE

ANOVA[b]

Model		Sum of Squares	df	Mean Square	F	Sig.
1	Regression	30863058	4	7715764.408	63.487	.000[a]
	Residual	18108456	149	121533.262		
	Total	48971514	153			

a. Predictors: (Constant), Av. EPS, Av. EVACE, Av. RONW, Av. ROCE

b. Dependent Variable: Av. SP

Coefficients[a]

Model		Unstandardized Coefficients		Standardized Coefficients	t	Sig.
		B	Std. Error	Beta		
1	(Constant)	-96.352	67.229	—	-1.433	.154
	Av. EVACE	-.851	1.277	-.049	-.666	.506
	Av. RONW	-.340	1.408	-.017	-.241	.810
	Av. ROCE	1.438	2.620	.039	.549	.584
	Av. EPS	17.281	1.143	.792	15.119	.000

a. Dependent Variable: Av. SP

Appendix VIII(A)
Correlation Results (EVA *vs.* RONW, ROCE and EPS)

Correlations

		Av. EVACE	*Av. RONW*	*Av. ROCE*	*Av. EPS*	*AV. SP*
(1)	*(2)*	*(3)*	*(4)*	*(5)*	*(6)*	*(7)*
Av. EVACE	Pearson Correlation	1	.67 (**)	.66 (**)	.13	.08
	Sig. (2-tailed)		.00	.00	.12	.34
	N	135	135	135	135	135
Av. RONW	Pearson Correlation	.67 (**)	1	.60 (**)	.18(*)	.11
	Sig. (2-tailed)	.00		.00	.03	.21
	N	135	135	135	135	135
Av. ROCE	Pearson Correlation	.66 (**)	.60 (**)	1	.23 (**)	.16
	Sig. (2-tailed)	.00	.00		.01	.01
	N	135	135	135	135	135
Av. EPS	Pearson Correlation	.13	.18 (*)	.23 (**)	1	.89 (**)
	Sig. (2-tailed)	.12	.03	.01		.00
	N	135	135	135	135	135
AV. SP	Pearson Correlation	.08	.11	.16	.89 (**)	1
	Sig. (2-tailed)	.34	.21	.06	.00	
	N	135	135	135	135	135

** Correlation is significant at the 0.01 level (2-tailed).
·Correlation is significant at the 0.05 level (2-tailed).

APPENDIX VIII(B)
Regression Results EVA and Share Price Behavior

SPSS Regression Output

Variables Entered/Removed(b)

Model	Variables Entered	Variables Removed	Method
1	Av. EPS, Av. EVACE, Av. RONW, Av. ROCE(a)		Enter

a. All requested variables entered.

b. Dependent Variable: Av. SP

Model Summary

Model	R	R-Square	Adjusted R-Square	Std. Error of the Estimate
1	.897(a)	.805	.799	217.33411

a. Predictors: (Constant), Av. EPS, Av. EVACE, Av. RONW, Av. ROCE

ANOVA[b]

Model		Sum of Squares	df	Mean Square	F	Sig.
1	Regression	25307120.535	4	6326780.134	133.945	.000[a]
	Residual	6140434.980	130	47234.115		
	Total	31447555.514	134			

a Predictors: (Constant), Av. EPS, Av. EVACE, Av. RONW, Av. ROCE

b Dependent Variable: AV. SP

Coefficients[a]

Model		Unstandardized Coefficients		Standardized Coefficients	t	Sig.
		B	Std. Error	Beta		
1	(Constant)	34.856	44.080		.791	.431
	Av. EVACE	.171	.823	.012	.208	.836
	Av. RONW	-.737	.914	-.044	-.806	.422
	Av. ROCE	-1.044	1.759	-.033	-.594	.554
	Av. EPS	14.098	.620	.909	22.730	.000

a Dependent Variable: Av. SP

Select Bibliography

Books

Arnold, G., Corporate Financial Management, London, *Financial Times,* Prentice Hall, 1998.

Arthur Anderson and Co., Accounting and Reporting Problems of the Accounting Profession, Chicago III: Arthur Anderson and Co., 1973 (5th Edition).

Benjamin Graham, David L. Dodd and Sidney Cottle Security Analysis: Principles and Technique, New York: McGraw Hill, Inc., 1962 (4th Edition).

Brealey, R.A. and Myers, S.C., Principles of Corporate Finance, McGraw Hill Inc., New York, 1991 (4th Edition).

Brigham, E.F., Financial Management—Theory and Practice, Hinsdle, 111, Dryden Press, 1994 (7th Edition).

Copeland, T.T., Koller and J. Murrin, Valuation: Measuring and Managing the Value of Companies, John Wiley and Sons, Inc., 1998 (2nd Edition).

Copeland, T.E., Weston, F.J., Financial Theory and Corporate Policy, Addison—Wesley Publishing Company, New York, 1992 (3rd Edition).

Damodaran, Aswath, Investment Valuation, John Wiley and Sons, Inc., 1996.

Ehrbar, A1., EVA: The Real Key to Creating Wealth, John Wiley and Sons, New York (1st Edition).

Higgins, C. Robert, Analysis for Financial Management, Irwin, McGraw Hill, New York (5th Edition).

Joel, M. Stern and Donald, H. Chew; Revolution in Corporate Finance, Blackwell Publishers, 1998 (3rd Edition).

Knight, A. James, Value Based Management: Developing a Systematic Approach to Creating Shareholder Value.

Leopold, A. Bernstein, Financial Statement Analysis: Theory, Application and Interpretation, Homewood, III; Richard D. Irwin, Inc., 1978.

Raiborn, A. Cecily, Barfield, T.T. and Kinney, R.M., Managerial Accounting, South Western College Publishing, 1999 (3rd Edition).

Rappaport, Alfred, Creating Shareholder Value: The New Standard for Business Performance, New York, The Free Press, A Division of Macmillan Publishers, 1986 (1st Edition).

Rappaport, Alfred, Creating Shareholder Value: A Guide for Managers and Investors.

Ross, S., R. Westerfield and B. Jordan, Fundamentals of Corporate Finance, Irwin, McGraw Hill, Inc., 2000, (5th Edition).

Roy, A. Foulke, Practical Financial Statement Analysis, New York, McGraw Hill, Inc. 1968 (6th Edition).

Samuels, John, Wolkes, M. and Brayshaw, Robin, Financial Management and Decision-making, International Thomson Business Press, London.

Stewart, Bennett, G. (III), The Quest for value, Harper Business, USA, 1991.

Vinay Kumar and Mohinder N. Kaur, "Executive Compensation and Corporate Performance: An EVA Approach", *South Asian Journal of Management*, Vol. 9, Issue 3, pp. 12-20.

Papers/Articles

Adhikari Anand, "Hind Lever's EVA Improves to Rs. 694 Crs. In 1999, Average Cost of Debt Down", *The Hindustan Times*, March 27, 2000.

Anand, Manoj, "Corporate Finance Practices in India: A Survey", *Vikalpa*, Vol. 27, No. 4, October-December 2002, pp. 29-56.

Anand, Manoj, Garg Ajay and Arora Asha, "Economic Value Added: Business Performance Measure of Shareholder Value", *The Management Accountant,* May 1999, pp. 351-56.

Bacidore, J.M. Boquist, J.A. Milbourn, T.T. Thakor, A.V., "The Search for the Best Financial Performance Measure", *Financial Analyst Journal,* May/June, 1997, pp. 11-20.

Banarjee, Ashok, "Economic Value Added: A Better Performance Measure", *The Management Accountant,* December, 1997, pp. 886-88.

Banarjee, Ashok, "Economic Value Added and Shareholder Wealth: An Empirical Study of Relationship", *Paradigm,* Vol. 1, January-June, 1999.

Banarjee, Ahsok, "Linkage Between Economic Value Added and Market Value Added: An Analysis, *Vikalpa,* Vol. 25, No. 3, July-September 2000, pp. 23-36.

Banarjee, Ashok and Jain, S.C., "Financial Variables: Measuring Performance", *The Chartered Accountant,* February, 1999, pp. 34-40.

Bhaskaranarayana, P., "Benchmarks for Profitability: RONA *vs.* EVA", *The Chartered Secretary,* Vol. XXX, No. 7, July, 2000.

Bhattacharya, K. Ashish, "Volunary Disclosures", *The Chartered Accountant,* May, 1997.

Bhattacharya, K. Ashish and Phani, B.V., "Economic Value Added: In Search of Relevance", *Decision,* Vol. 27, No. 2, July-December, 2000, pp. 25-54.

Bhattacharya, Sudipta, "The Feel of Real Value", *The Economic Times,* December 27, 1998.

Biddle, G., Bowen, R.M., Wallace, J.S., "Abstract of Evidence on Relative and Incremental Information Content of EVA, Residual Income, Earnings and Operating Cash Flow", University of Washington, Seattle, WA.

Biddle, G.C., R.M. Bowen and J.S. Wallace, G., "Does EVA Beat Earnings? Evidence on Association with Stock Returns and Firm Values", *Journal of Accounting and Economics,* 24, December 1997, pp. 301-06.

Blair, Alistair, "Watching the New Metrics", *Management Today,* April, 1997, pp. 48-50.

Booth, Rupert, "EVA as a Management Incentive", *Management Accounting,* October, 1997, Vol. 75(9), p. 48.

Clinton, Douglas, Band Chen, Shimin, "Do New Performance Measures Measure up?", *Management Accounting*, October, 1998, pp. 38-47.

Deveshwar, Y.C., "Managing Shareholder Value", *Business Today*, September 7-21, 1999.

De Villiers, J., "The Distortions in Economic Value Added", *Journal of Economics and Business*, Vol. 49, No. 3, May/June, 1997, pp. 285-300.

Dodd, James, L., Chen Shimin, "EVA: A New Panacea?", *Business and Economic Review*, Vol. 42, July-September, 1996, pp. 26-28.

Drucker, Peter, F., "The Information Executives Truly Need", *Harvard Business Review*, January-February, 1995.

Dyal, Bhatnagar and Chandra, Shekhar, In Search of A Potent Measure of Financial Performance among Indian Industries, www.jimsindia.org, pp. 1-9.

Eric, Armour and Michael, C. Mankins, "Back to the Future", *Journal of Business Strategy*, July/August, 2001, pp. 22-27.

Eric, E. Olsen, "VBM Strategies : An Investor Can Love", *Journal of Business Strategy*, November/December, 2002, pp. 14-19.

Eric, E. Olsen, "New Direction in Value Management", *ICFAI Reader*, June 2003, pp. 52-55.

G. Bennett Stewart III, "How to Fix Accounting Measure and Report Economic Profit", *The Journal of Applied Corporate Finance*, Vol. 15, No. 3, Spring 2003, pp. 63-82.

Gerald, T. Garvey and Todd, T. Milbourn, "EVA *versus* Earning: Does It Matter which is More Highly Correlated with Stock Returns", *Journal of Accounting Research*, Vol. 38, Supplement 2002, pp. 209-54.

Goswami, Omkar, Karthikeyan, M., Srivastava, G., "Measuring Shareholder Value", *The Economic Times*, June 3, 1999.

Grant, J.L. "Foundation of EVA for Investment Managers", *The Journal of Portfolio Management*, Vol. 23, Fall 1996, pp. 41-48.

Gupta, K. Dinesh, "Future of Traditional Performance Measures", *Productivity*, Vol. 39, No. 2, July-September, 1998.

Hamel, Gary, "Killer Strategies that Make Shareholders Rich", *Fortune*, June 23, 1997.

Ittner, C.D. and D.F. Larcker, "Innovations in Performance Measurement: Trends and Research Implications", *Journal of Management Accounting Research,* 10, 1998, pp. 205-38.

Jensen, C., Murphy, K.J., "CEO Incentives: Its Not How Much You Pay, But How", *Harvard Business Review,* May-June, 1990, pp. 138-53.

Kolay, M.E., "Measuring the Total Performance of an Organization", *Productivity,* Vol. 34, No. 2, July-September, 1993, pp. 274-80.

Kondragunta, C.S., "Winning with EVA", *Business Today,* February 22, 2000.

Kumar, Atul, "Economic Value Added: What it is and How does it Help in Internal Management", *The Management Accountant,* July 1999.

Kumar, Vinod, M.P. "Economic Value Added: Creating Wealth, The EVA Way", *Chartered Financial Analyst,* July 1994.

Lehn, K.K., Makhija, A.K., "EVA and MVA: As Performance Measures and Signals for Strategic Change", *Strategy and Leadership,* Vol. 24, May-June, 1996, pp. 34-38.

Luber, R.B., "Who are the Real Wealth Creators", *Fortune,* December 9, 1996.

Mayfield, John, "Economic Value Management", *Management Accounting,* September 1997, pp. 32-33.

Mayura, R. Jaiswal, "Shareholders' Wealth Maximisation: A Global Perspective", *Effective Executive,* April 2004, pp. 52-54.

Nemivant, R. Tanuja, "Economic Value Added—What Time India?", *Chartered Financial Analyst,* November, 1998.

O'Hanlon, J., Peasenell, K., "Measure for Measure", *Accountancy,* International Edition, February, 1996, pp. 44-46.

Pablo Fernandez, "Three Residual Income Valuation Methods and Discounted Cash Flow Valuation", *The ICFAI Journal of Applied Finance,* April 2004, pp. 75-93.

Pattanayak, J.K., Mukherjee, Kampan, "Economic Value Added-Adding Value to Money", February, 1998.

Rai, Asha, "HLL's EVA Rises to Rs. 694 crores in 1999", *The Economic Times,* April 20, 2000.

Raul, R.K., "The Shareholder Value Creation and The Market Movement—A Strategy in Interrelation", *The Management Accountant*, Vol. 35, No. 3, March 2000.

Saha, Gurudas, "Shareholder Value and EVA—New Corporate Goals", *The Chartered Accountant*, April, 2000.

Saha, Gurudas, "Shareholders' Value—Banking Companies", *The Management Accountant*, November, 2000, pp. 849-54.

Saksena, Pankaj, "Economic Value Added and Performance Evaluation", *The Management Accountant*, May 1998, pp. 341-42.

Salmi, Timo and Ilkka Virtanon, "Economic Value Added: A Simulation Analysis of the Trendy", Owner Oriented Management Tool, Acta Wasaensia, No. 90, 2001, pp. 1-33.

Satya, R., "Value Creation in Banks", *The Financial Times*, June 23, 1999.

Sengupta, A.K., "Strategic Management: A Tool for Value Management", *The Management Accountant*, January 2001, pp. 7-18.

Shyam, G. Menon, Latha Venkatraman, "Economic Value Added is Back to Basics Seriously", *The Hindu Business Line*, Internet Edition, September 2003, pp. 1-4.

Stanley Paulo, "Is EVA Fiction?—An Academic Comment", The ICFAI Reader, December, 2002, pp. 48-50.

Stern, M. Joel, "EVA is Working", *Business Today*, September 22/ Oct. 6, 1997.

Stewart, Bennett, G. (III), "EVA Works-But not if You Make These Common Mistakes", *Fortune*, May 1, 1995.

Swain, N. Mishra, C.S. Kumar, M. and Vijaylakshmi, S., "Shareholder Wealth Maximization In Indian Pharmaceutical Industry: An Economic Analysis", *ICFAI Journal of Applied Finance*, November, 2002, pp. 31-52.

Tatikonda, Lakshmi U., and Tatikonda, Rao J., "We need Dynamic Performance Measures", *The Management Accounting*, September, 1998.

Teitelbaum, Richard, "America's Greatest Wealth Creators", *Fortune*, November 10, 1997, pp. 265-76.

Topkis Maggie, "A New Way to Find Bargains", *Fortune*, Dec. 9, 1996.

Tully, Shawn, "How do CEOs like You Create and Sustain an Organisational Adding Value Culture that is Sharply Focused on Shareholder Value?", *Business Today*, Sept. 22-Oct. 6, 1997.

Tully, Shawn, "The Real Key to Creating Wealth, *Fortune*, Sept. 20, 1993.

Uyemura, Kantor and Petitt, Justin, "EVA for Bank Value Creation, Risk Management and Profitability Measurement", *Journal of Applied Corporate Finance*, Vol. 9, No. 2, Summer, p. 94.

Walker, Fred, H., "Cost Justification of Capital Equipment Using Economic Value Added Analysis", February-April, 1999, Vol. 15, No. 2, pp. 1-6.

Wallace, J.S., "Adopting Residual Income-based Compensation Plans: Evidence of Effects on Management Actions", Working Paper, University of California, Irwin, CA, 1997.

Weaver, S.C., "Measuring Economic Value Added: A Survey of the Practices of EVA Proponents", *Journal of Applied Finance*, Fall/Winter, 2001, pp. 7-17.

Wood, A. Nicholas, "Economic Value Added (EVA): Uses, Benefits and Limitations—A South African Perspective", *Southern African Business Review*, pp. 1-12.

Index